PAST & PRESENT

NORTHGLENN

Huron Junior High School opened its doors to 450 junior high and 120 elementary students in the fall of 1964. Architects Wheeler & Lewis and the Pinckard Construction Company completed the $450,000 complex that boasted two science laboratories, a foreign language laboratory, an arts center, and a gymnasium among the amenities. Also visible in this c. 1974 image are churches along Kennedy Drive and the Northglenn Mall complex. (Courtesy of Adams 12 Five Star Schools.)

PAST & PRESENT

NORTHGLENN

Elizabeth Moreland Candelario

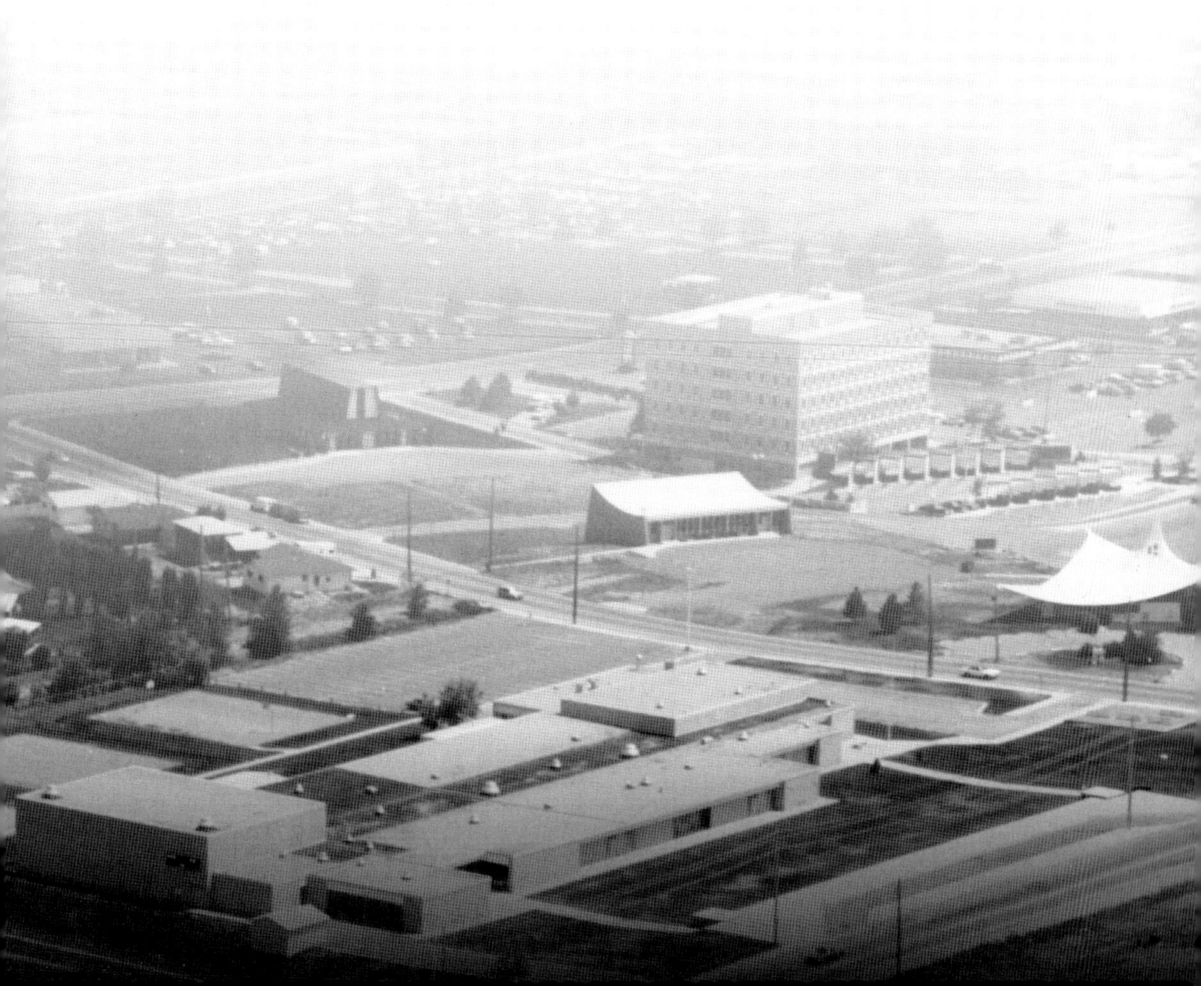

To Ben, thank you for being my "After All." Your support and love cannot be measured.

ISBN 978-1-4671-6052-0

Library of Congress Control Number: 2023943636

Published by Arcadia Publishing
Charleston, South Carolina

Printed in the United States of America

For all general information, please contact Arcadia Publishing:
Telephone 843-853-2070
Fax 843-853-0044
E-mail sales@arcadiapublishing.com

Visit us on the Internet at www.arcadiapublishing.com

On the Front Cover: St. Stephen's Lutheran Church held the ground breaking for its building near the corner of Huron Street and Kennedy Drive on June 2, 1963. Designed by Boulder architect Charles A. Haertling, the building is an example of midcentury Neo-Expressionist architecture. The unique, swooping concrete arched roof appears to float above the walls and windows while resting on reinforced concrete beams that meet at the center of the building. It was listed in the National Register of Historic Places in 2019. (Courtesy of St. Stephen's Lutheran Church.)

On the Back Cover: On June 30, 1959, Perl-Mack Homes hosted an open house of the five homes at 104th Avenue (background) and Grant Drive (foreground). The prices, ranging from $11,600 to $30,000, were so popular that the sales staff was overwhelmed by the orders, with 110 sales in a single day. Perl-Mack's goal was to have a minimum of 1,000 families living in North Glenn by 1960. (Courtesy of History Colorado, Robert Schott Collection, Box 4, Scan No. 10041425.)

Contents

Acknowledgments

Writing another book about Northglenn has been my pleasure. A city is merely a dot on the map if not for the stories that make it a community. While these images focus on locations and buildings, it is the people that use them that make them unique and their stories worth remembering.

My biggest thanks go to a number of people who gave their advice, support, time, stories, and photographs to make this book possible. In no particular order, I appreciate the residents of Northglenn, the City of Northglenn, the Northglenn Senior Center, the Northglenn Historic Preservation Commission, Joyce Downing, Jerry Gavette, Jack White, Dianne Cooksey, Sara Dusenberry, Johanna Small, John Eisel, Debbie Tuttle, Lillian Frey, Kate Fisher, Chief Jim May, Madeline Norconk, Bernd and Patty Hegel, Anthony Abeyta, Phil Carney, Jane Viers, Caron Horner, Betty Painter, Joe Lachermeier, Dolores Gallegos, Barb Meier, Jerry Meier, Susi Rice, Kasey Nunn, Marisa Philips, Joe Ferdani of Adams 12 Five Star Schools, and David Frasman of Beck Archives. I was blessed to work with the following churches: Gethsemane Lutheran Church, Calvary Northglenn, Calvary Community Baptist, Northglenn United Methodist, Northside Baptist, St. Stephens Lutheran Church, Good Shepherd Presbyterian Church, and Immaculate Heart of Mary. Warm appreciation goes to Myron, Derrick, Jonathan, Justin, and Spencer, who let me share my stories and pictures during many work lunches and meetings. I would like to thank Lindsey Givens, Stacia Bannerman, and Arcadia Publishing for bringing this book to life.

I can never thank my family enough for their support during the time that I spent focused on buildings instead of them. Ben wandered all around Northglenn with me, often looking for the correct spot to take a picture. Brian and Kathie Moreland, Magan and Coe Kunz, and John and Jamie Moreland listened to me and supported every step of this process. I hope that Brian, Traven, Adelaide, and Kateri will read this book and know that they inspired me to chase my dreams, as I will always cheer them on while they chase theirs.

Most of the present-day pictures are by the author. Special recognition to Xavier Culp for taking the Interstate 25 picture. Historical photographs are credited in the captions.

Introduction

A small city of approximately seven square miles about 20 minutes north of downtown Denver, what we know today as the city of Northglenn had humble roots as farmland that became a suburban community with nearly 39,000 residents. In 1959, Jordon Perlmutter, Samuel Primack, and William Morrison of Perl-Mack Enterprises looked upon the fertile farmland in unincorporated Adams County and envisioned a place where parents could raise children in a self-contained community—a community named North Glenn. The developers used their previous experiences in building the surrounding suburbs to create what they deemed a perfectly planned community of homes, shopping centers, churches, schools, and parks.

Knowing that they faced the challenge of selling homes in a newly established area, Perl-Mack worked with Flesher Advertising to embark on a media campaign that included multiple newspaper and television ads showcasing their Rocky Mountain Home Fair. Printed promotional materials highlighted driving times rather than distance to popular front-range locations including downtown Denver, Stapleton Airport, Rocky Flats, and the Denver Federal Center. On June 30, 1959, Perl-Mack hosted an open house to present the five model homes that had been built on the corner of 104th Avenue and Grant Drive. Drawn by the reasonable prices that ranged from $11,600 to $30,000 with names such as Matchless, Eureka, Summit, Alpine, and Lark, thousands of people visited and purchased homes. Perl-Mack received numerous awards between 1960 and 1963 for the development of Northglenn. Awards included Excellence in Merchandizing by *Practical Builder Magazine*, Certified for Better Living Features by *McCall* magazine, Most Perfectly Planned Community in America by *Life* magazine, Best Home for the Money in Southwestern United States by *American Home* magazine, Good Housekeeping Citation by *Good Housekeeping* magazine, and Best in Nation Award for Home Marketing by *Look* magazine. Chapter three of this book explores examples of Perl-Mack homes along with original farmland and homes by other developers in areas later annexed into Northglenn.

Initially voting down incorporation in 1963, residents were encouraged by the North Glenn Civic Association to go back to the polls in 1969 to vote for incorporation rather than face annexation from neighboring Thornton. After a brief court battle, the City of North Glenn was officially incorporated on April 18, 1969, with the installation of officials in a ceremony held at Northglenn High School. Records indicate that the city name changed to Northglenn in 1970. The housing communities of Deza Estates and Northmor were annexed in 1970, while the Hillcrest subdivision and the Hinkhouse-Mowery property followed in 1971. However, neighboring Thornton and Westminster annexed land surrounding Northglenn, limiting the city to its current borders. Despite being landlocked, the city has continued to explore growth through further development of existing areas, most recently the Hinkhouse property, which until recently was among the last remaining underdeveloped areas in the city. City master plans are adapted every few years to maximize space while providing needed services to residents.

Building city infrastructure commenced after incorporation. Mayor Hugh Danahy and the original city council members set out to create a budget, make plans for a city building, which was completed in 1970, and set up a police force. Through town hall meetings, the city council sought the input of residents on city issues, with the most pressing being public safety. Early in 1970, fifteen Northglenn police officers were sworn in, patrolling the streets in two cars borrowed from the Adams County Sheriff's Department. The Northglenn Ambulance continued to operate on a volunteer basis, as it had since 1963. The fire department remained under the control of the West Adams County Fire Protection District, with Northglenn being the home of two fire stations—one on Irma Drive and the other on Huron Street. The Northglenn Metropolitan Recreation District, initially responsible for all the recreational needs of the Northglenn community, purchased a home at 1710 Leroy Drive, which would remain its home until it merged with the city in 1972. Under the leadership of the district, two community centers were built, and adult and youth sports programs were instituted. After 1972, the city took charge of the recreation district, continuing the development of the park system and a 28-mile greenway path system that winds through the city. Chapter four explores the buildings and park system created during the years following incorporation.

Initial promotional materials distributed by Perl-Mack promised a "Better Life" for people who chose Northglenn. Part of that plan included conveniently placed schools and churches. The speed at which Perl-Mack completed houses kept Adams 12 School District racing to complete schools to accommodate the growing student population. Churches incorporated quickly and often used those schools for meeting places while their buildings were erected. The pages of chapters one and two focus on the development and changes of these institutions.

Making it easier to live and work in Northglenn are the various businesses that were introduced during the community's development. Retail was established early with the construction of the Garland Shopping Center and the Northglenn Mall. However, commerce was not limited to retail. Restaurants, banks, car dealerships, hotels, gas stations, and office buildings are among the various industries that took up residence in the city. The Northglenn Urban Renewal Authority has sought to keep commerce areas alive through new development and redevelopment of aging infrastructure, as seen with the demolition of the aging Northglenn Mall and its redevelopment into the Northglenn Marketplace. Multiple examples are provided in chapter five to explore the variety of commerce and industry supporting the city since its inception.

Photographs give us a snapshot of a single moment. However, a single snapshot can never tell the whole story; rather, it is a multitude of moments that make up an individual's or a city's history. While not an all-encompassing history of Northglenn, this book sets out to give a glimpse into life in "the city that pride built." Hopefully, through these pages, these images will remind the reader of stories about schools, church events, that game in the park, mud being tracked into a new house, or a first date at the mall. As Northglenn continues to change, these photographs will serve to document the past and share the present, all while looking to the future.

CHAPTER 1

PLACES OF WORSHIP

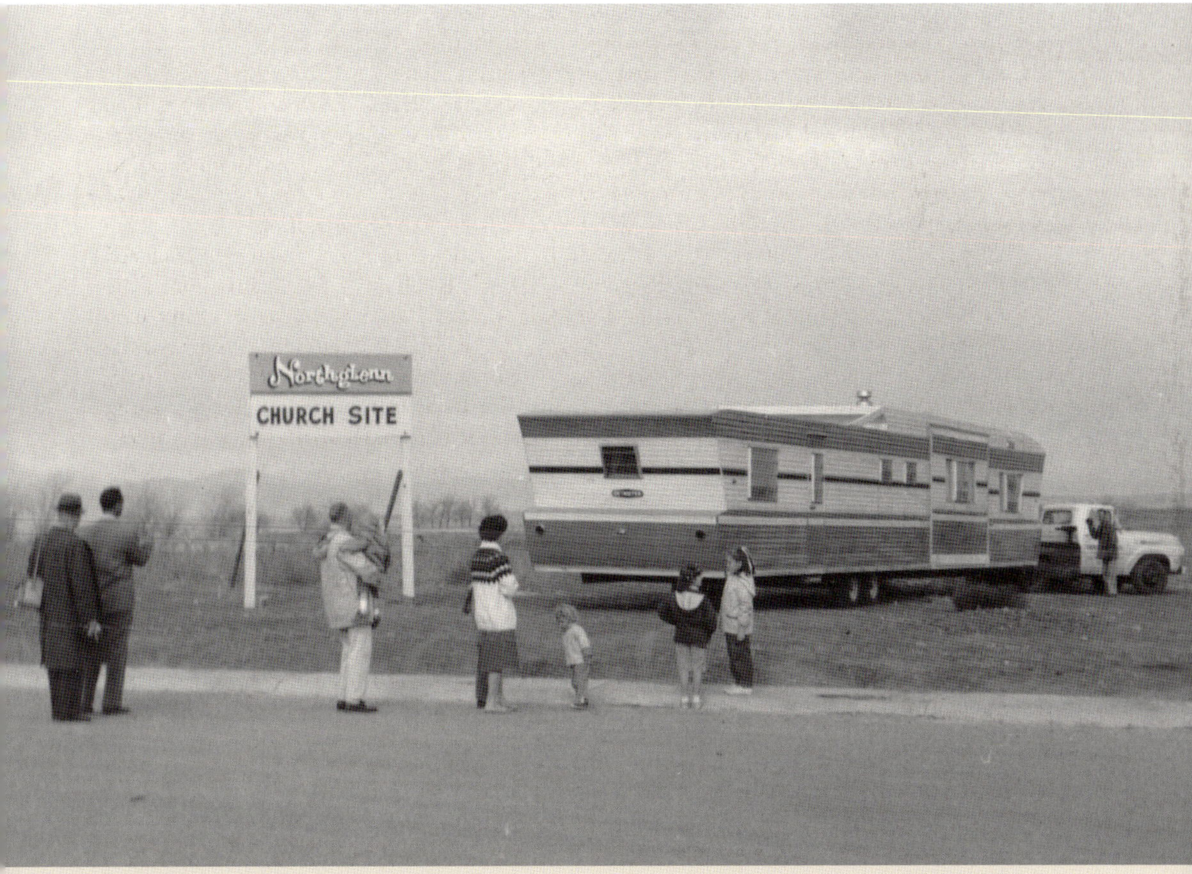

In January 1963, the Northglenn United Methodist Church officially organized and needed a location other than the parsonage for meetings. With construction underway on its permanent location, it used this mobile unit from February 1963 until April 1965. This was considered a "modern solution" for a congregation awaiting a permanent structure. As Rev. William Youngblood and his family watch, the trailer is moved onto the empty lot. (Courtesy of Northglenn United Methodist Church.)

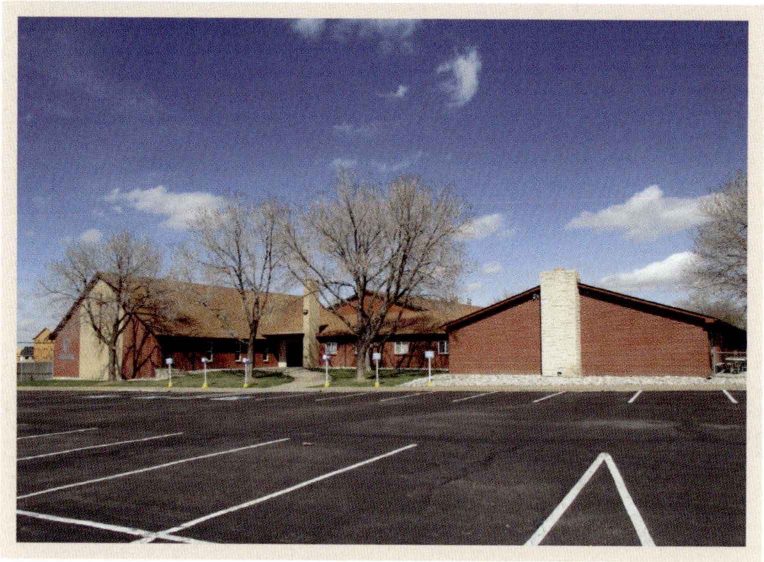

Calvary Community Baptist Church started as Sunny Acres Community Church on January 22, 1967, when Rev. Howard Herbst led nine people in services at Sunny Acres Villa. Moving to Northglenn Junior High in September 1967, it changed its name to Calvary Community Church and finally Calvary Community Baptist in 1974. The church purchased three acres of property at 11980 Irma Drive in 1968 and held a ground breaking on April 6, 1969, and a dedication in November 1969. A 20,000-square-foot education wing was added in 1984. (Past image, courtesy of Calvary Community Baptist Church.)

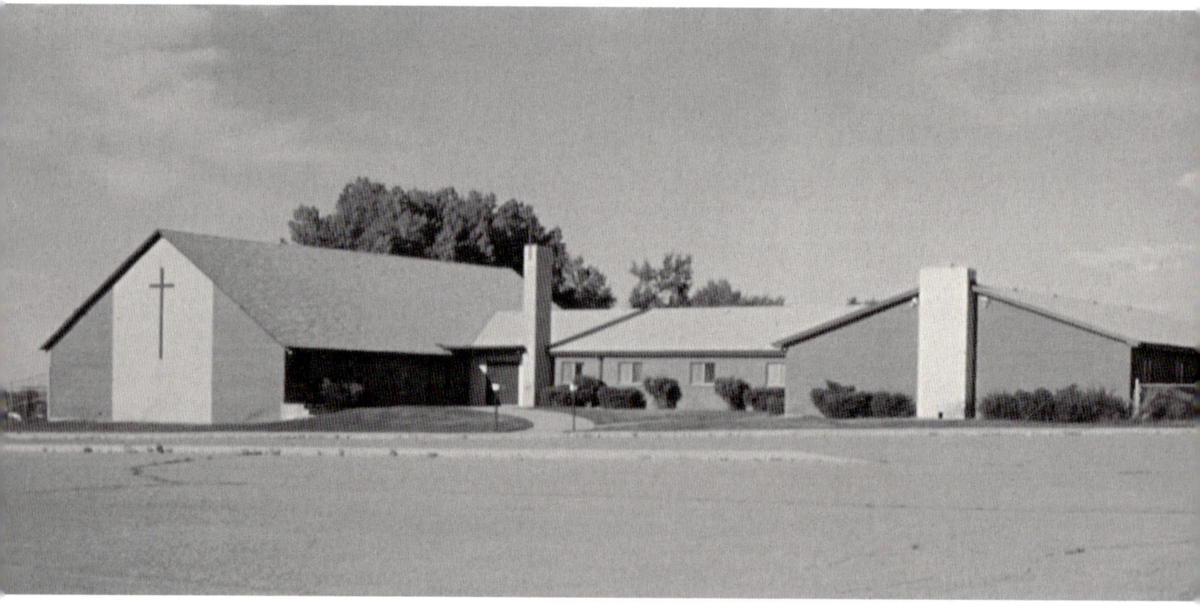

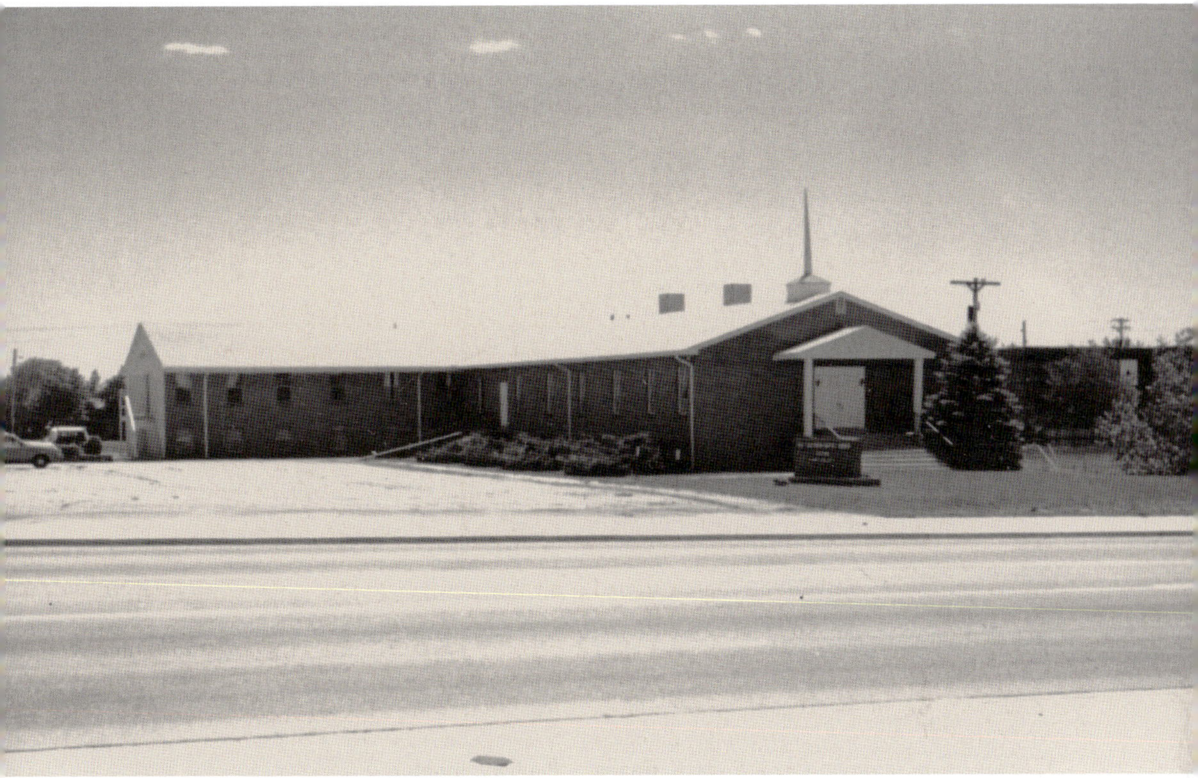

Northglenn First Southern Baptist Church began in 1960 when members of the First Baptist Church of Thornton purchased land at 10620 North Washington Street. Members of the church met in local homes while waiting for the building's dedication on October 15, 1961. The structure, which includes classroom and office space in addition to the sanctuary, remains the same today. The church was renamed Calvary Northglenn in 2022 and continues to have weekly services. (Past image, courtesy of Calvary Northglenn.)

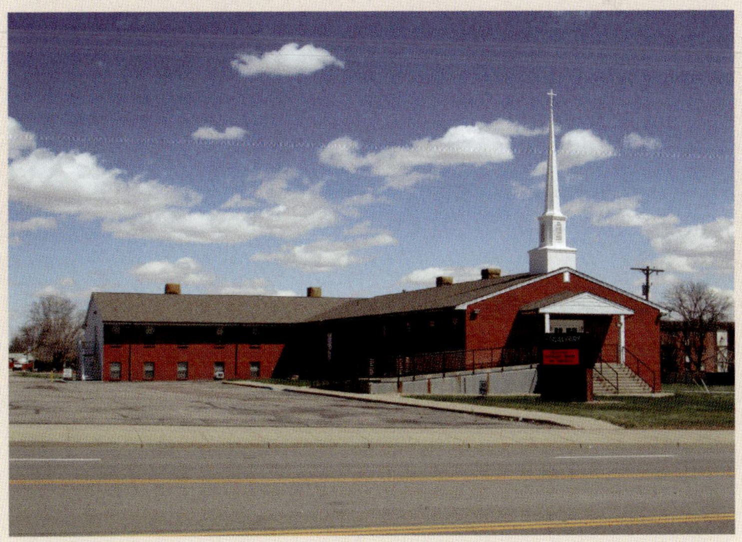

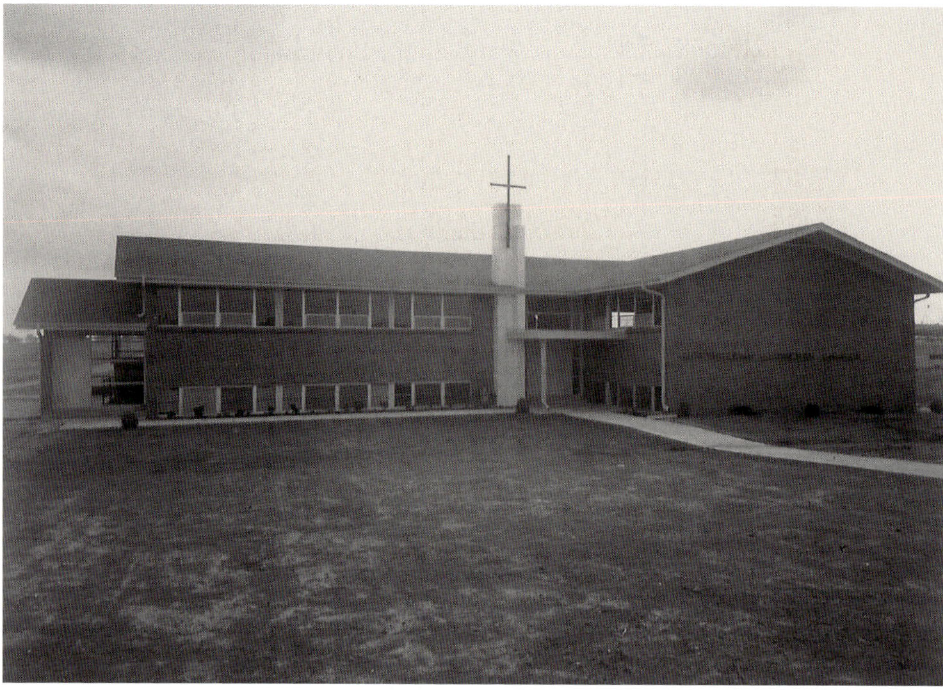

Northglenn Lutheran Church, later renamed Gethsemane Lutheran Church, held its first service in this building at 10675 Washington Street on July 9, 1961, with 257 people in attendance. A classroom addition was added in 1965 to the right of the original sanctuary when a school was added. An additional sanctuary, constructed to hold up to 600 people on the east side of the building, was dedicated on April 4, 1971, and remains in use today. (Past image, courtesy of Gethsemane Lutheran Church.)

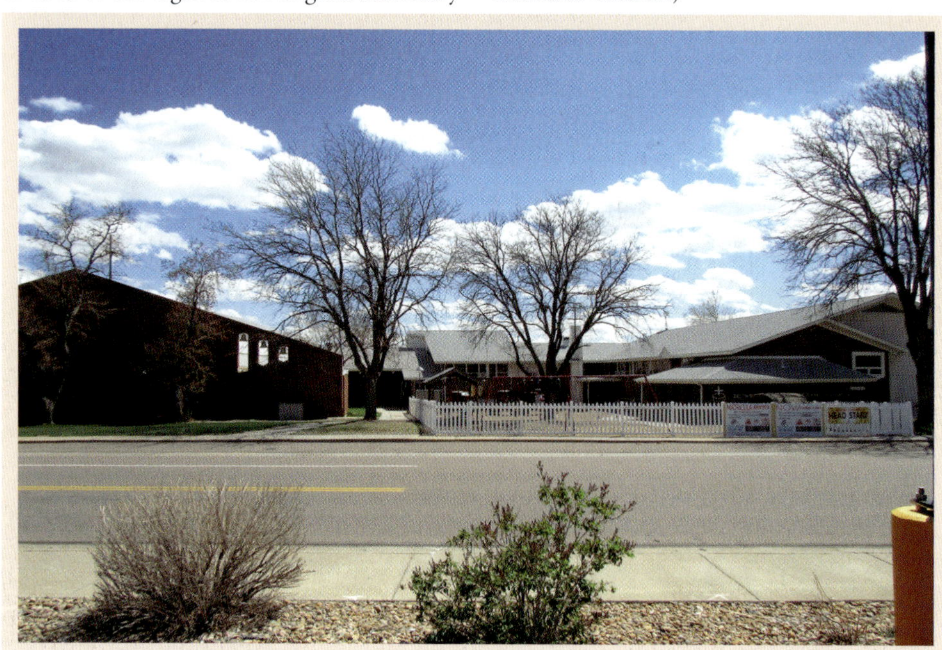

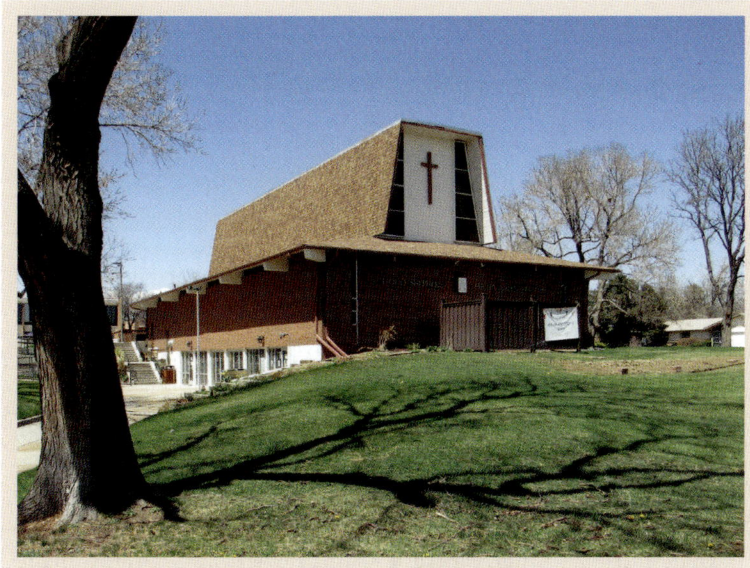

Chartered in 1967, Good Shephard Presbyterian Church chose John Anderson of Wheeler and Lewis to design this building at 10785 Melody Drive. Completed in October 1968, the sanctuary had seating for 350 people. In 1969, artist Jan Myers was commissioned to paint the Plexiglas windows for the front of the church. Additional congregation members created offices, classrooms, and a kitchen in the basement. In 1986, the congregation opened a food bank, still in operation, in the basement of the church. (Past image, courtesy of Good Shephard Presbyterian Church.)

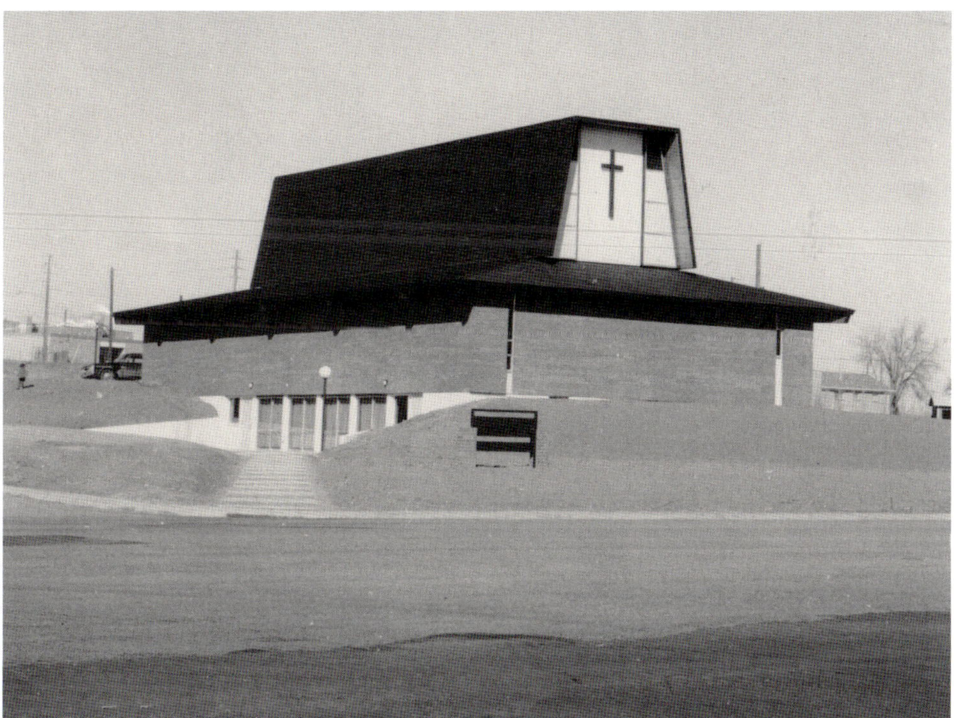

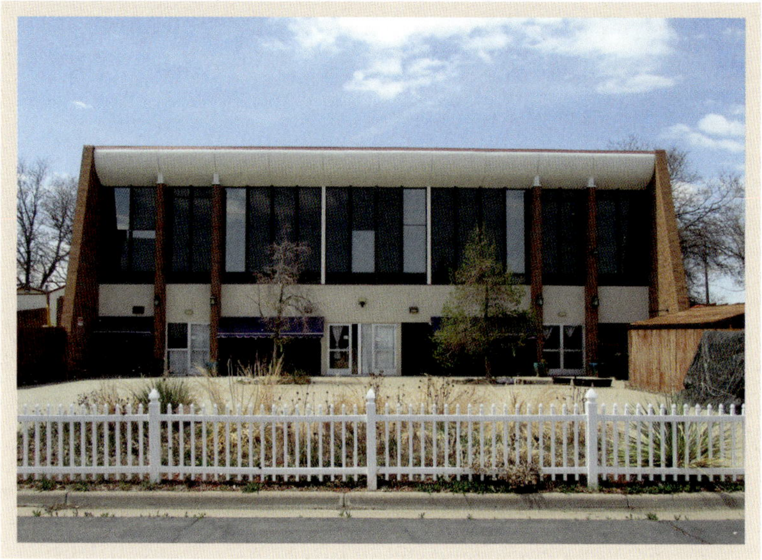

Good Shepherd Presbyterian Church and St. Stephen's Lutheran Church entered into a joint financial corporation called PAL Inc. (Presbyterians and Lutherans) to complete this structure in 1973. It was used by both congregations for classroom and event space until 2003, when Good Shepherd purchased St. Stephen's portion of the building and renamed it Shepherd's Hall. Educational space continues to be the building's primary use, with Purple Moon Early Learning Center taking over in 2018. (Past image, courtesy of St. Stephen's Lutheran Church.)

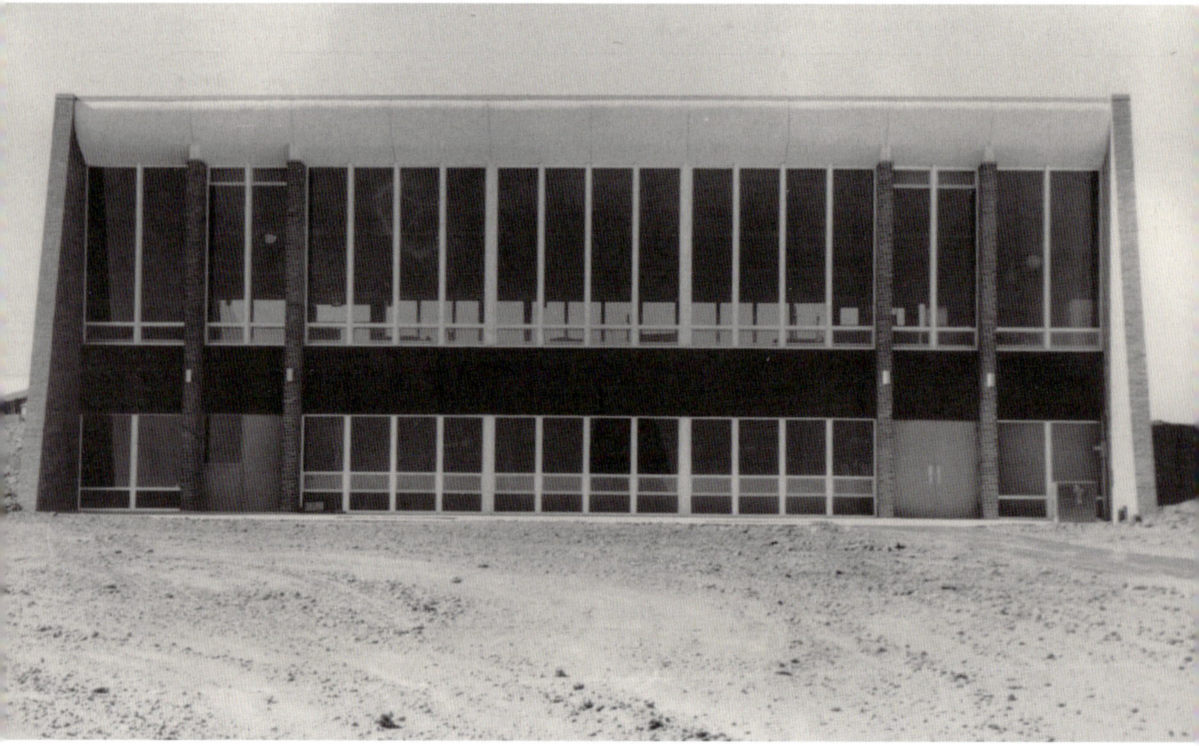

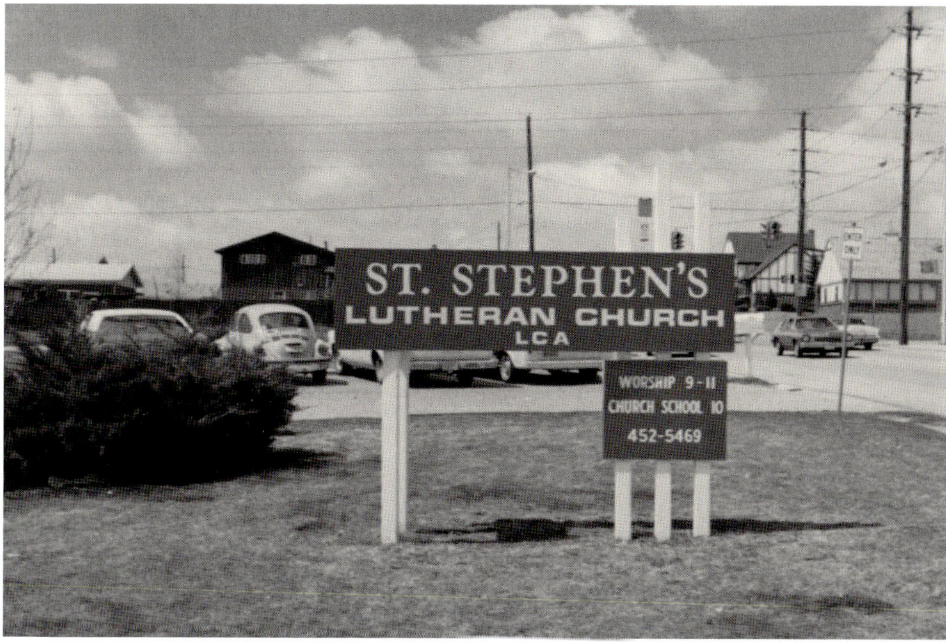

St. Stephen's Lutheran Church is primarily known for the Heartling building, shown on the front cover. Here, one can see the sign welcoming guests to the church complex. By 2001, St. Stephens had outgrown the Heartling building. With the help of United Church Structures, the congregation built a new building on the corner of Huron Street and Kennedy Drive. This structure was dedicated in November 2001 and continues to be the primary place of worship. (Past image, courtesy of St. Stephen's Lutheran Church.)

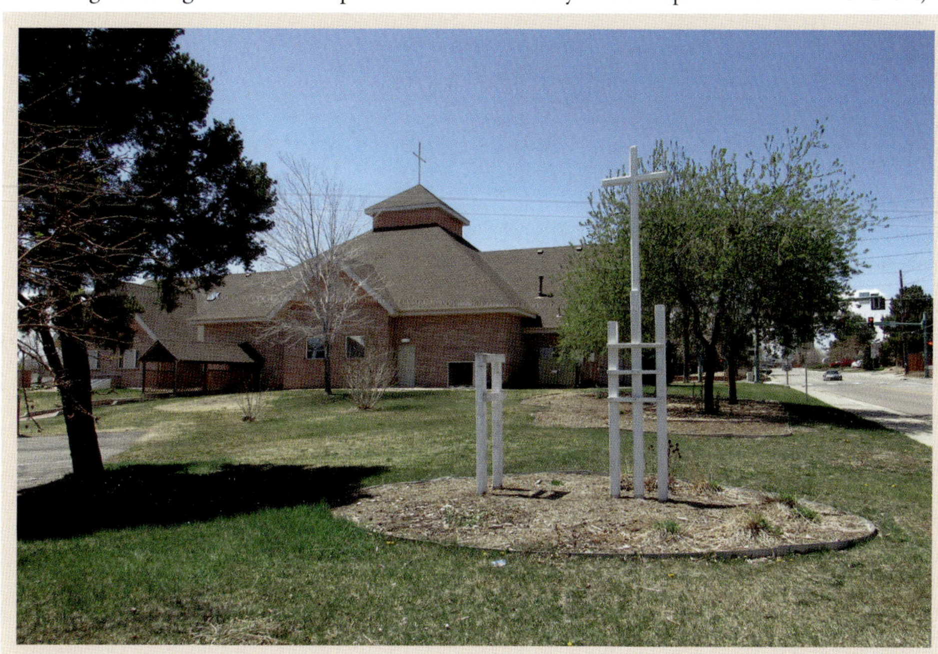

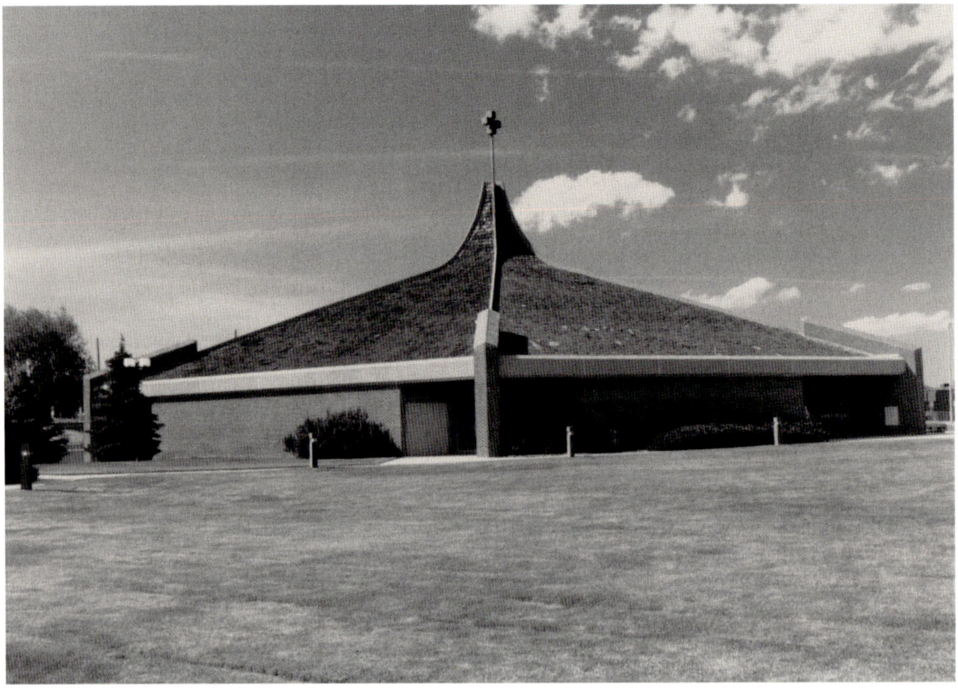

In 1967, a total of 380 Catholics met at Leroy Elementary, dubbed "St. Leroy," to discuss building a church. Members of the parish council, including Northglenn resident Joe Lachermeier, helped raise funds to build this ultra-modern structure designed by Everett-Zeigel Architects. The church at 11385 Grant Drive was dedicated on April 30, 1970, by Archbishop James V. Casey and Rev. Martin J. McNulty. Multiple renovations and additions have increased its size, and the parish currently serves over 6,000 families. (Past image, courtesy of Caron Horner.)

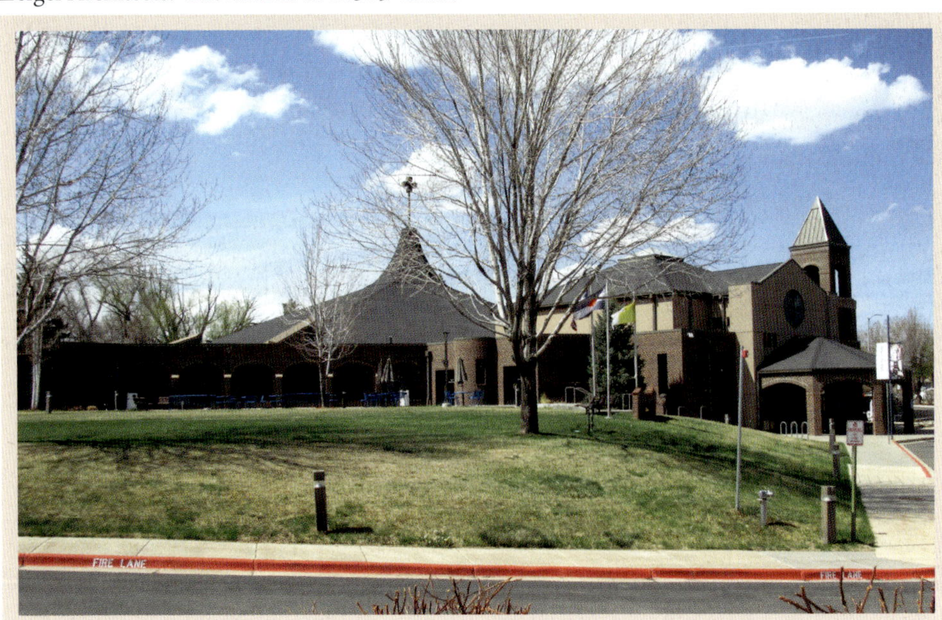

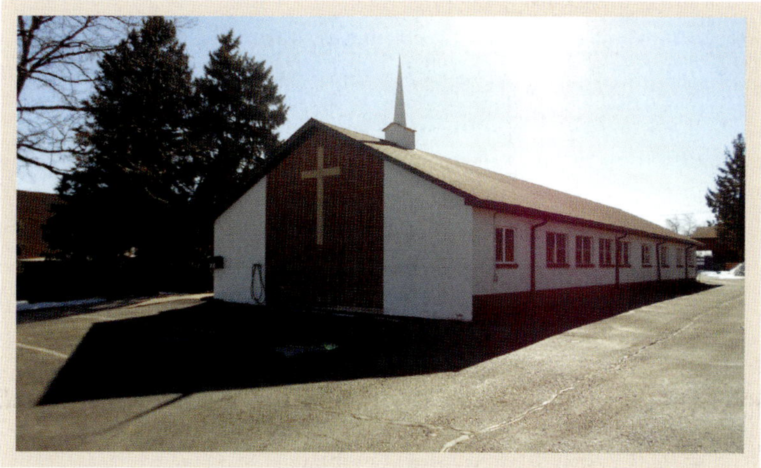

After holding meetings at Highland Mortuary and Northglenn Junior High School from 1960 to 1966, Northglenn Christian Church purchased two acres at 1800 East 105th Place and held the dedication of its worship auditorium on July 19, 1966. An additional two acres were purchased in 1970 for a new sanctuary dedicated in 1971. A two-story educational building constructed in 1982 connected the original auditorium to the 1971 sanctuary. Two additional remodels are obscured by the large trees beside the original structure. (Past image, Courtesy of Northglenn Christian Church.)

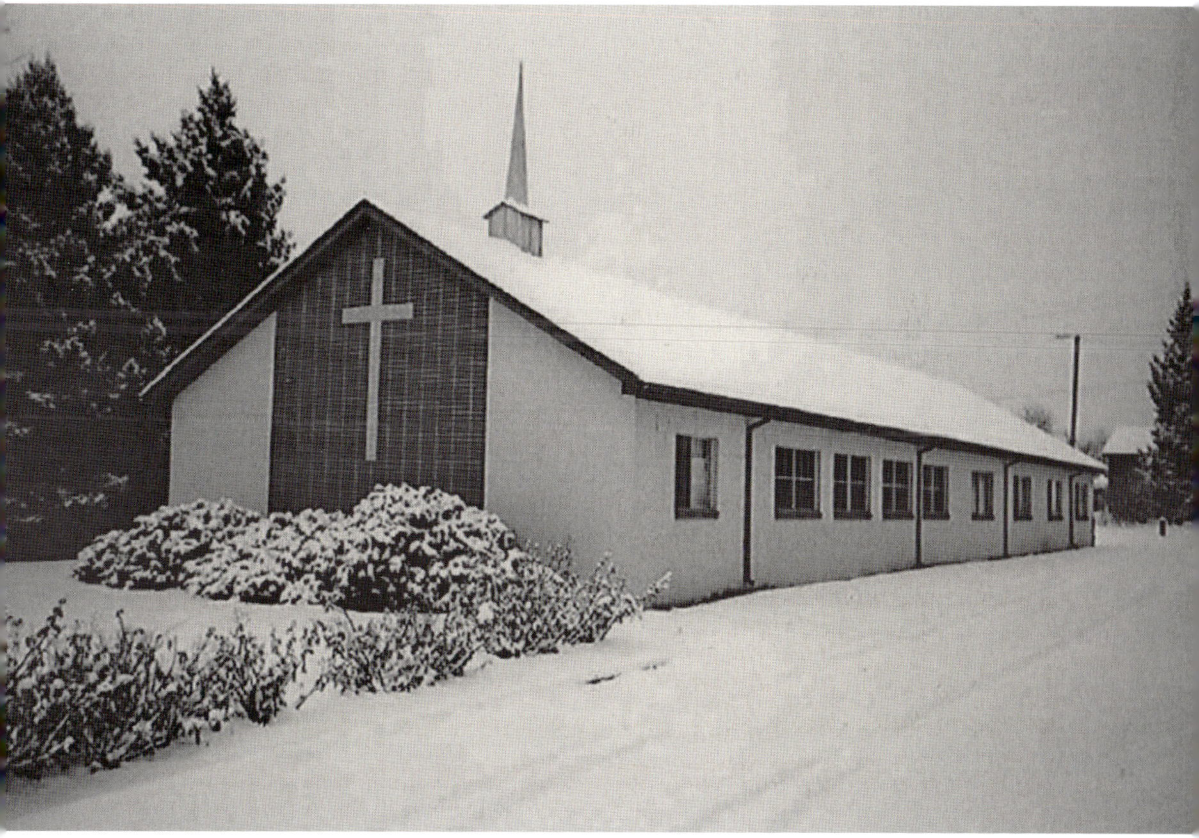

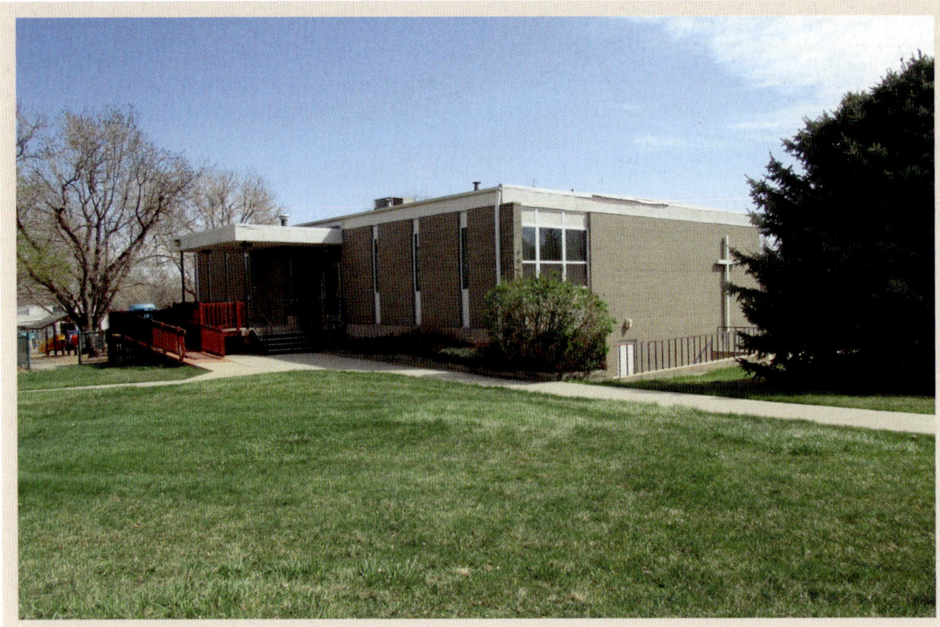

Northglenn United Methodist Church broke ground on the first of a planned three-building complex at 1551 West 106th Avenue on August 16, 1964. The building, designed by the architectural firm Arter and Speece, was completed in time for Palm Sunday services on April 11, 1965. When the congregation moved into the newer, larger building in 1973, this building became the church's education building, still used today as part of its Early Education Center. (Past image, courtesy of Northglenn United Methodist Church.)

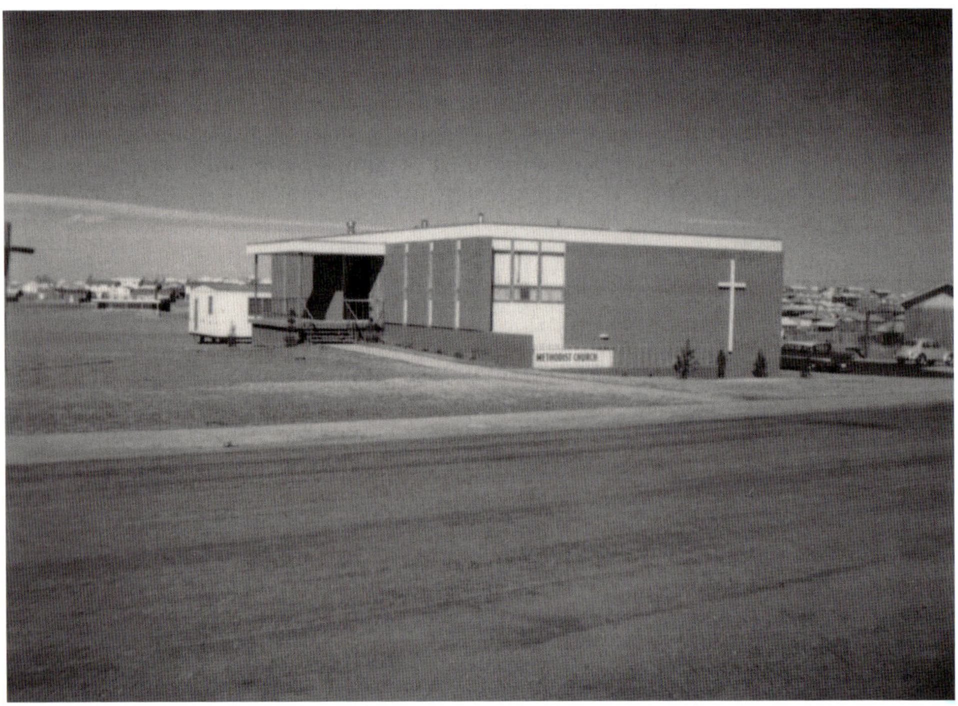

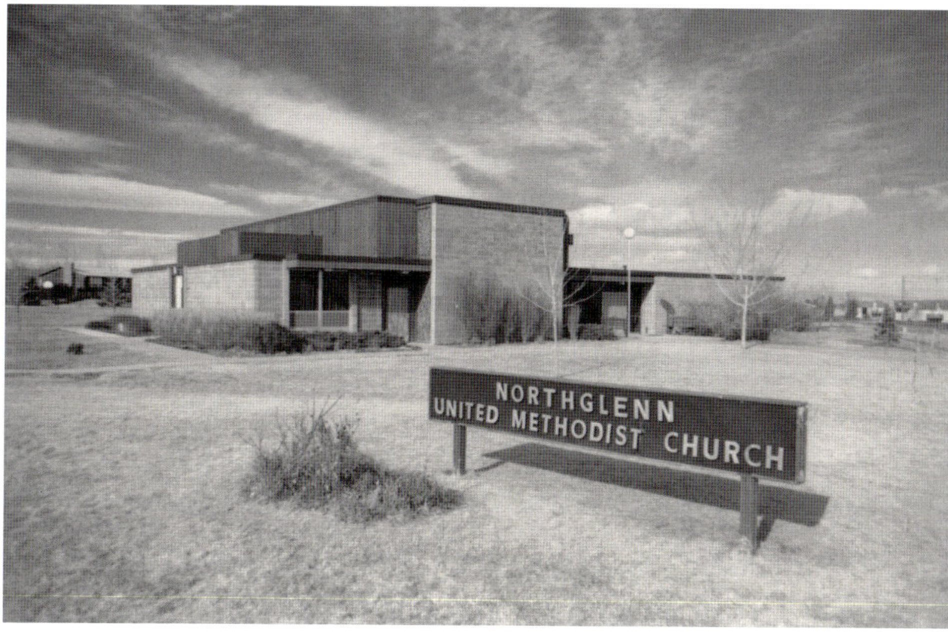

In August 1972, Northglenn United Methodist Church broke ground on its 6,600-square-foot building housing the new sanctuary, offices, and classrooms designed by architect Orville Anderson and dedicated on April 15, 1973. Analyzing long-range plans and growth needs, another expansion began in 1984. Additional renovations, largely performed by congregation members, began in August 1996 and were dedicated on April 13, 1997. The final addition created the entrance and bell tower seen in the present image. (Past image, courtesy of Northglenn United Methodist Church.)

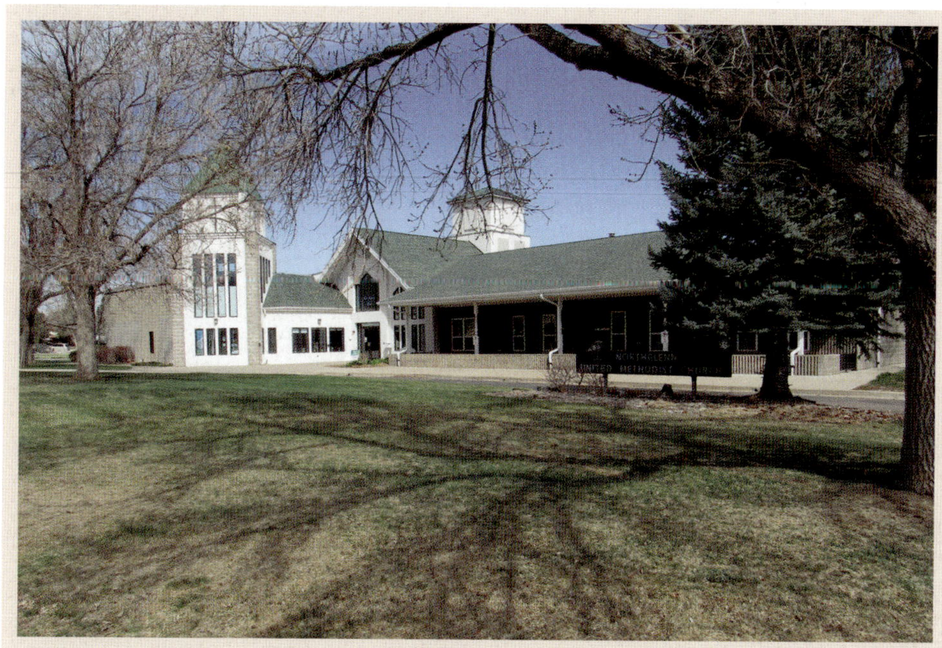

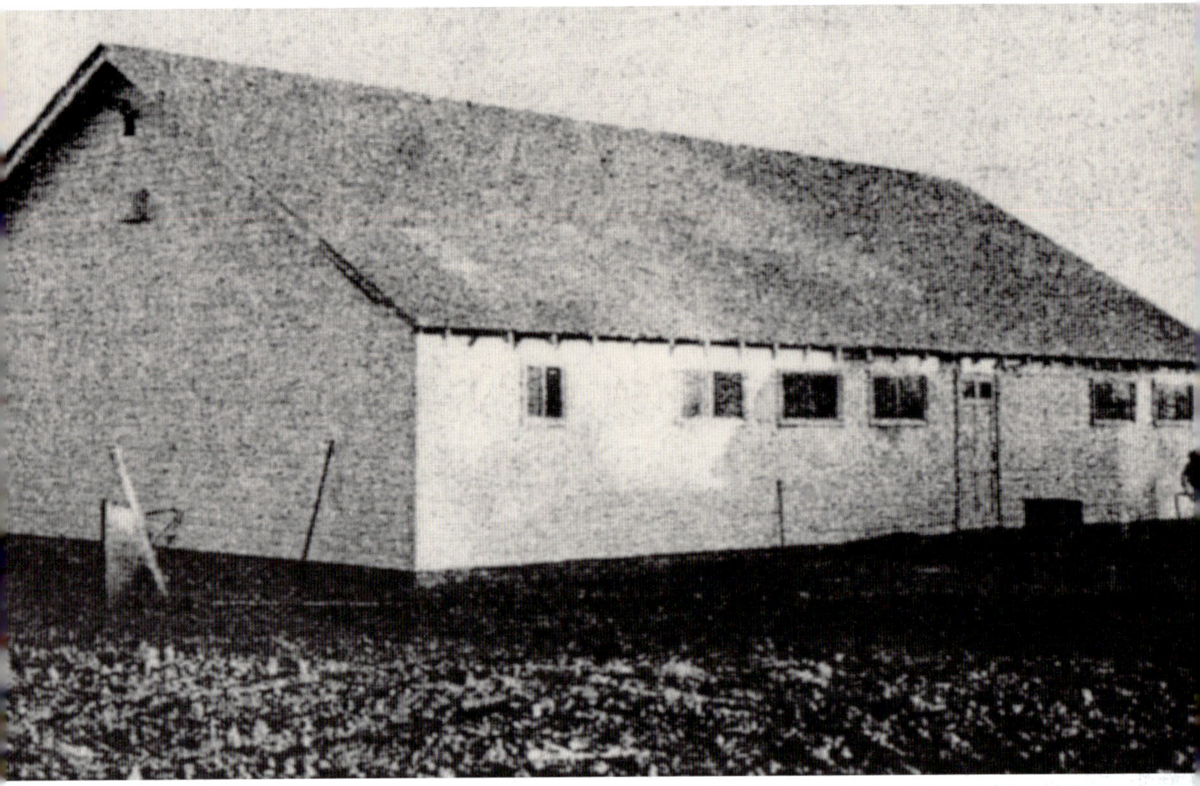

Northside Baptist Church converted this barn into an auditorium in 1964 by adding theater seats bolted to the floor. A two-story education wing was connected to the auditorium in 1972. In 1985, construction began on a geodesic dome that rests on a brick wall reinforced with a steel band around the top. Completed in 1987, the congregation moved into this new auditorium with seating for 400 people. The original barn auditorium is still used by Northside Christian Daycare. (Past image, courtesy of Northside Baptist Church.)

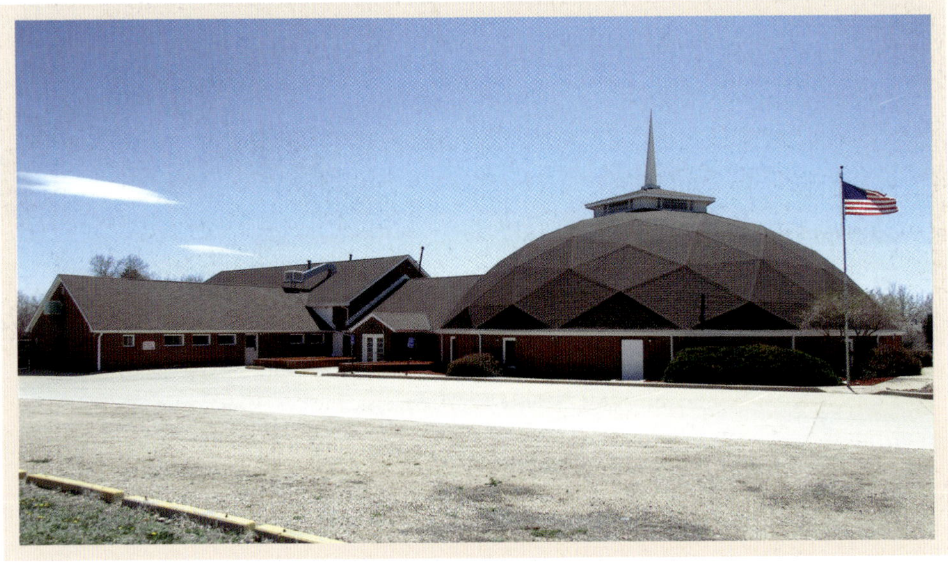

CHAPTER 2

Institutions of Learning

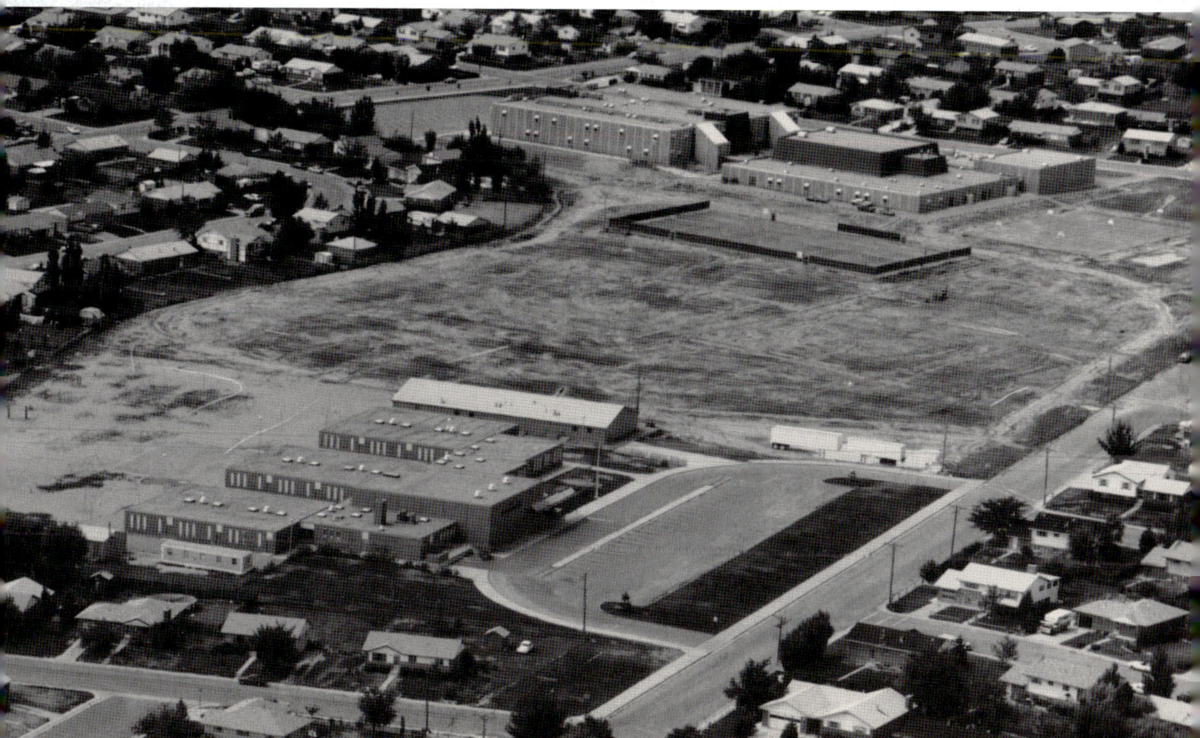

Wyco Drive Elementary School (left), now Hulstrum K-8, was one of three schools completed for Adams 12 Schools in 1965. The 20-classroom building was designed by Denver architects Atchison, Kloverstrom, Saul, and Atchison and featured a television antenna wired into each classroom. Northeast Junior High School (right) opened in 1971. Northeast, now STEM Lab, was partially demolished and renovated, upgrading the aging building for increased school attendance. (Courtesy of Adams 12 Five Star Schools.)

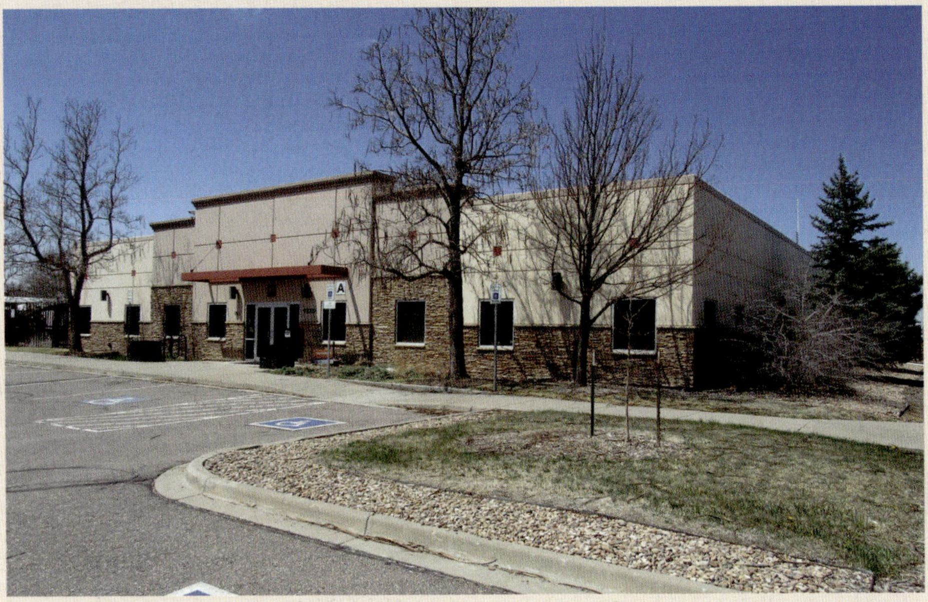

Eastlake School at 12323 Claude Court was constructed in 1920 and opened with a combined 110 students from Block School (120th Avenue and Colorado Boulevard) and Webster School (112th Avenue and Washington Street). In 1980, Eastlake School became home to the district's alternative junior and senior high schools. Attempts to preserve the structure as a historical site failed and the school building was demolished in 2002, making way for the Northglenn Maintenance and Operations Building constructed in 2003. (Past image, courtesy of Northglenn Historic Preservation Commission.)

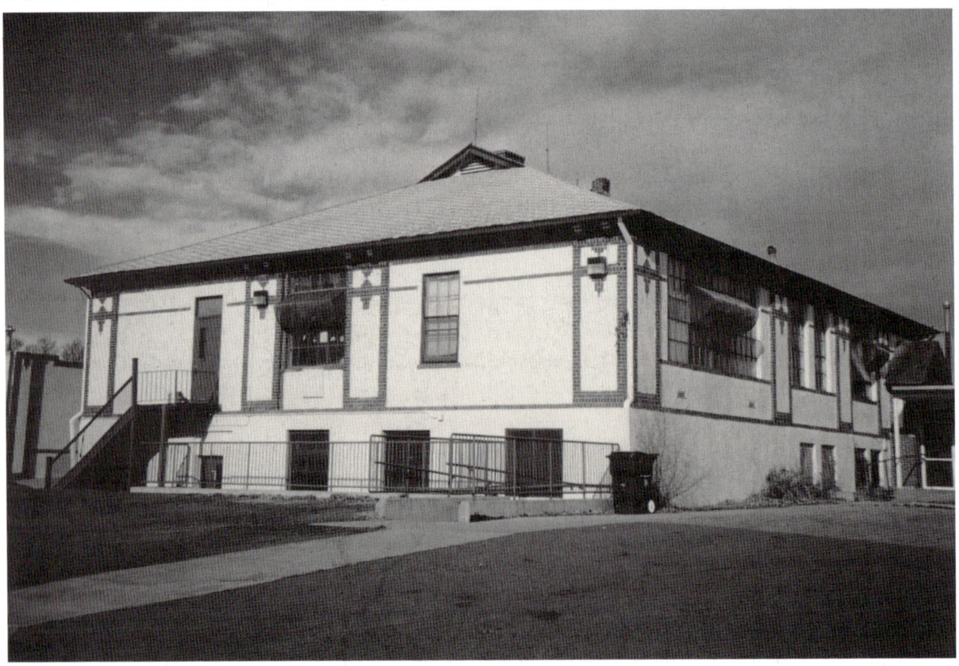

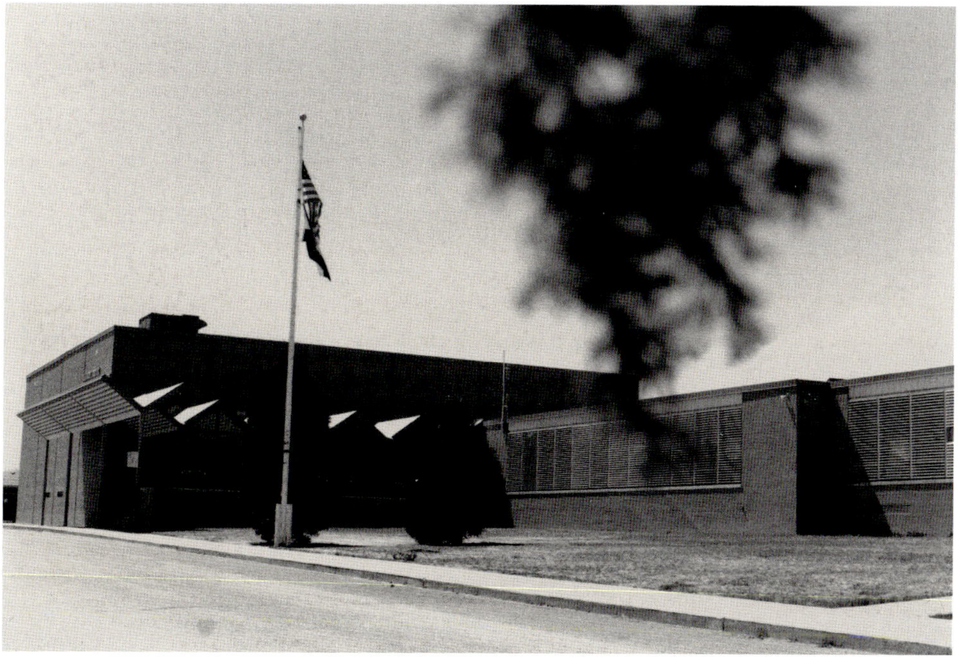

Leroy Drive Elementary School held its dedication on April 25, 1963, even though students had been attending class in the building since the fall of 1962 while builders completed the offices, kitchen, and all-purpose rooms. Designed by the architectural firm of Atchison, Kloverstrom, Saul and Atchison, the 33,425-square-foot school design reflected the importance of the overall physical, mental, and social environment in education. Later renovations added additional educational space and changed the main entrance to the building. (Past image, courtesy of Leroy Drive Elementary School.)

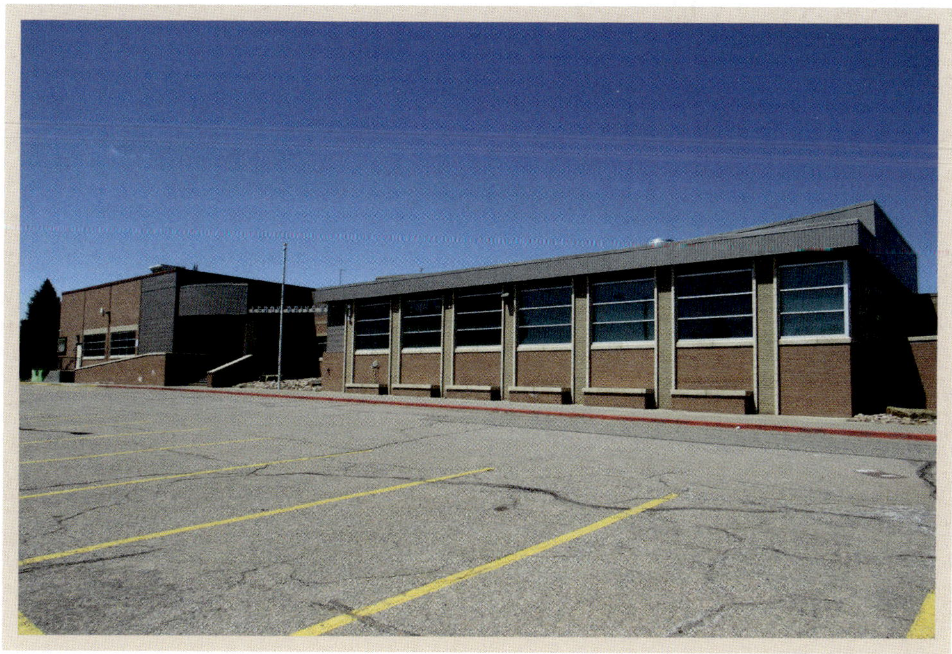

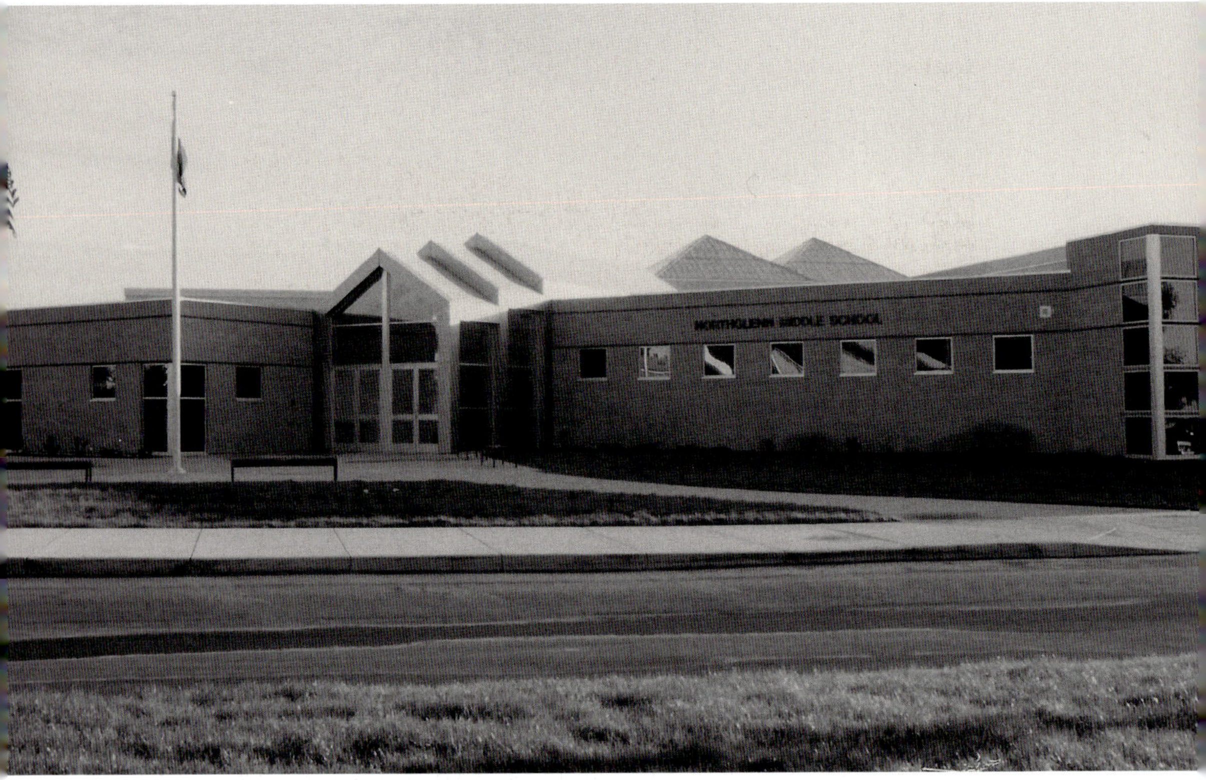

Opening its doors on December 1, 1961, Northglenn Junior High at 1123 Muriel Drive was designed by architects Ditzen, Rowland, Mueller and Associates and constructed by the Robbins Construction Company. The building's 13 classrooms, gymnasium, library, and science laboratory were designed to be home to around 900 seventh- and eighth-grade students. A second wing of classrooms and a shop facility were added in 1963. The school was remodeled in 2007, resulting in the front entrance seen here. (Past image, courtesy of Adams 12 Five Star Schools.)

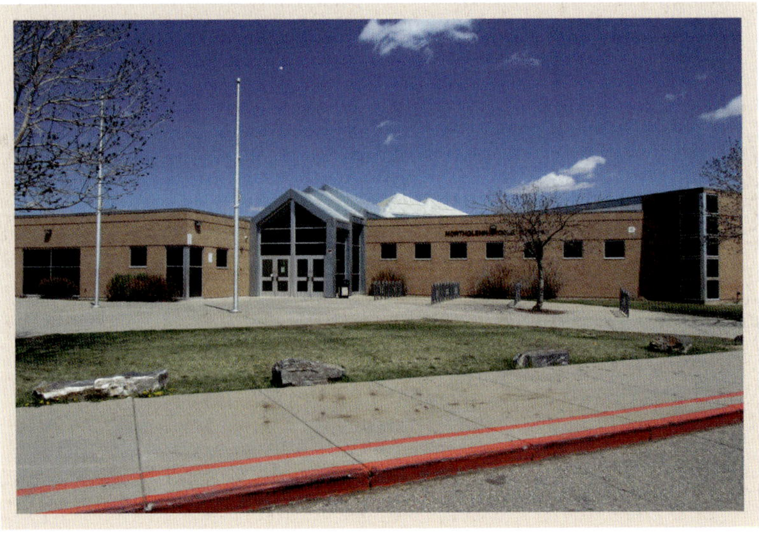

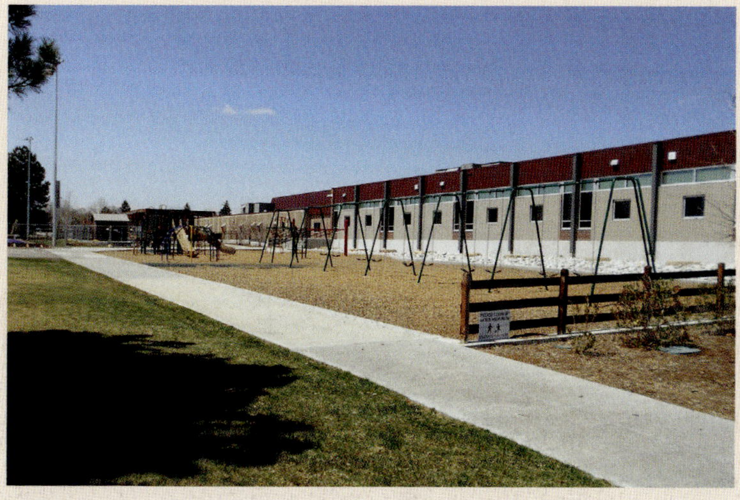

Northeast Junior High, now STEM Lab, opened to students in 1971. Popularly called "Northeast Jail" by decades of students, the school underwent a two-year, partial demolition and reconstruction starting in 2018 to upgrade the aging building. Portions of the original walls can be seen in the center of the present picture. The park adjacent to the school was established as a joint ownership between the Adams 12 School District and the North Glenn Recreation Department. (Past image, courtesy of Northglenn Senior Center.)

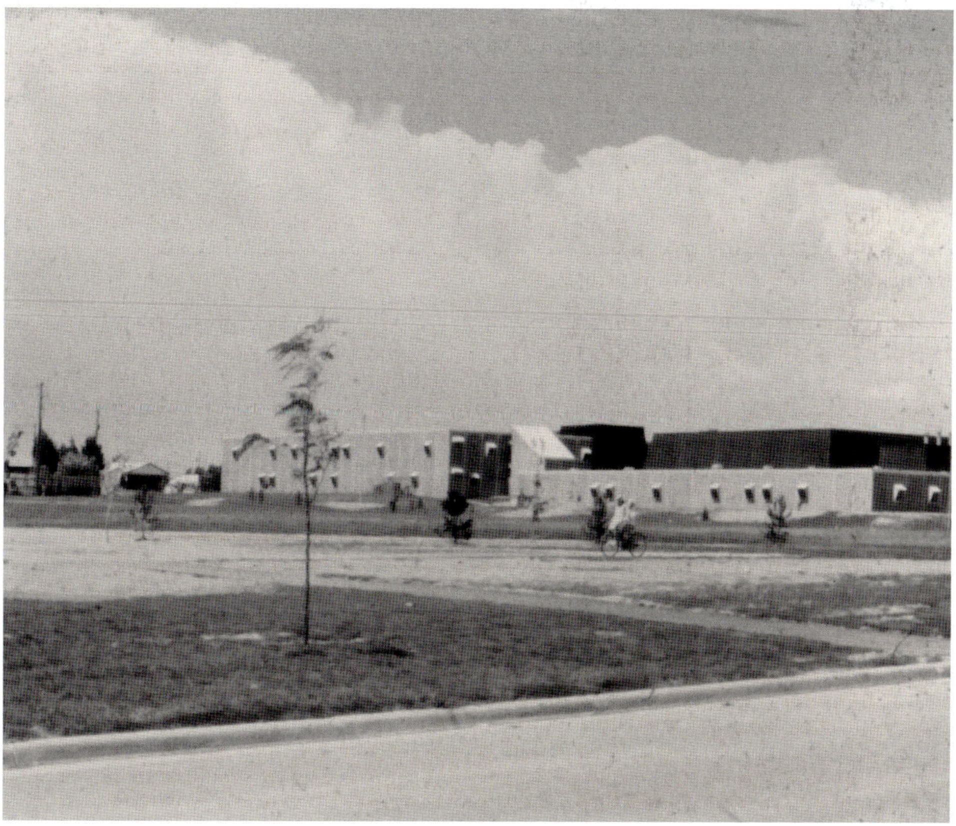

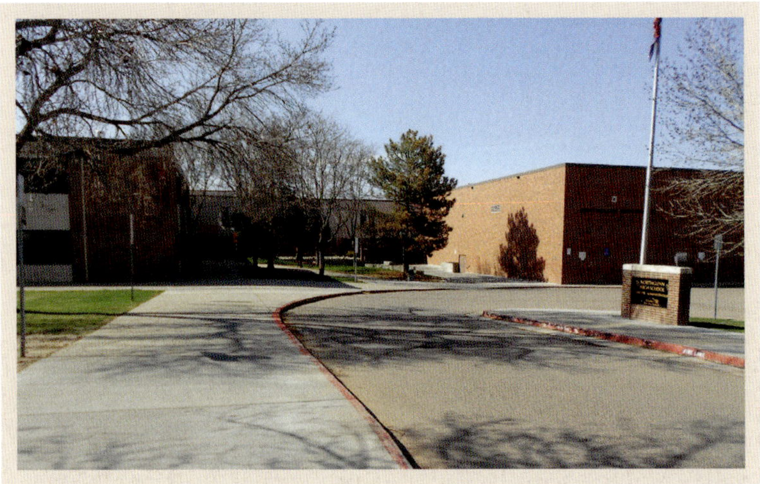

Northglenn High School was built on 32 acres of land donated by Perl-Mack Construction Company. Architects Atchison, Kloverstrom, Saul and Atchison designed the multi-structure complex with the Phase I construction (left side) completed by Cyrus G. DeLano Company of Denver. The first sophomore class occupied the building on August 30, 1965, and together, they selected the red and gold school colors and the Norseman mascot. Further additions to the campus were completed in later years. (Past image, courtesy of Northglenn Senior Center.)

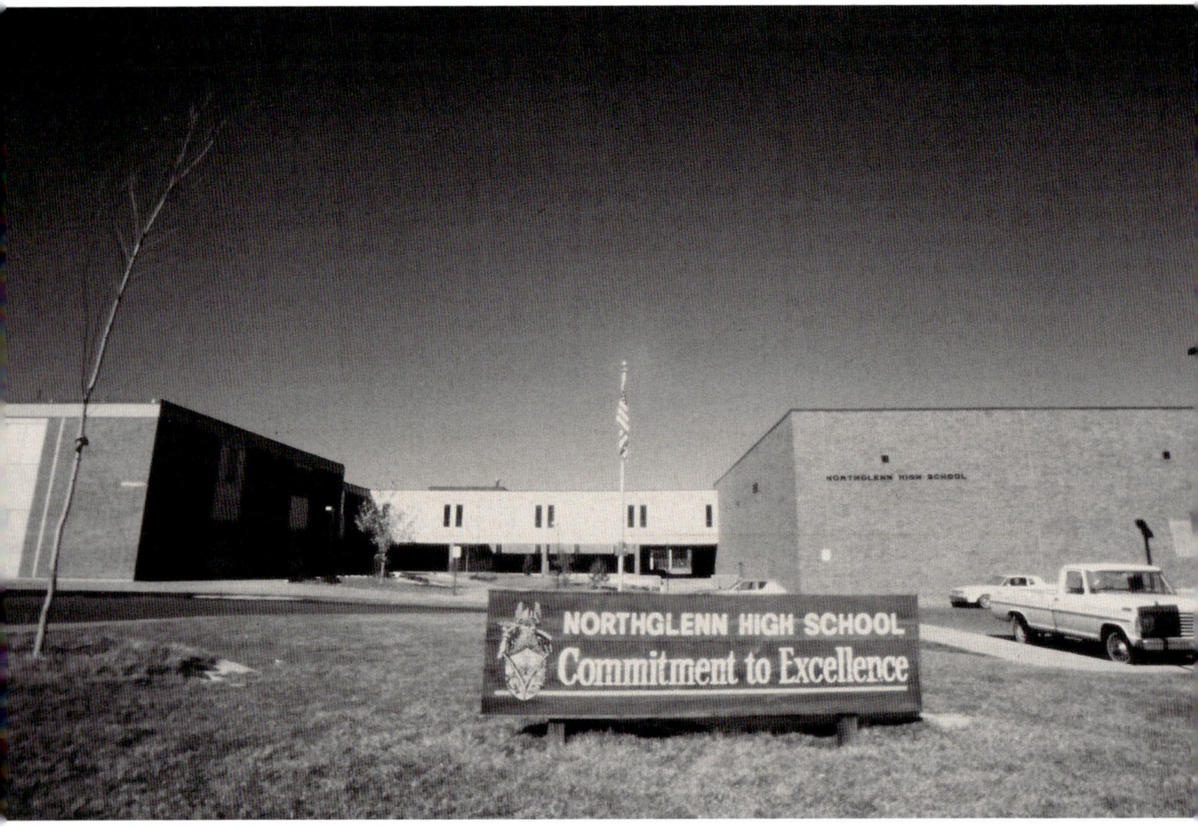

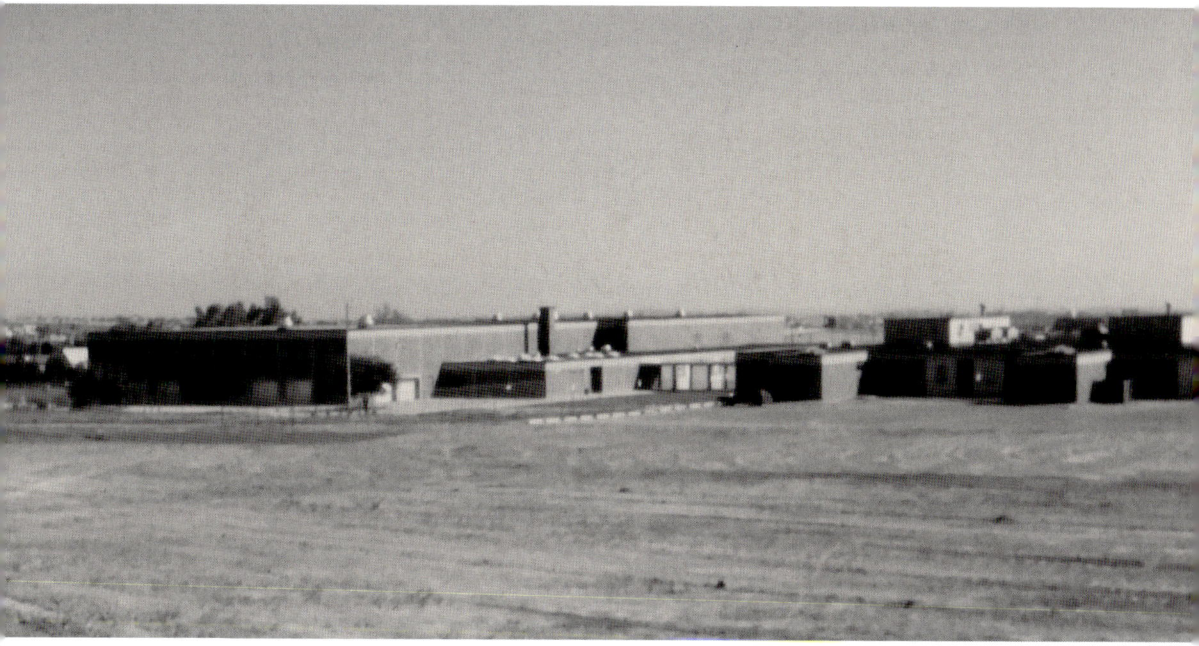

The Northglenn High School natatorium was a joint venture of the North Glenn Recreation District and Adams 12 schools to provide an indoor swimming facility that could be used for the school and city residents. The natatorium was redesigned in 2018 by RBB Architects into a new STEM building for Northglenn High School. The pool was filled with a foam material, with a new concrete floor poured on top, allowing for the space to be divided into labs, studios, and presentation space. (Past image, courtesy of Northglenn Senior Center.)

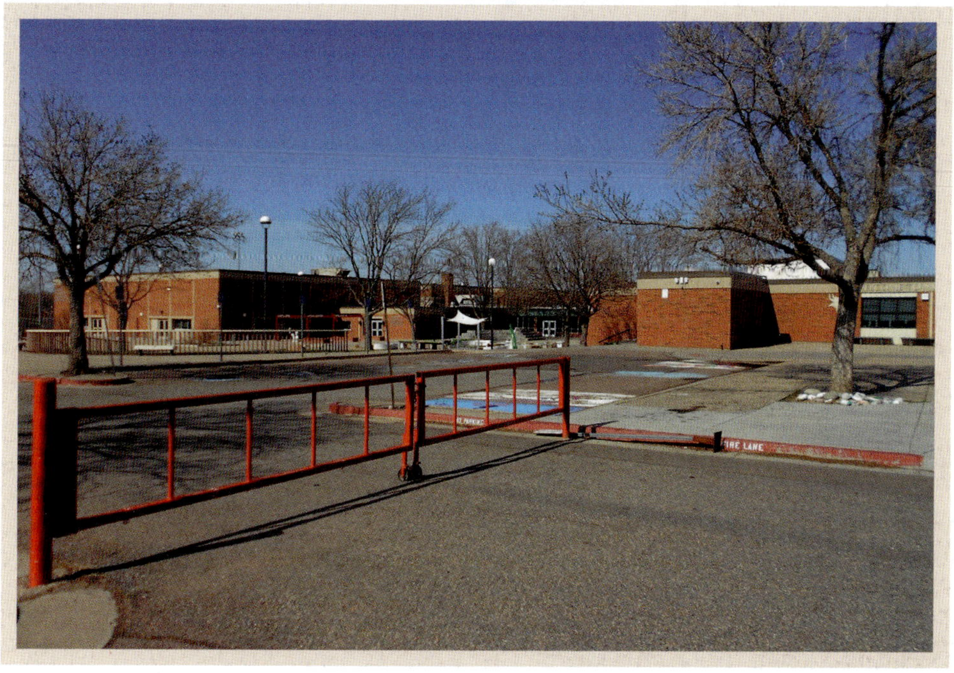

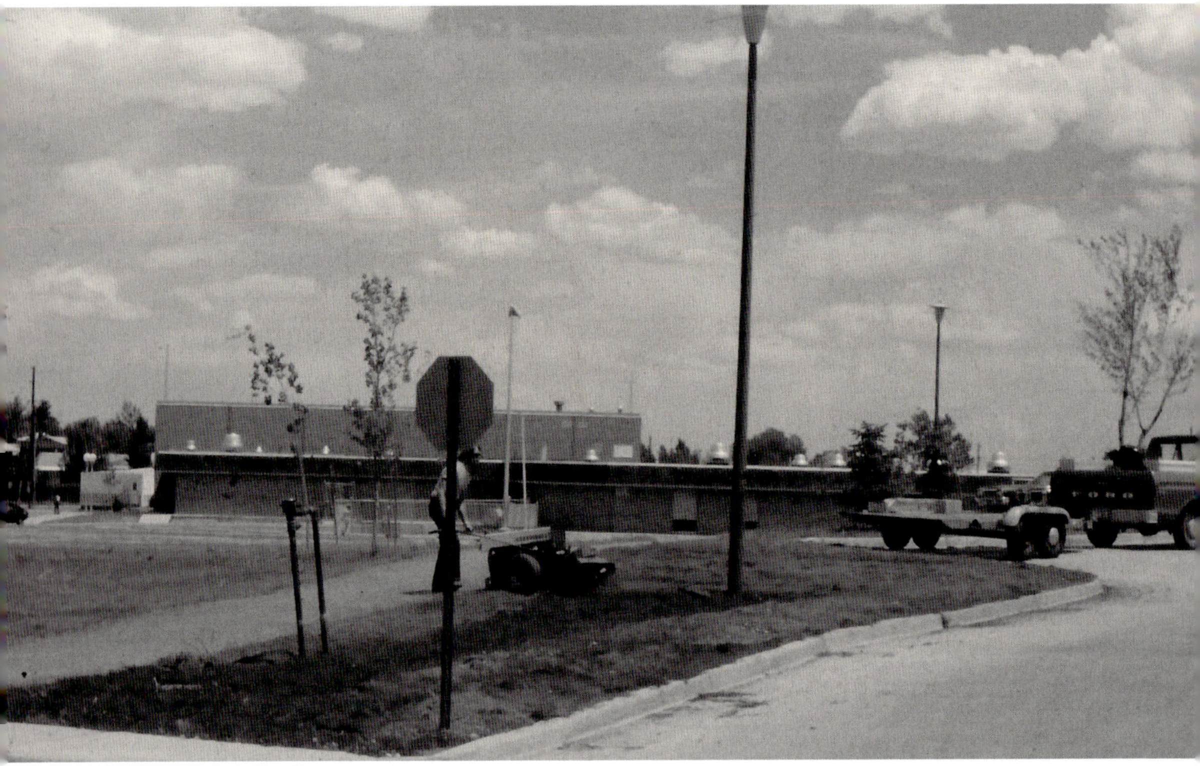

Westview Elementary School at 1284 Roseanna Drive, designed by architects Wheeler and Lewis, was constructed by Hayward Construction Company in 1969. The modern design had classrooms grouped in units of three triads, allowing teachers to have flexible groupings, integrate activities, and share instructional talents. This design also allowed students to have a less-regimented school day and promoted a broadening learning experience. The present view shows a later edition to the west side of the school. (Past image, courtesy of City of Northglenn.)

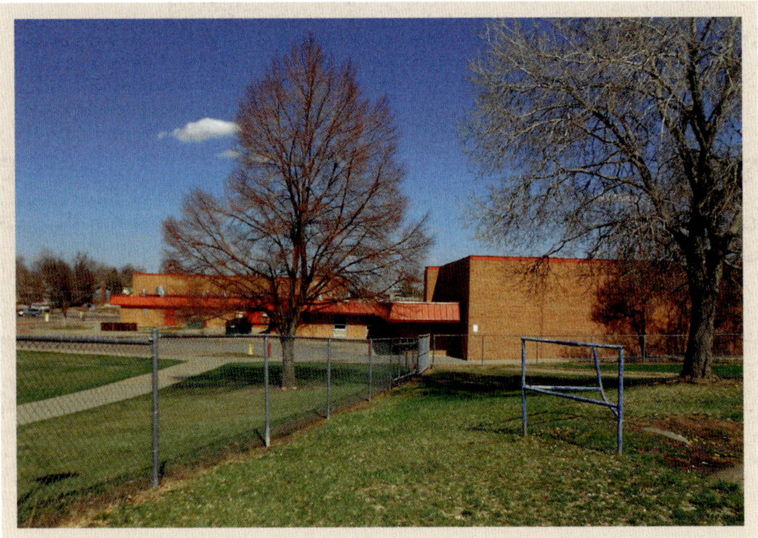

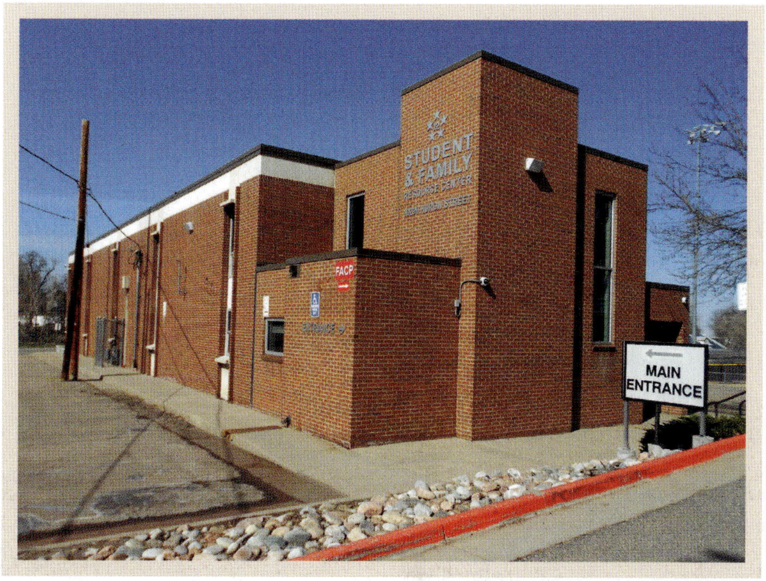

This brick building at 10290 Huron Street has been used for multiple purposes in the Adams District 12 School system. A longtime resident of the building was the School District 12 Credit Union (now Horizons North Credit Union). Located near Northglenn High School, the structure was also used as an administration building and as the district media and federal programs building. It currently is used as the Adams District 12 Student and Family Resource Center. (Past image, courtesy of City of Northglenn.)

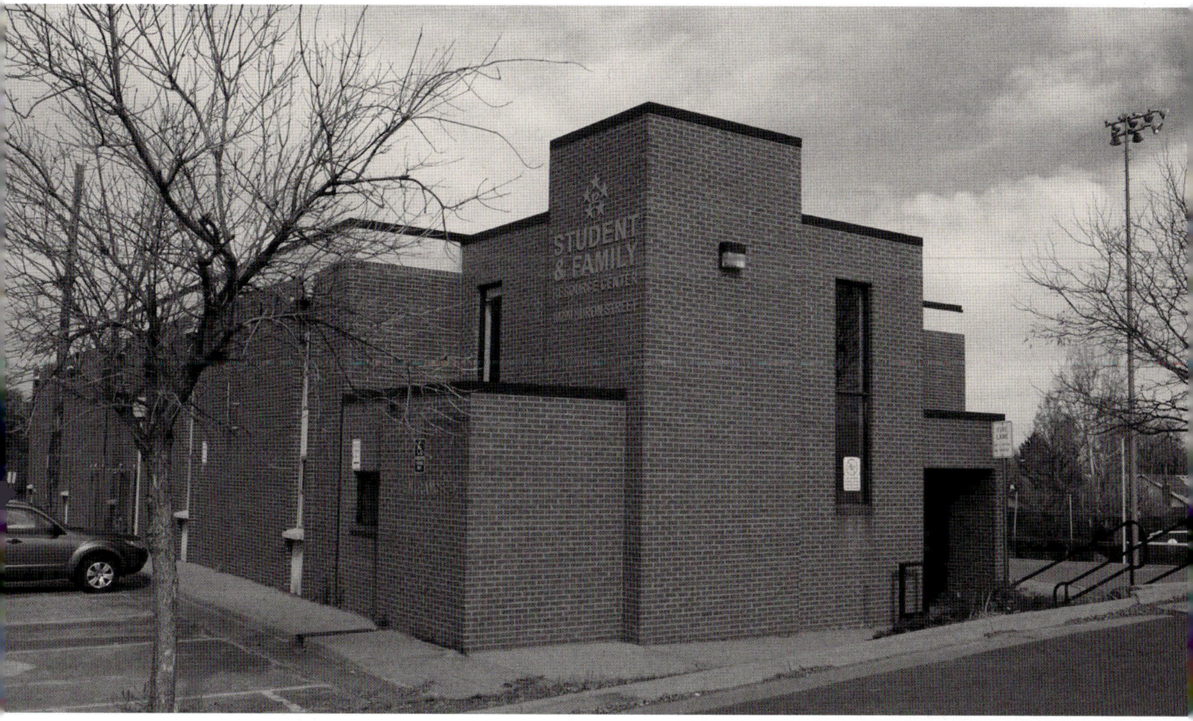

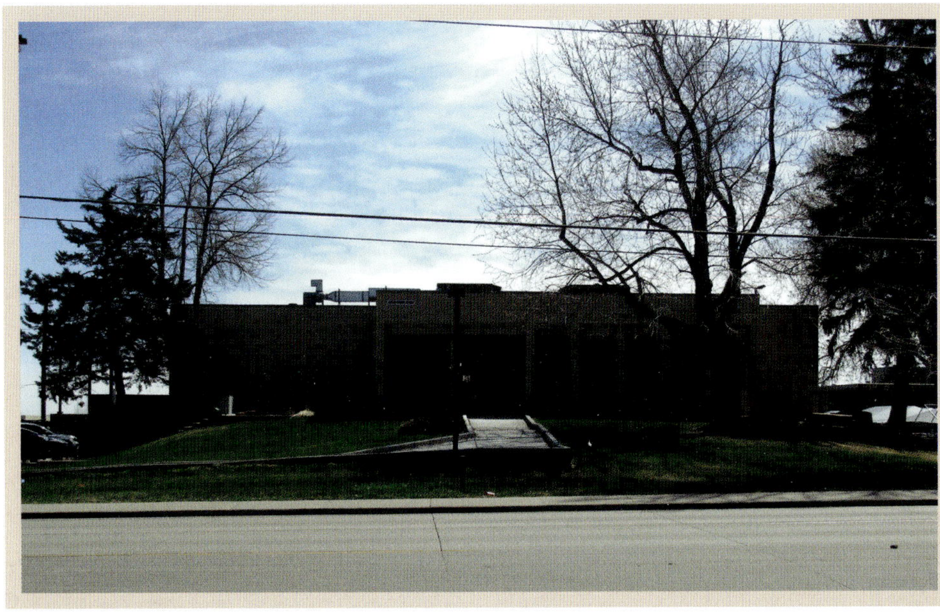

In 1969, the Adams County commissioners asked architect Donald Patton to design a branch library in Northglenn north of 104th Avenue on Huron Street. The two-story, 14,100-square-foot building constructed of beige brick was built on land donated to Adams County by Perl-Mack Industries. Members of the Northglenn Jaycees assisted in collecting thousands of books to stock the shelves. Adams County eventually closed this branch, and the building is now in use as Anythink Libraries' Internal Support Services. (Past image, courtesy of City of Northglenn.)

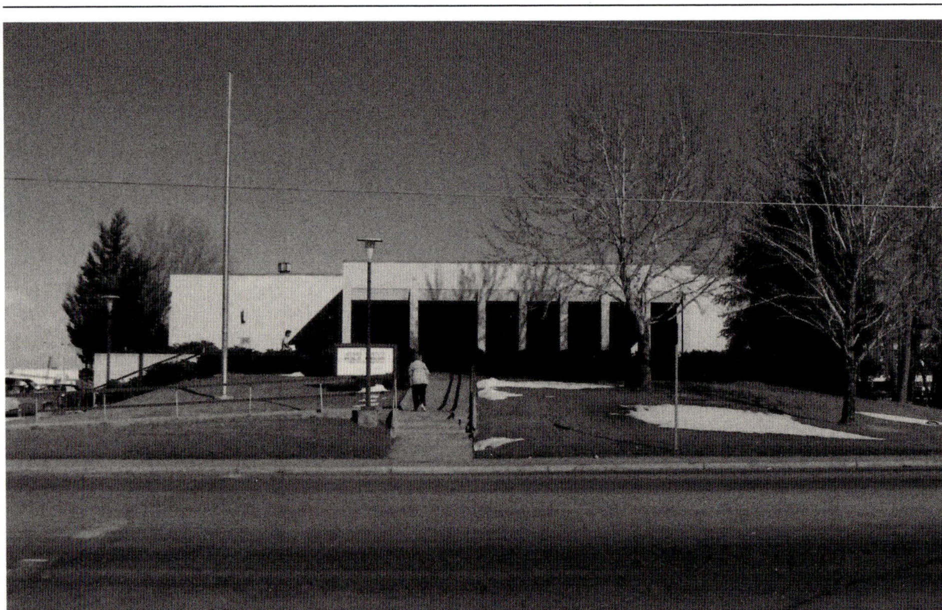

CHAPTER 3

Residences

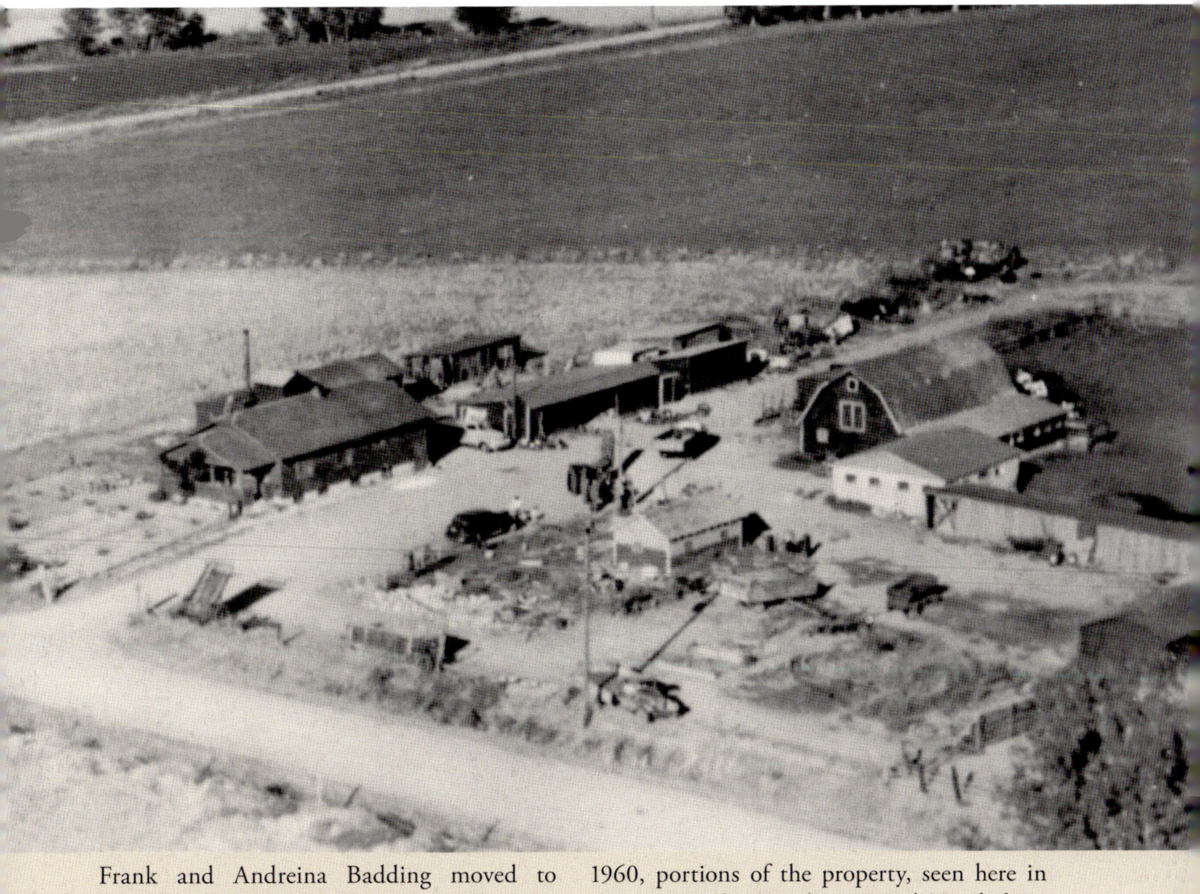

Frank and Andreina Badding moved to property starting on the corner of 104th Avenue and Huron Street in 1931, operating the Badding Dairy until 1946. Selling his route in 1946, Badding continued to sell raw milk to the Sunset Dairy in Denver. When Badding sold his property to Perl-Mack in 1960, portions of the property, seen here in about 1950, became houses and Northglenn High School. In this image, the farmhouse is facing a dirt Huron Street (left) with 104th Avenue to the north. (Courtesy of Caron Horner.)

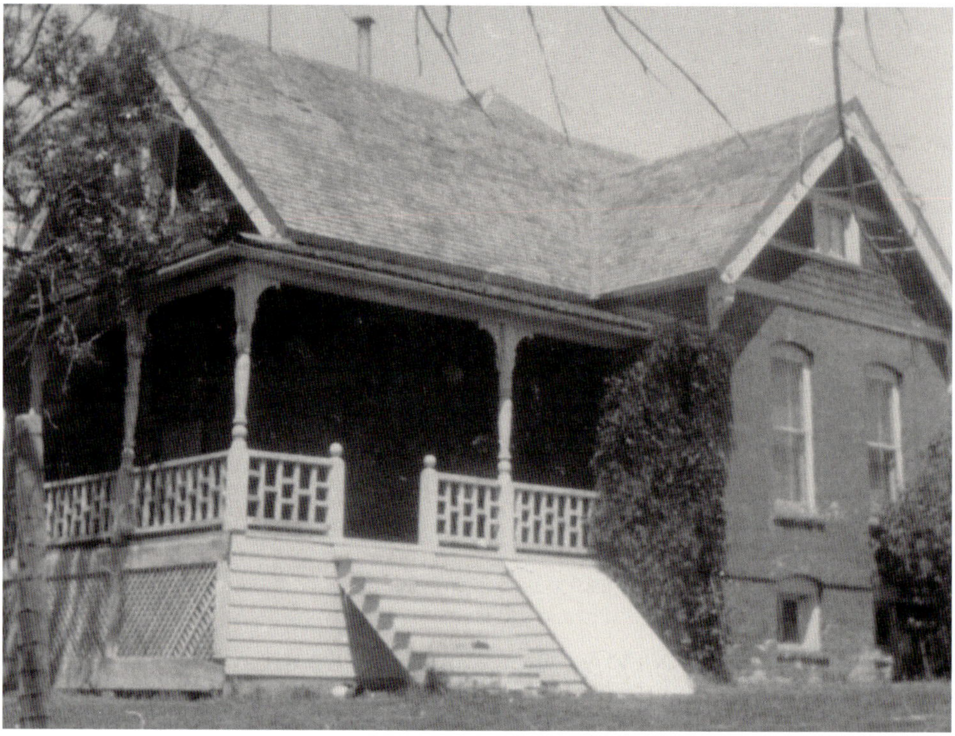

Built around 1903 by John Thede, this brick, Queen Anne–style farmhouse is the oldest standing structure in Northglenn. Multiple families resided in this house, farming the surrounding 160 acres prior to the North Glenn Recreation District purchasing it in 1973 with plans for ballfields, a golf course, and a park. The farmhouse was preserved and listed in the National Register of Historic Places in 1998. The Northglenn Historic Preservation Commission continues to oversee use of the building and the remaining 9.9-acre Stonehocker Park. (Past image, courtesy of Northglenn Historic Preservation Commission.)

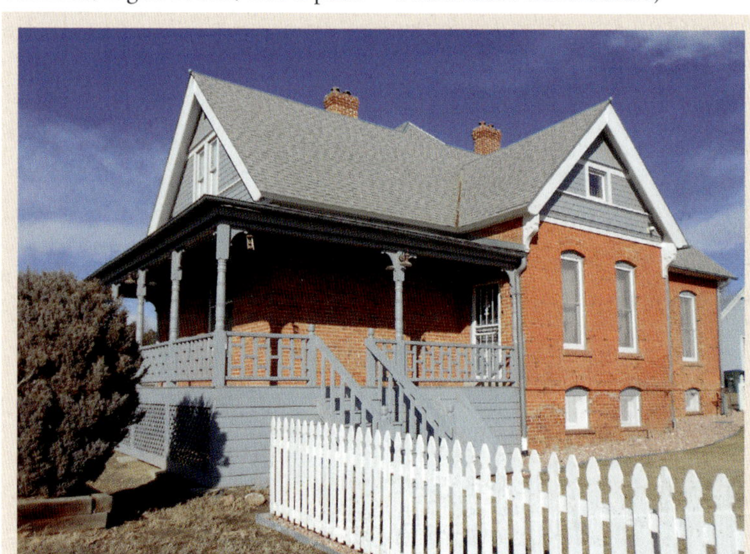

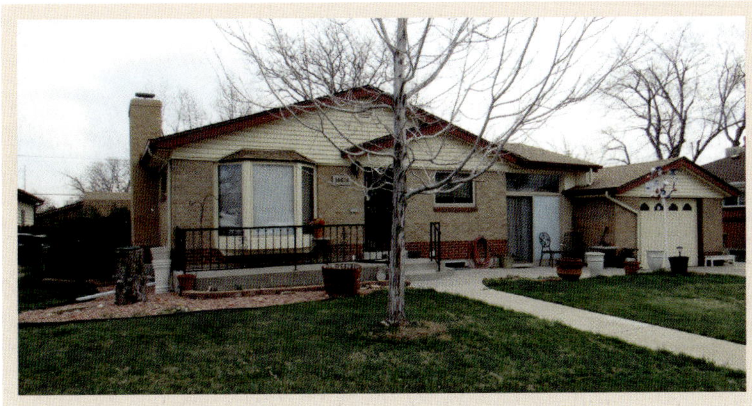

Robert and Dolores Gallegos were driving along 104th Avenue when they spotted the Perl-Mack model homes on Grant Street. The Gallegos family liked the area and having a view of the mountains when they selected the Alpine model house where they raised a son and daughter. This image of Dolores and her son Robert Jr. was taken after the foundation on Northglenn Drive was laid in 1959. The fields behind them filled in with houses and the Garland Shopping Center. (Past image, courtesy of Gallegos family and City of Northglenn.)

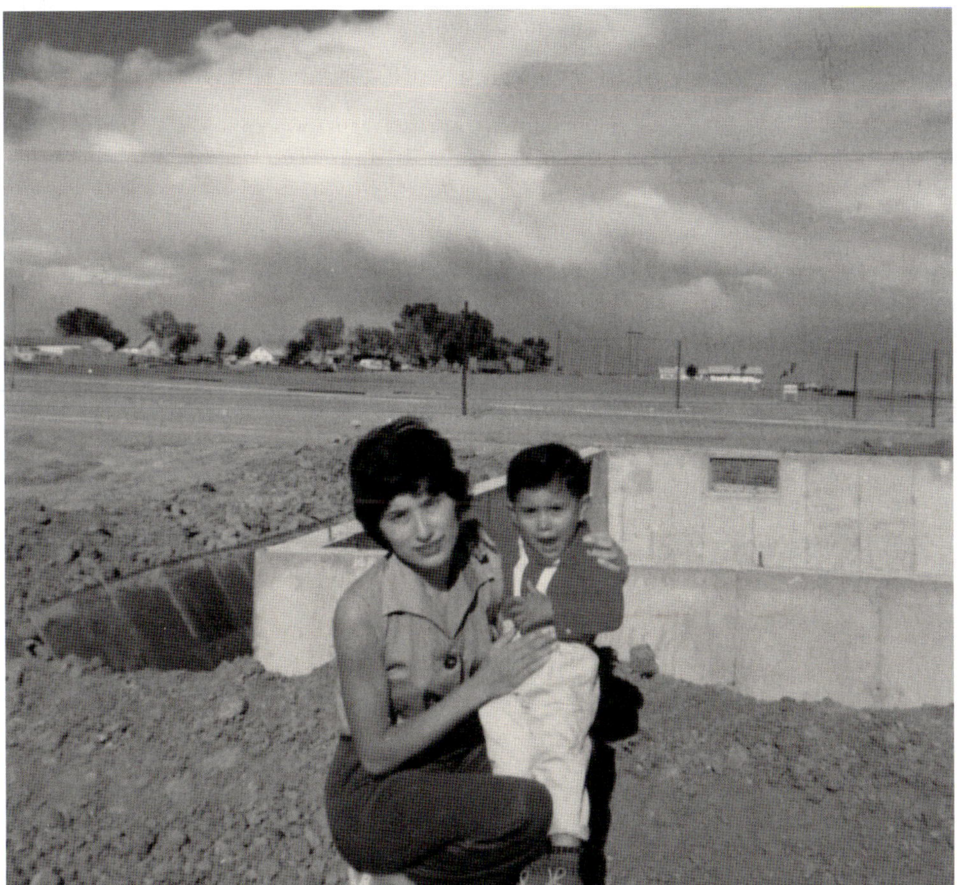

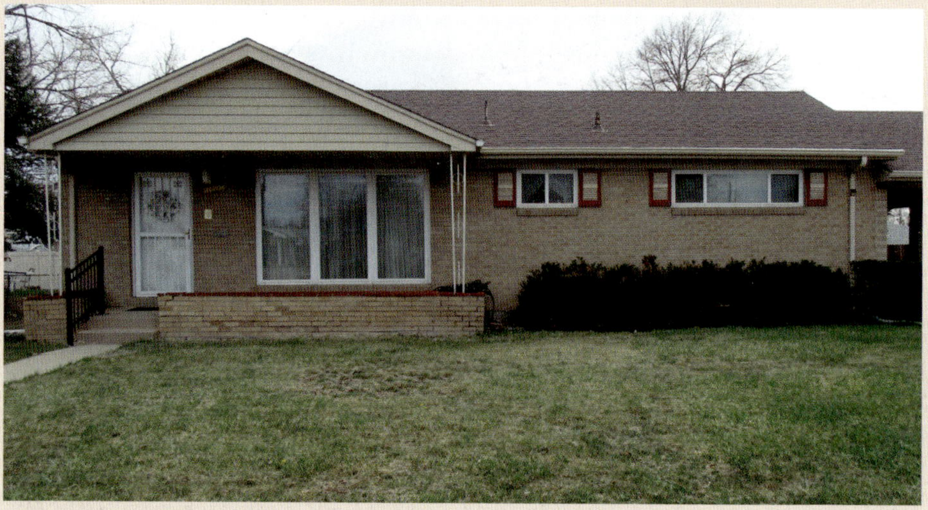

Betty Painter helped her husband, Doyle, pick out this Perl-Mack Summit model home at 10708 Northglenn Drive when they moved to Northglenn in 1968. The ranch-style house was built in 1959. Betty was a substitute teacher in Adams 12 School District for one year. She has been working at First Southern Baptist Church in Northglenn for the last 53 years and still lives in this house. (Past image, courtesy of Betty Painter.)

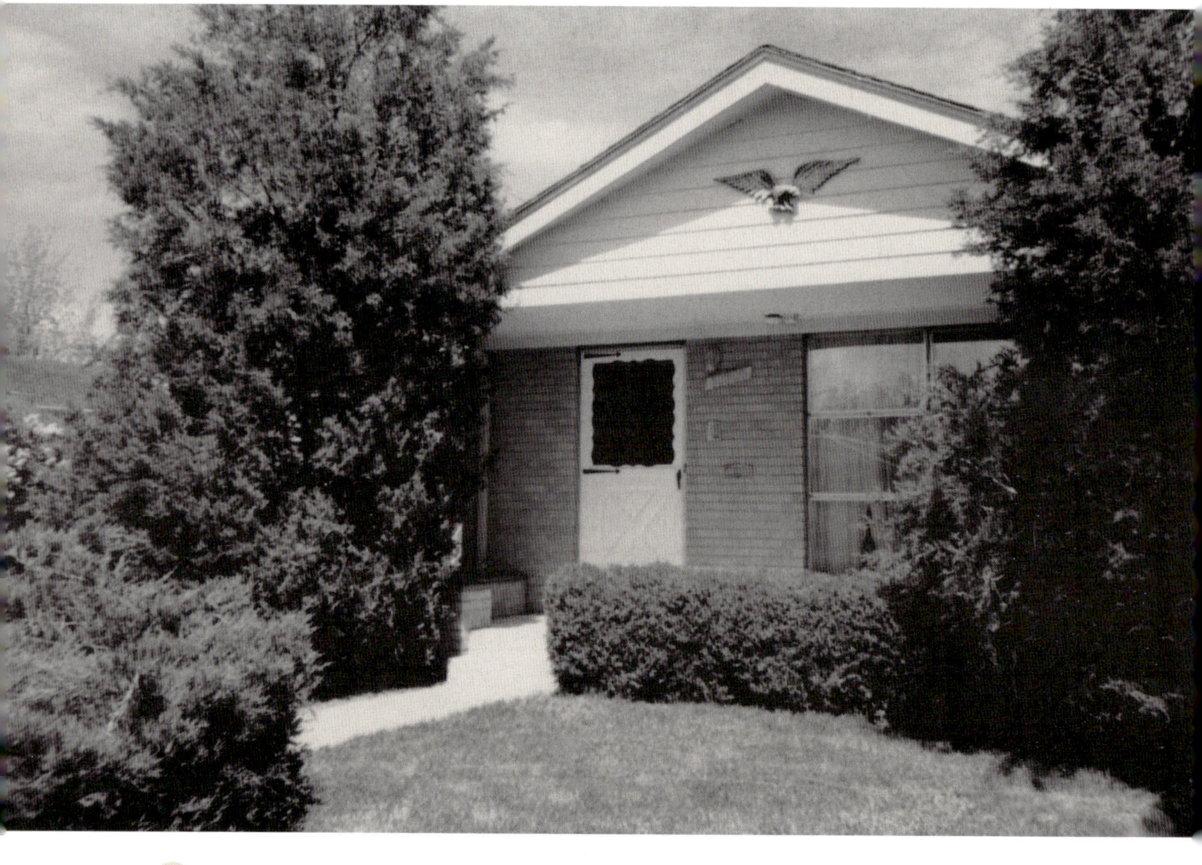

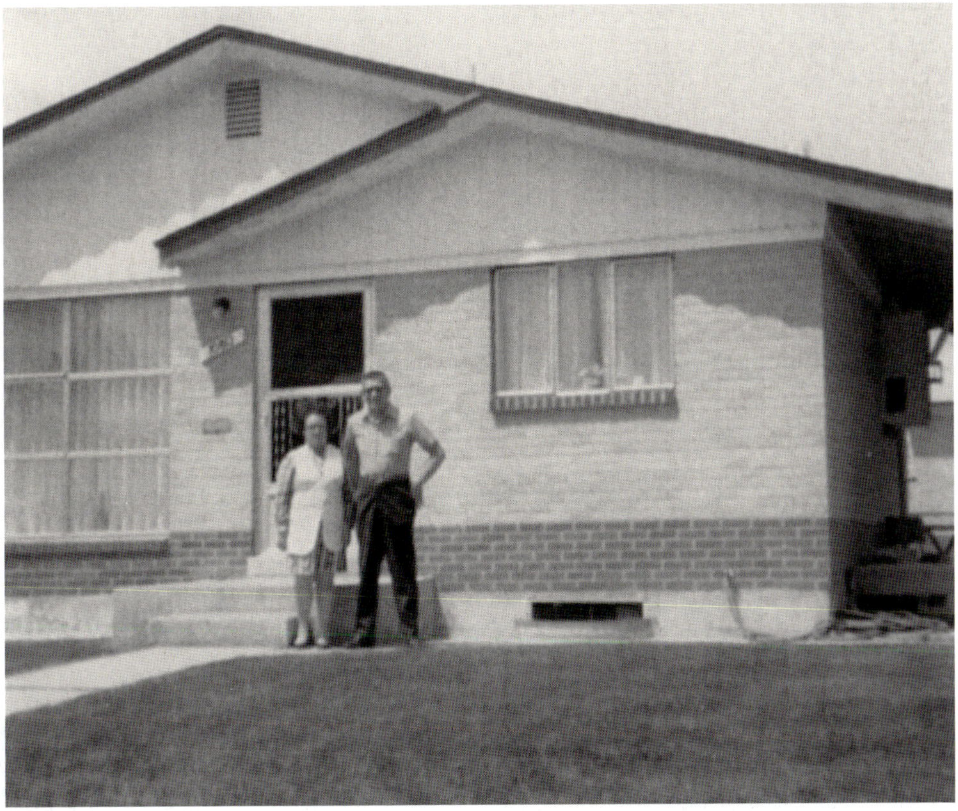

Leroy and Ruth Meier, seen here in front of their home at 10813 Larson Drive, were familiar with Perl-Mack homes prior to purchasing theirs. Appreciating the good lots at reasonable prices, the Meiers chose a corner lot near the farmhouse once owned by the Larson family. Together with their children, they moved into this ranch home on September 3, 1961, during an early fall snowstorm. The family still owns the house and remains one of the few original families on Larson Drive. (Past image, courtesy of Meier family and City of Northglenn.)

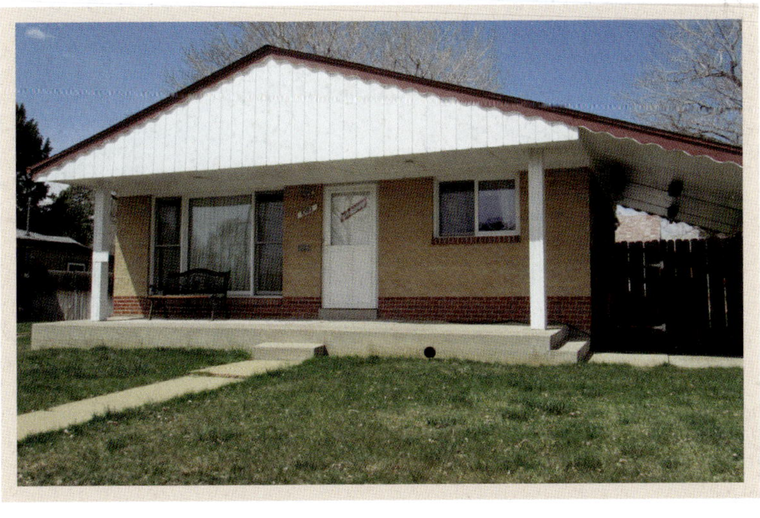

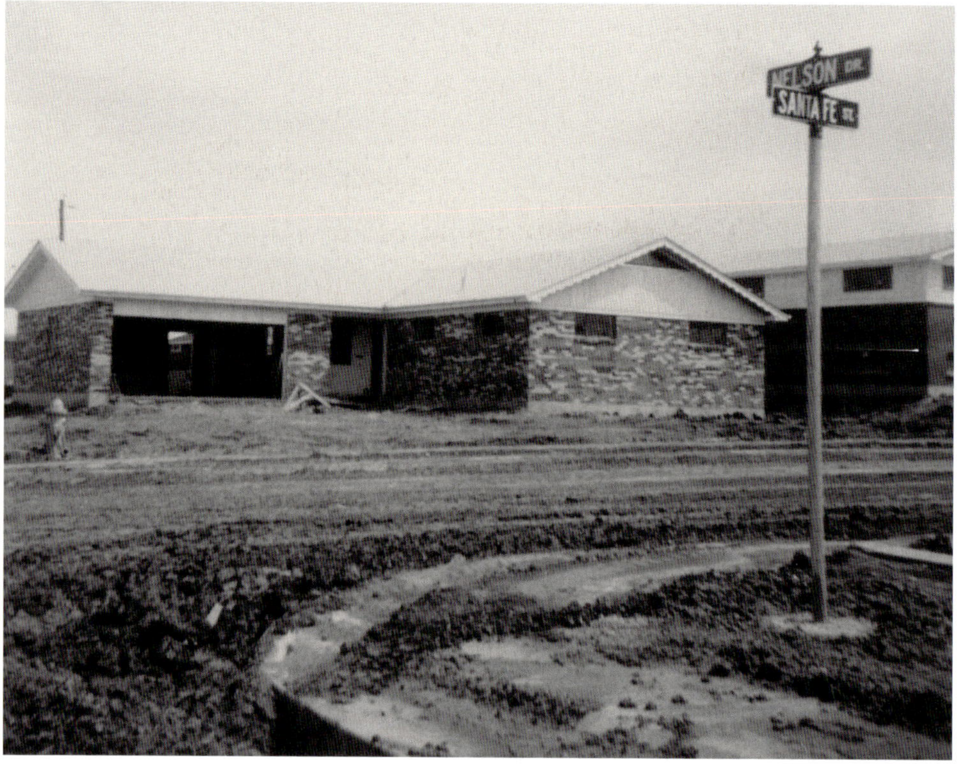

This Perl-Mack Elmwood model featured brick construction with steel I-beams. According to the sales brochure, the amenities included a large living room, three bedrooms, two bathrooms, and a deluxe kitchen. Richard Frear, a longtime art teacher in the Mapleton School District, moved into this home on 10542 Santa Fe Street with his wife and son in July 1961. The extension of the garage alters the overall look of the house. (Past image, courtesy of City of Northglenn.)

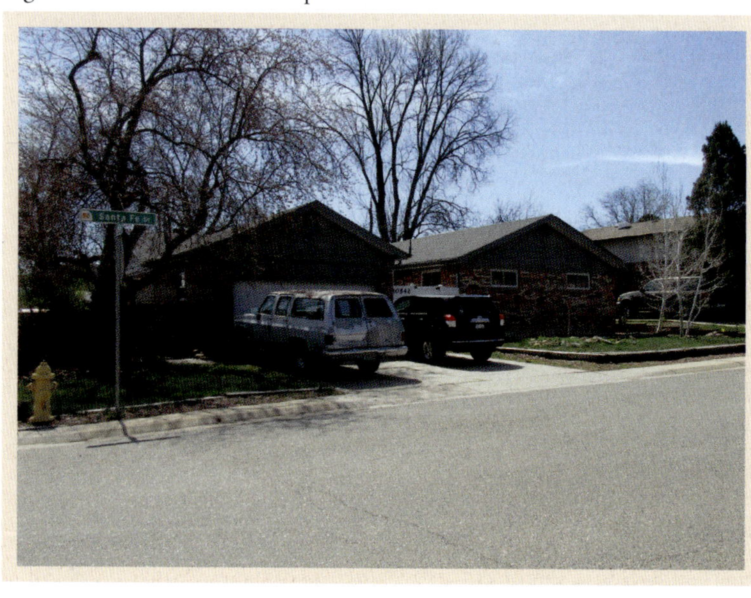

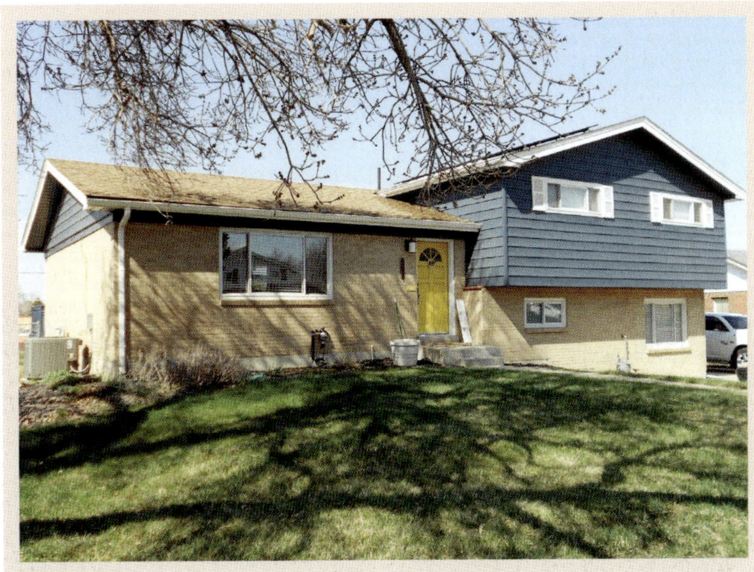

Rev. William and Betty Youngblood and their children moved into the Northglenn United Methodist Church's parsonage on November 23, 1962. Betty Youngblood recounted that vandals had damaged the house at 1481 West 106th Avenue prior to their arrival, and broken glass and mud covered the floors. The church held its first service in the living room of the parsonage on December 2, 1962. The church sold the house in 1971, opting instead to give pastors money for housing as part of their salary. (Past image, courtesy of Northglenn United Methodist Church.)

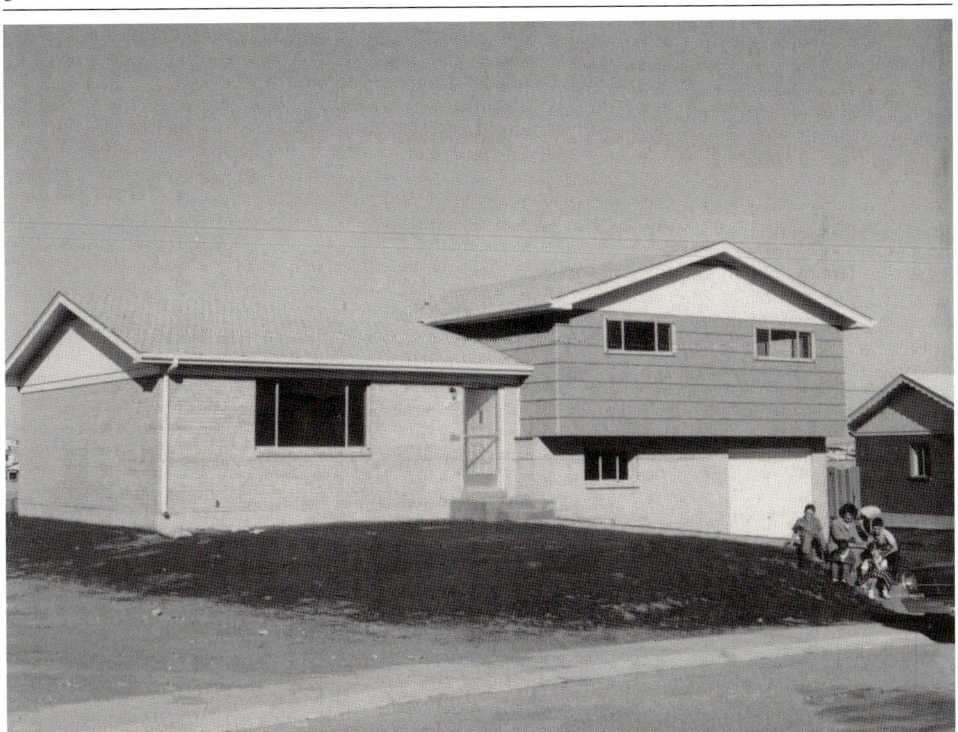

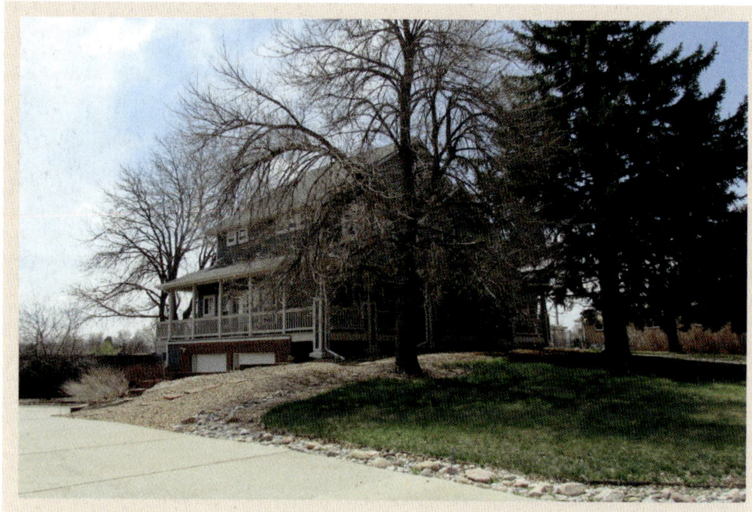

Prior to Northglenn's incorporation, recreation activities in the city were provided by the North Glenn Recreation District. Responsible for overseeing all sports activities and the development of the city park system, the Recreation District used this house at 1710 Leroy Drive constructed in 1964 as an administration building. Today, the house looks nothing like the original brick structure since it was remodeled as Northglenn's Urban Renewal Authority's example of how to adapt a Perl-Mack ranch home. (Past image, courtesy of City of Northglenn.)

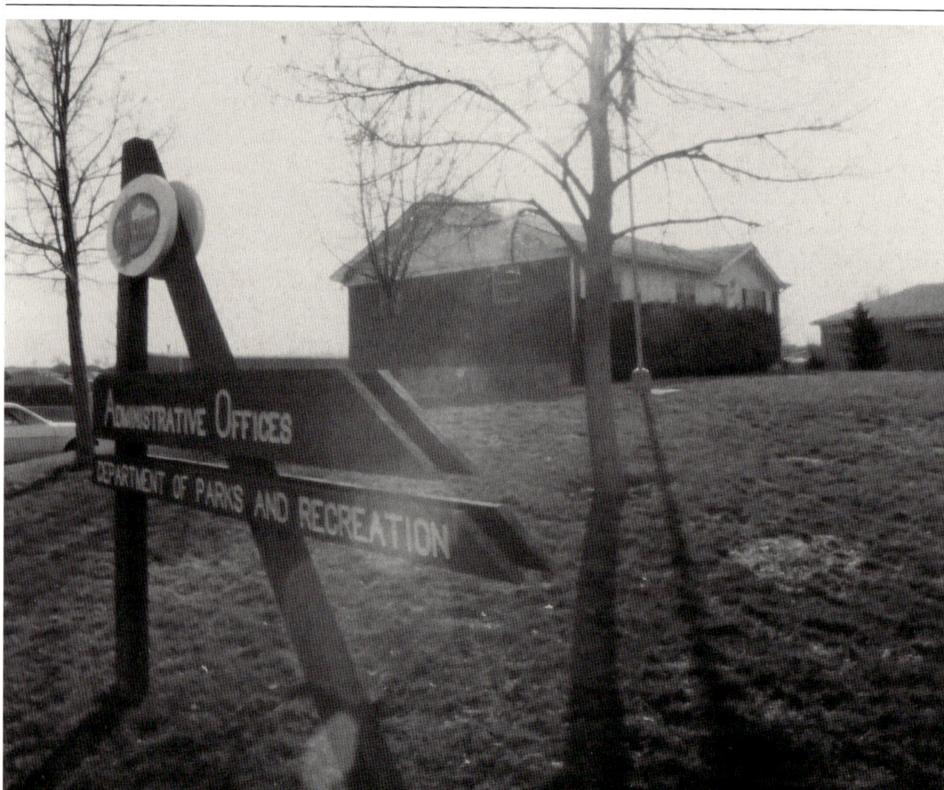

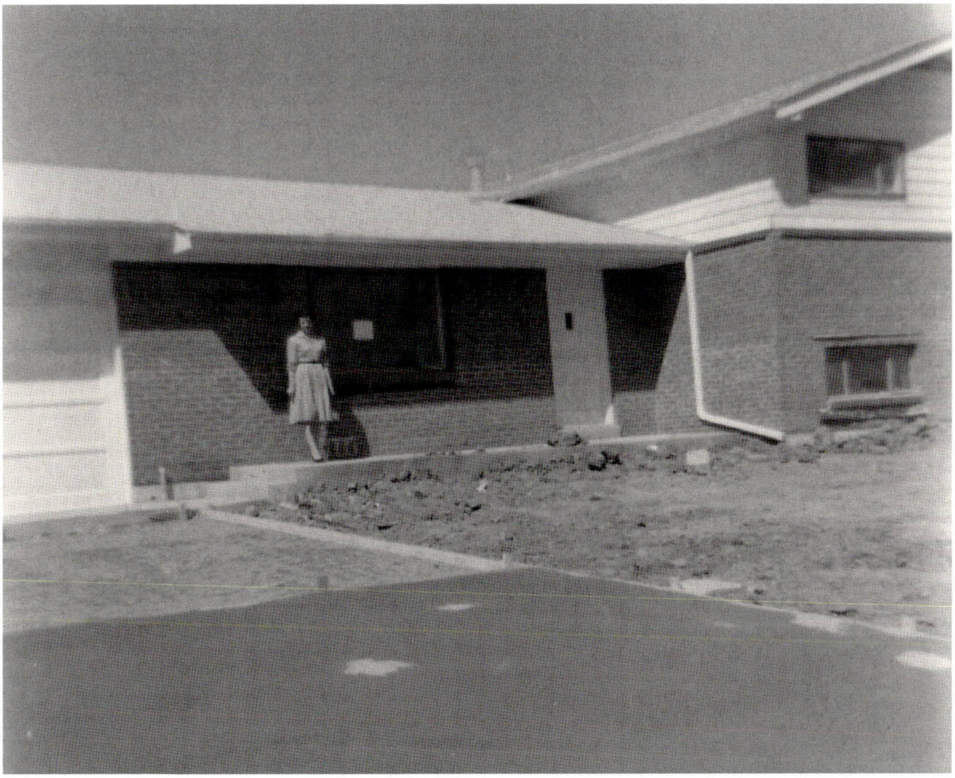

Lillian Frey stands by the front window of this trilevel house at 10517 Lipan Street just prior to her family moving in on October 15, 1961. The Frey family made many memories in this home, including watching additional homes in the neighborhood be built, constructing a covered patio on the back of their house, and digging out during the 1982 blizzard. Vegetation now partially obscures the house. (Past image, courtesy of Lillian Frey.)

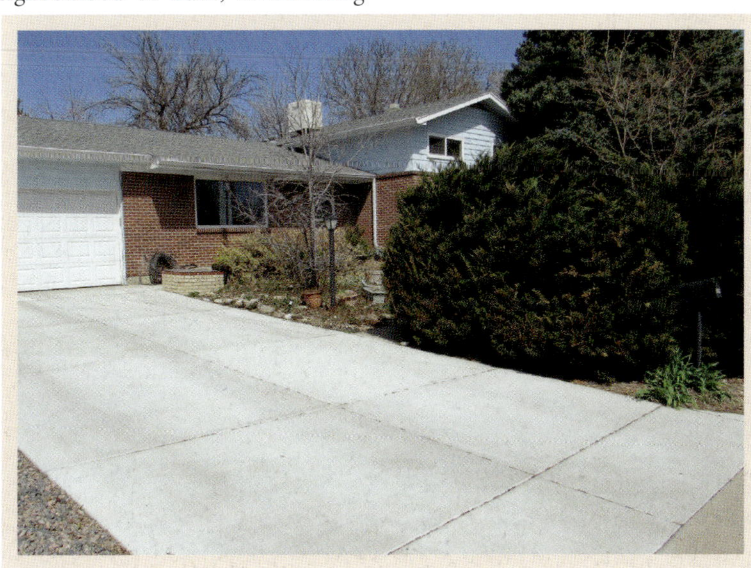

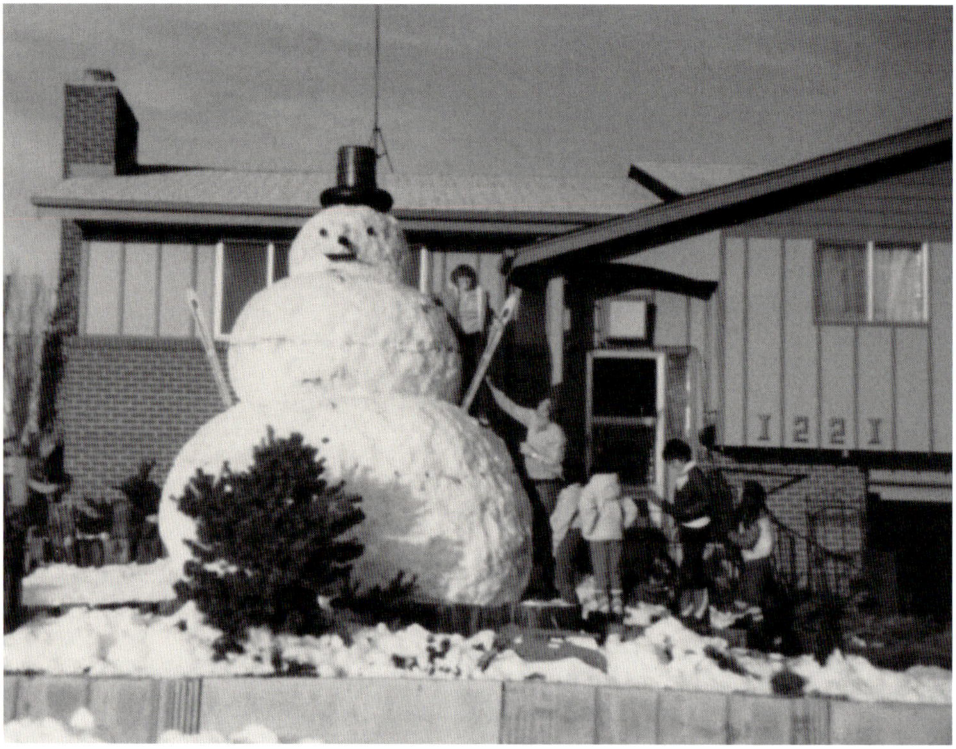

Bernd Hegel bought this Heftler Hillcrest bilevel house in 1972. One of the early residents on his street, Hegel watched the cities of Northglenn and Thornton grow around him. In 1982, a snowstorm during his children's winter break encouraged the family to go outside; together with neighborhood children, they built a snowman as tall as the house. In addition to planting the sapling trees, now taller than the house, Hegel built an awning above the front door and an addition on the back of the house. (Past image, courtesy of Bernd Hegel.)

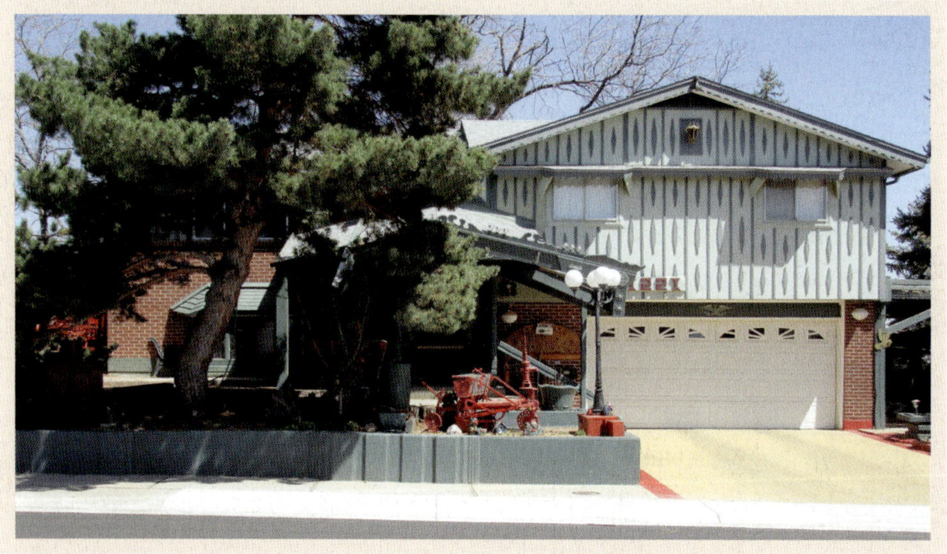

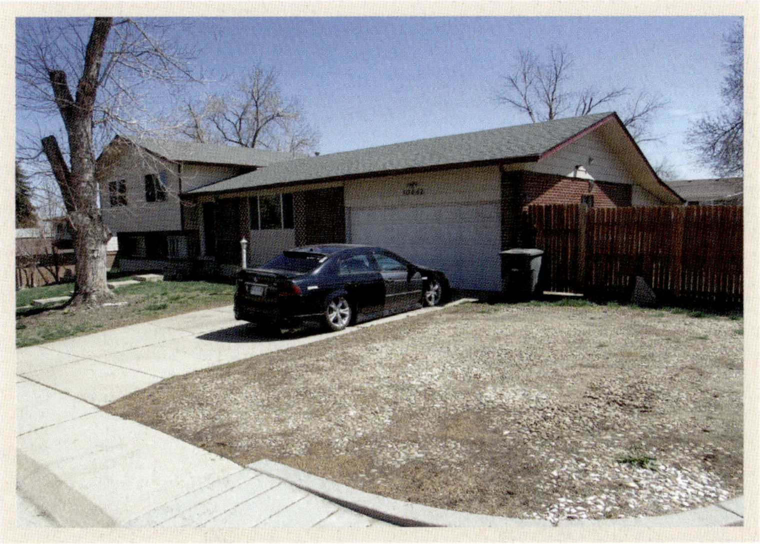

This trilevel Perl-Mack Bedford model house at 10442 Sperry Street was built in 1968 and is seen here in 1980 when Jane and Del Viers lived in the home. Both Jane and Del worked for Adams 12 schools, including some in Northglenn. At one point, the Viers family invited an executive for the auto dealerships on 104th Avenue to their home for dinner so they could see how bright the dealership lights were shining in the neighborhood. (Past image, courtesy of Jane Viers.)

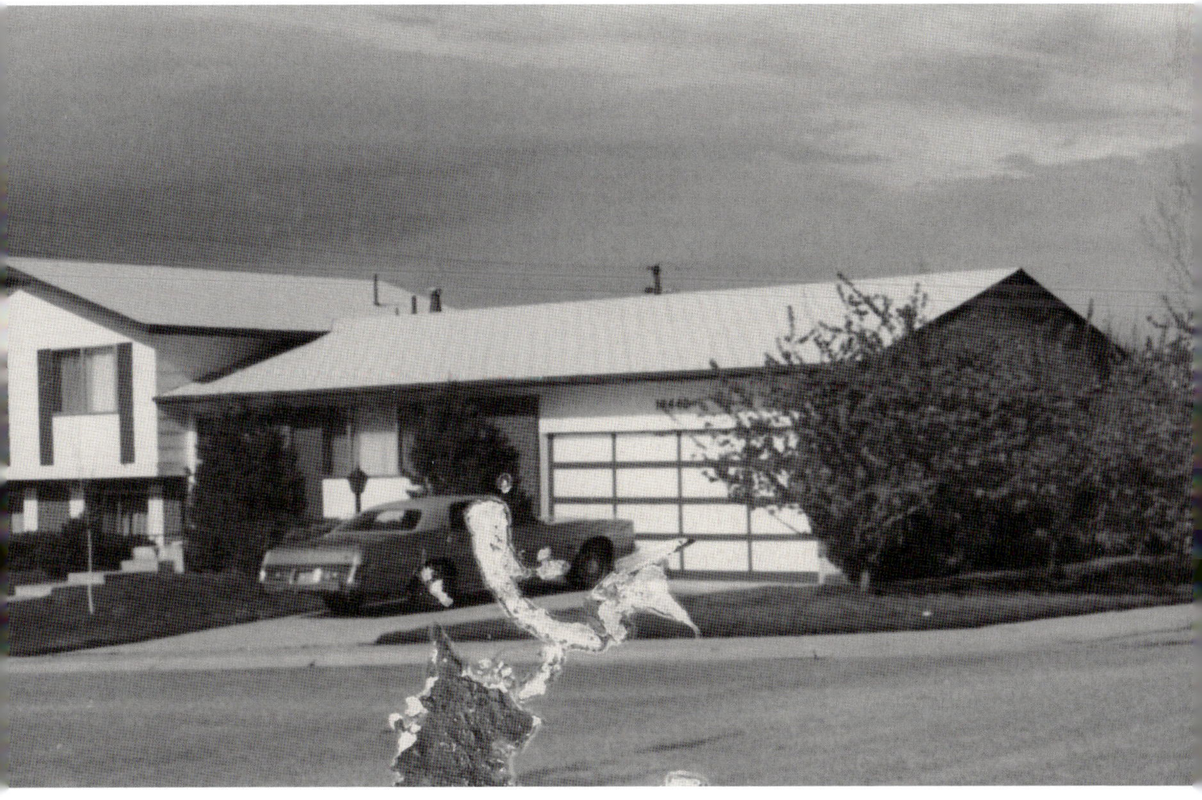

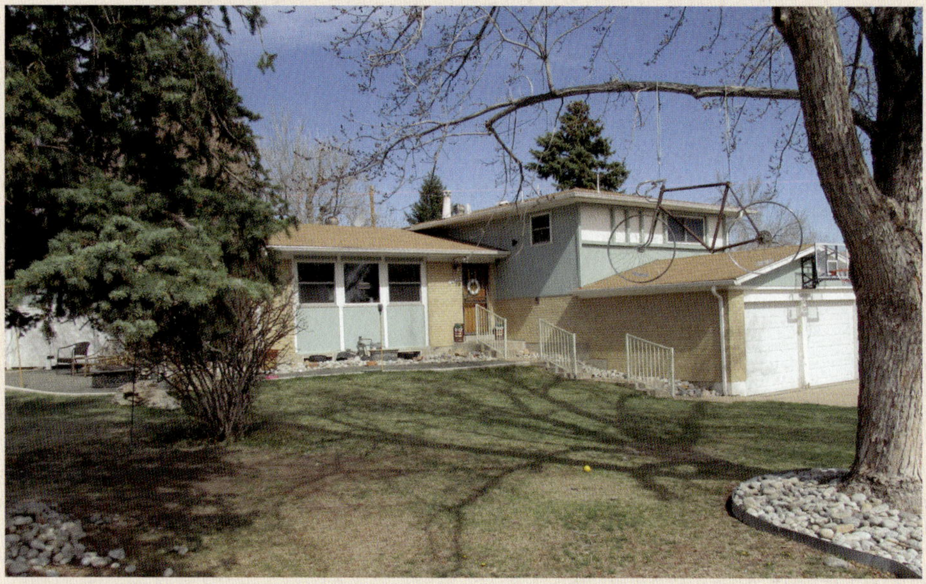

Very few changes have been made to this Perl-Mack Sherborn model, split-level house at 10609 Quivas Street. Mary Ann and Charles Bulis moved into the house in January 1968. The brochure listed amenities including four bedrooms, a two-car garage, acoustically sprayed ceilings, and aluminum windows. The neighborhood was still growing and neither the nearby Westview Recreation Center nor Westview Elementary had been built yet. (Past image, courtesy of Mary Ann Bulis and the Northglenn Senior Center)

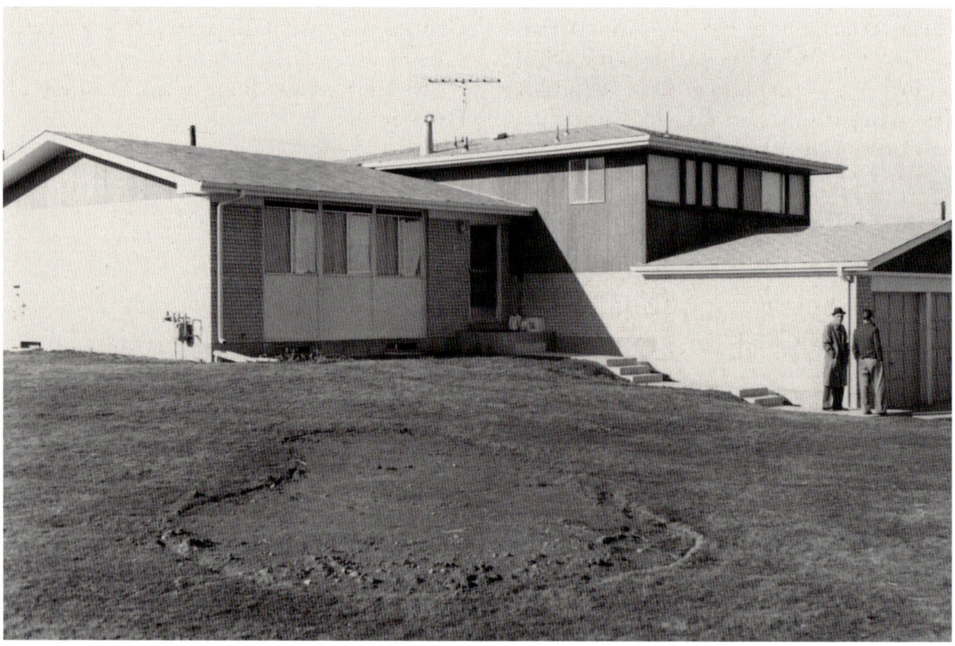

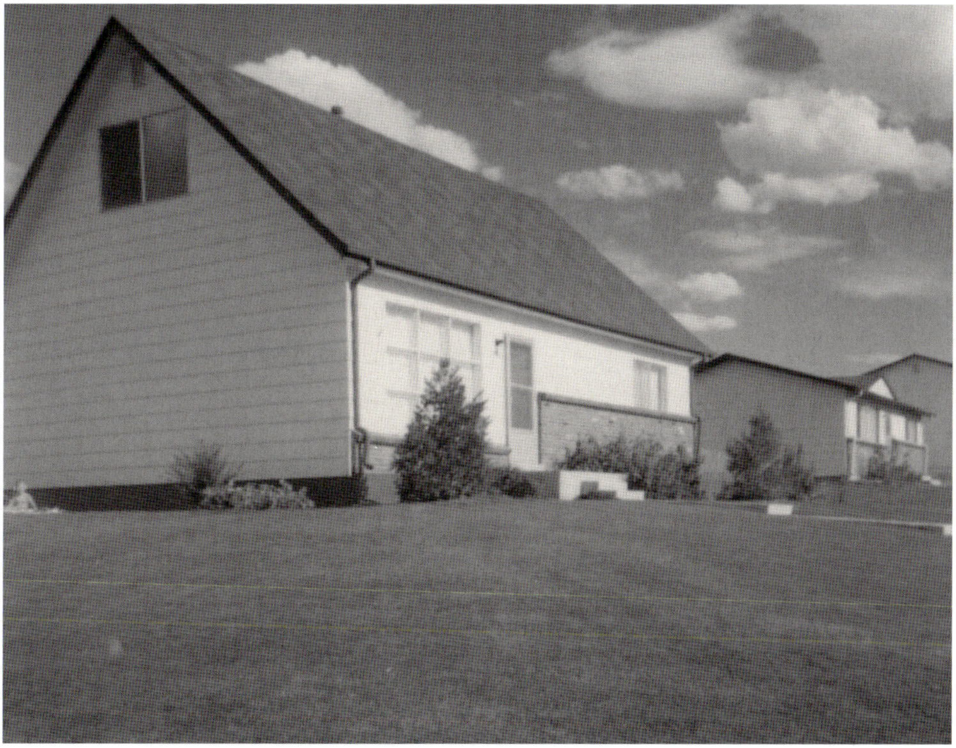

In 1968, Phil and Elaine Carney moved into this home on Melody Drive built by B&B Home Builders Inc. in the Huron Heights subdivision. Phil Carney completed all the landscaping for the lot, in addition to finishing the basement and attic. An addition was built on the left side of the house to give more room for their three sons and one daughter. Phil Carney served on the Northglenn City Council and the Northglenn Urban Renewal Authority. Trees mostly obscure the view of the house today. (Past image, courtesy of Phil Carney.)

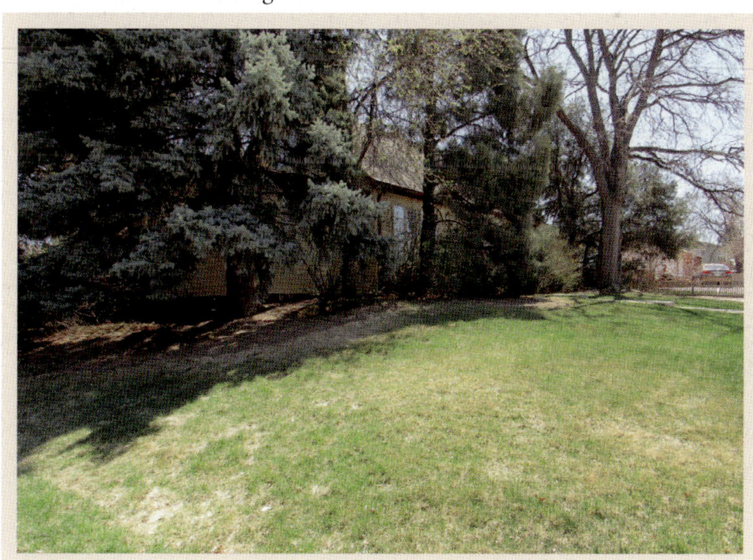

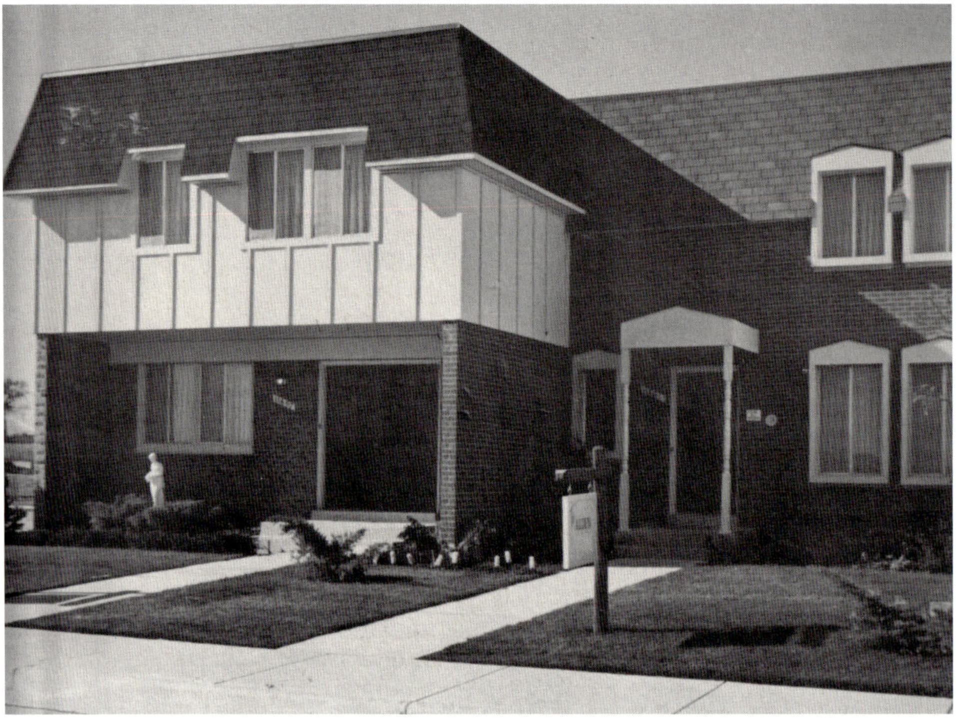

Perl-Mack entered the townhouse market with the construction of Meadowlake Village Townhomes, now Village Greens, including these models near 117th Avenue and Washington Street. All were built with eight inches of masonry to guarantee soundproofing and privacy from neighbors. The two-, three-, and four-bedroom townhomes were marketed as "living in a park" not only for the proximity to Webster Lake, but also for the multiple village parks distributed between house groupings. (Past image, courtesy of City of Northglenn.)

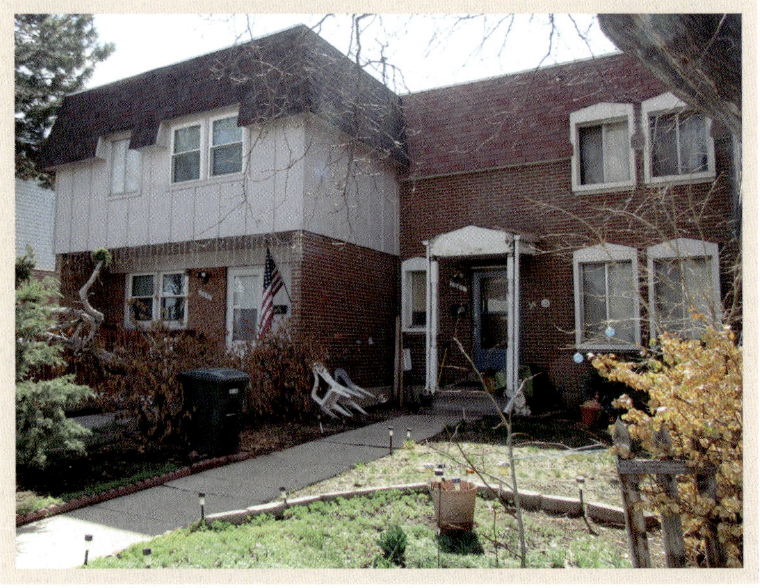

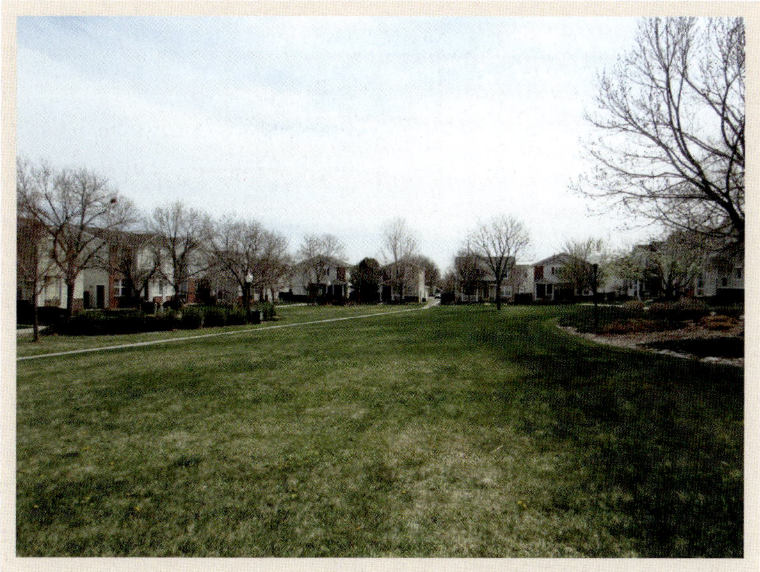

In the late 1990s, Signature Fox Run LLC designed a newly planned community of homes, trails, and parks to be developed on approximately 250 acres, partly on what once was the Stonehocker Property. Partnering with PrideMark Homes, construction began with families in mind. Pictured here are two-story homes built in 2000 in the Kimblewyck Village area of Fox Run. (Past image, courtesy of City of Northglenn.)

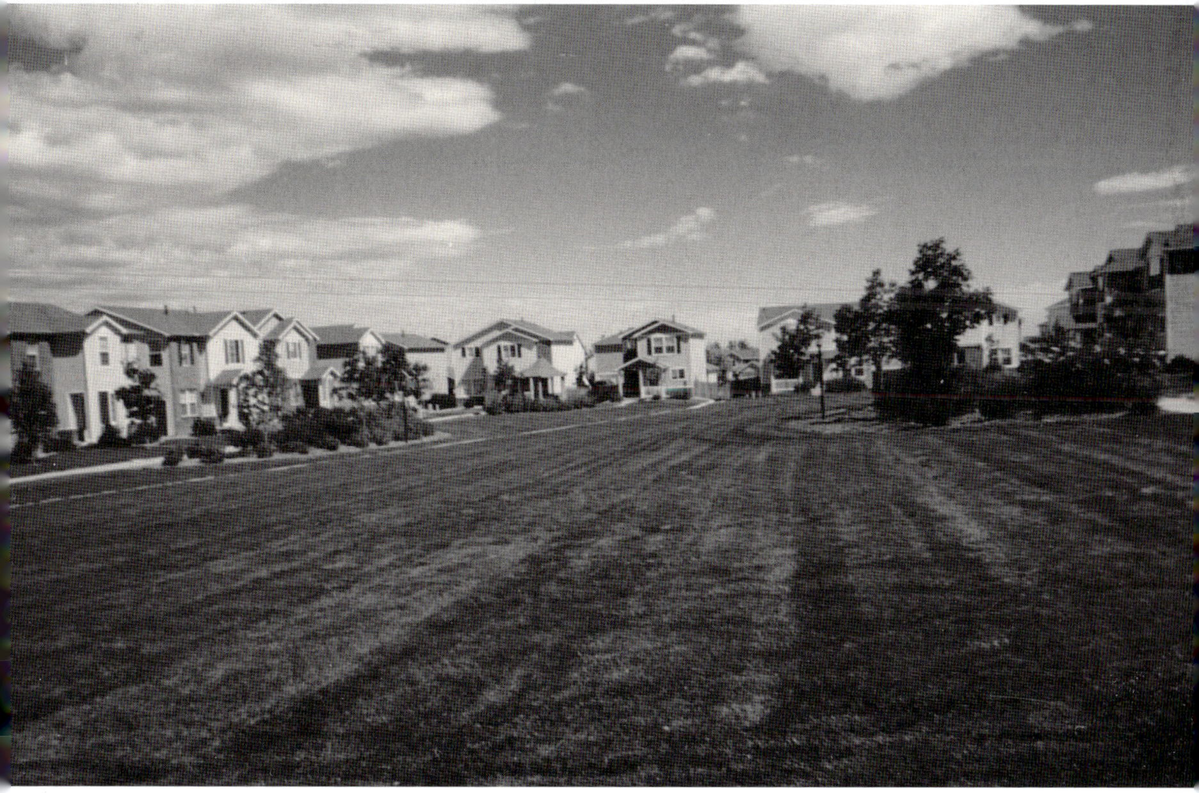

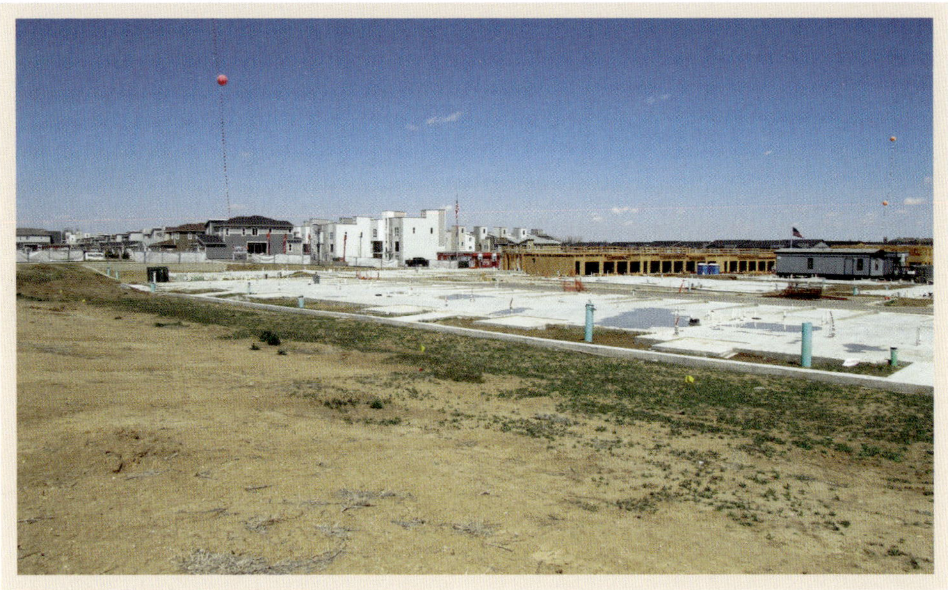

Bud and Fern Hinkhouse operated Karl's Farm Dairy starting in 1947, their home tucked amongst the trees at the back of their property. Annexed to Northglenn in 1971, visitors were once able to see cows grazing in the pasture. In 2016, the city partnered with the family creating a master plan designed to promote the redevelopment of the property while respecting the heritage of the land. In 2022, KF Developers in conjunction with Richmond American Homes and Meritage Homes began construction on single-family and multi-unit housing. (Past image, courtesy of City of Northglenn.)

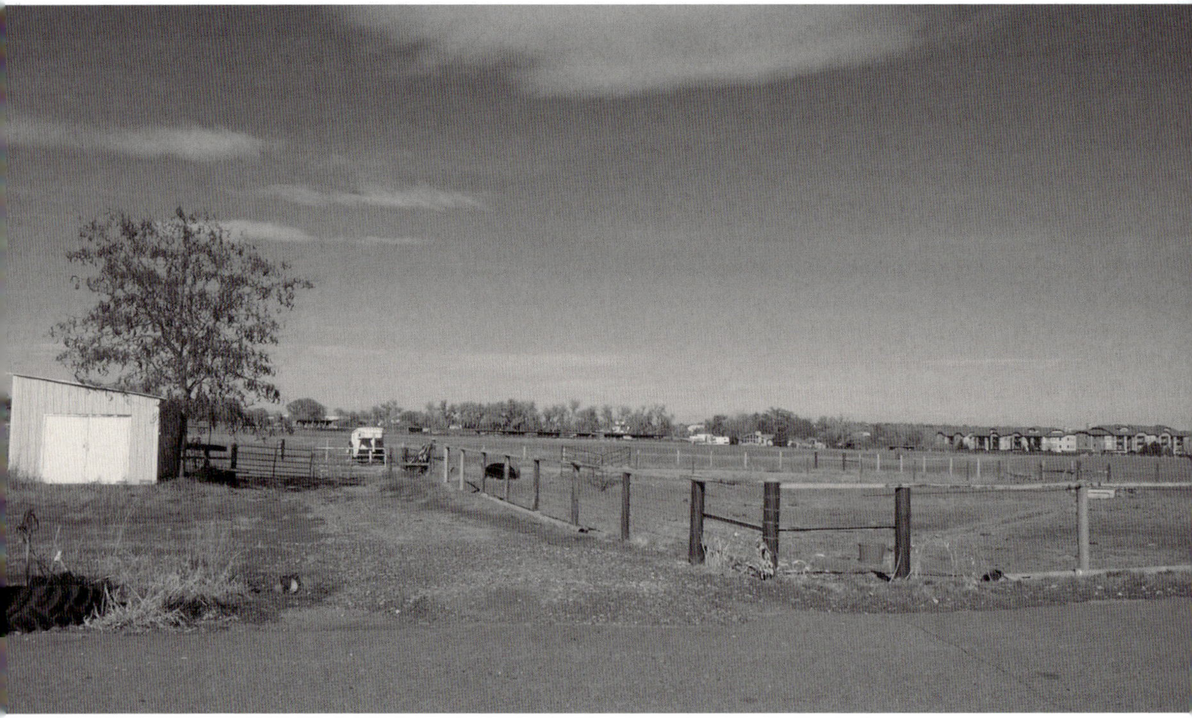

CHAPTER 4

Government, Parks, and Recreation

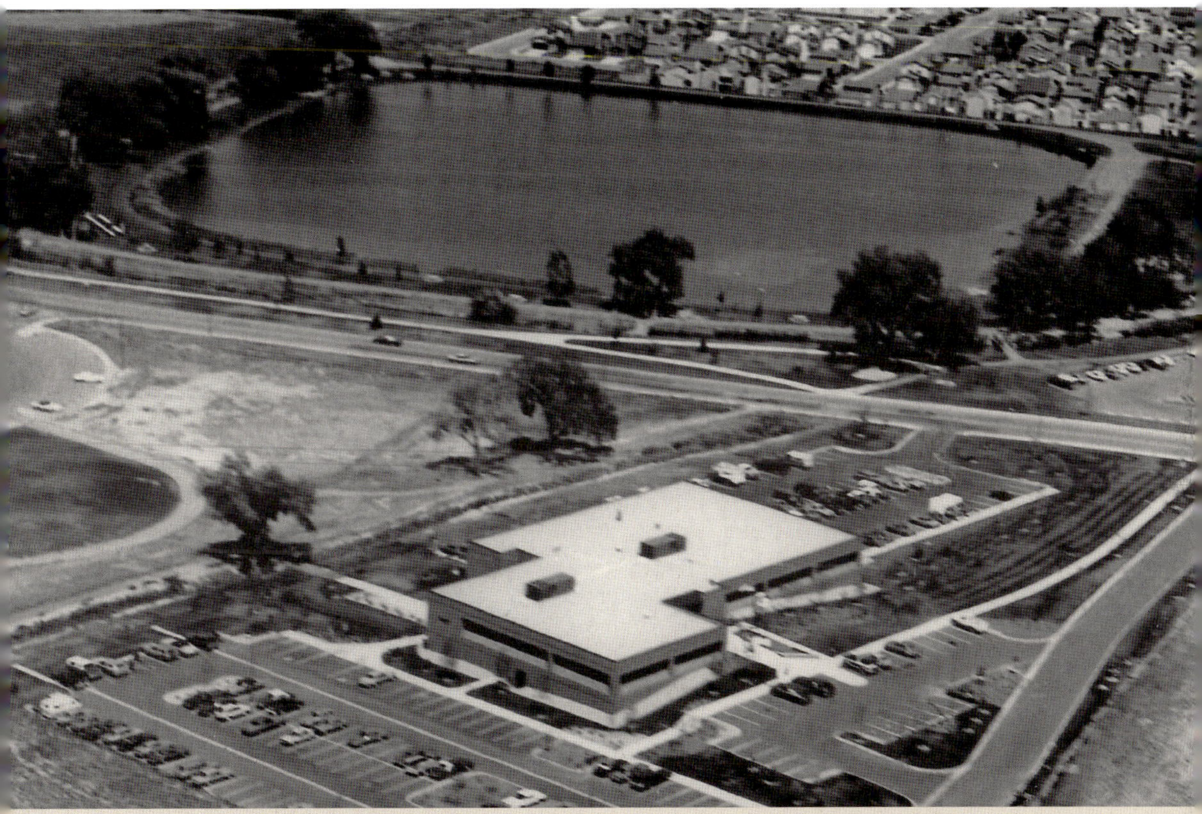

This aerial view shows Northglenn City Hall designed by architects R.V. Lord and Associates and constructed by Roche Construction Inc. in 1981 for $2.5 million, along with Webster Lake. Community Center Drive, seen between city hall and Webster Lake, is often the site of city events that utilize the entire municipal and park property. (Courtesy of Northglenn Police Department.)

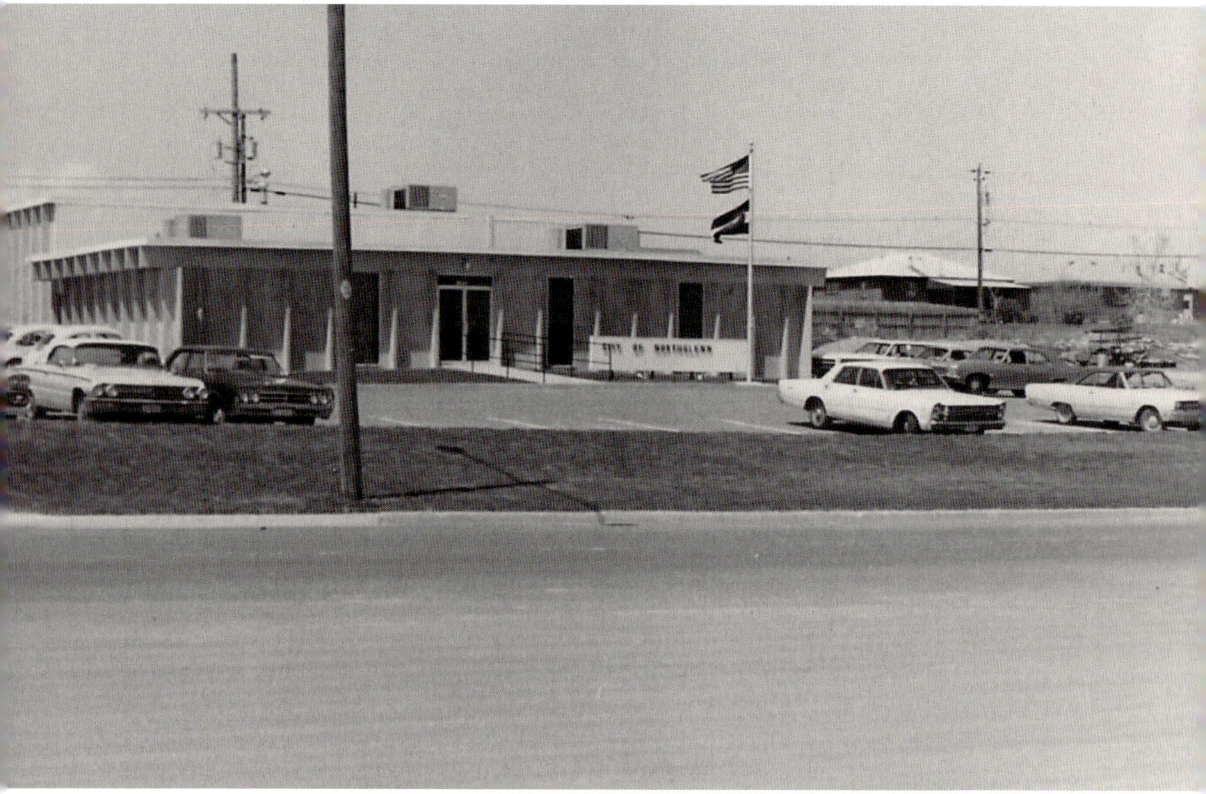

Mayor Hugh Danahy dedicated this structure, designed by Ronald Gordon Dougherty and built by Hunt Construction Company in July 1970, as Northglenn's first municipal building. The building at 10969 Irma Drive housed city government offices and the police department. In 1981, the city government moved to city hall on Community Center Drive resulting in Northglenn Elks Lodge No. 2438 purchasing the building from the city and moving from its previous location. Remodeled inside, the lodge is still active in the community. (Past image, courtesy of Northglenn Police Department.)

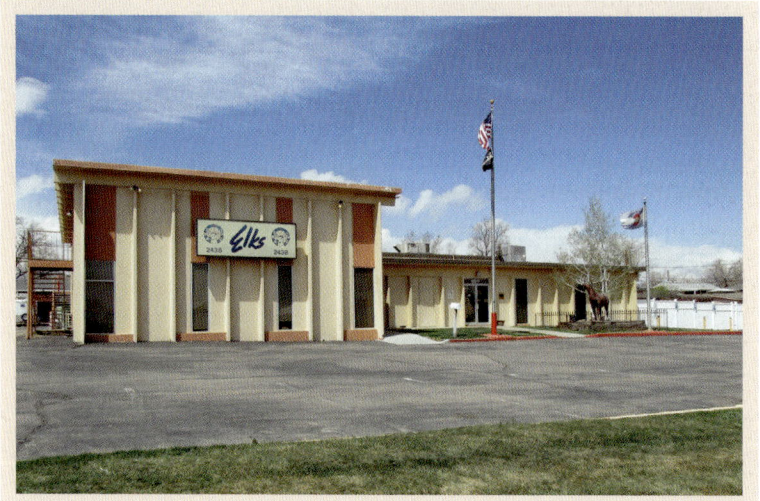

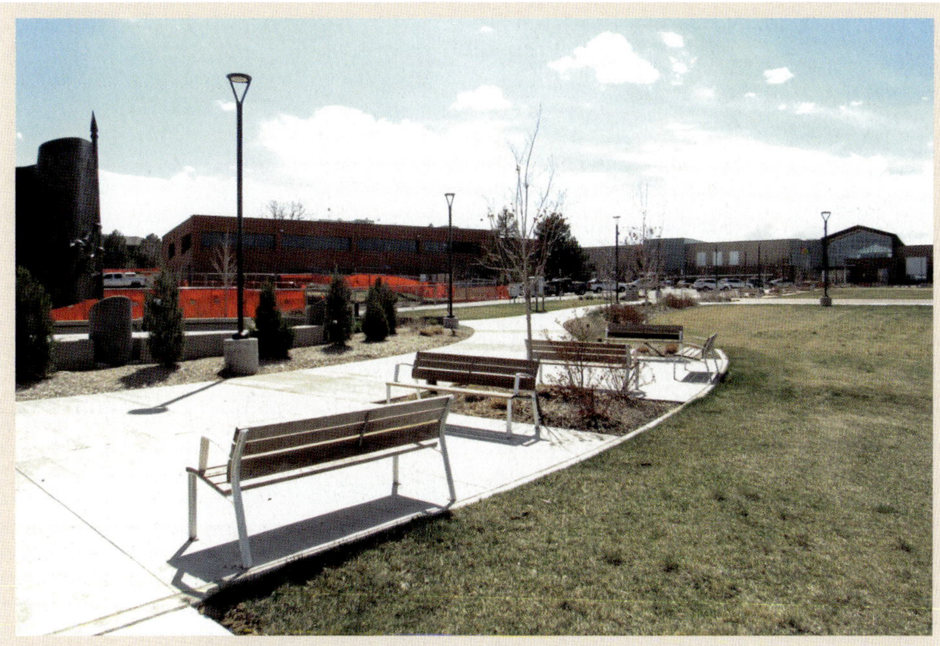

Northglenn City Hall was dedicated on October 17, 1981, by Mayor Odell Barry. The building reflected the architectural style of the neighboring recreation center. The new recreation center, visible in the present picture, was designed by architects Barker Rinker Seacat and architects Semple Brown and opened on October 9, 2021. Current city plans include a redevelopment of the municipal complex with a new city hall built in the lot in front of the current building. (Past image, courtesy of City of Northglenn.)

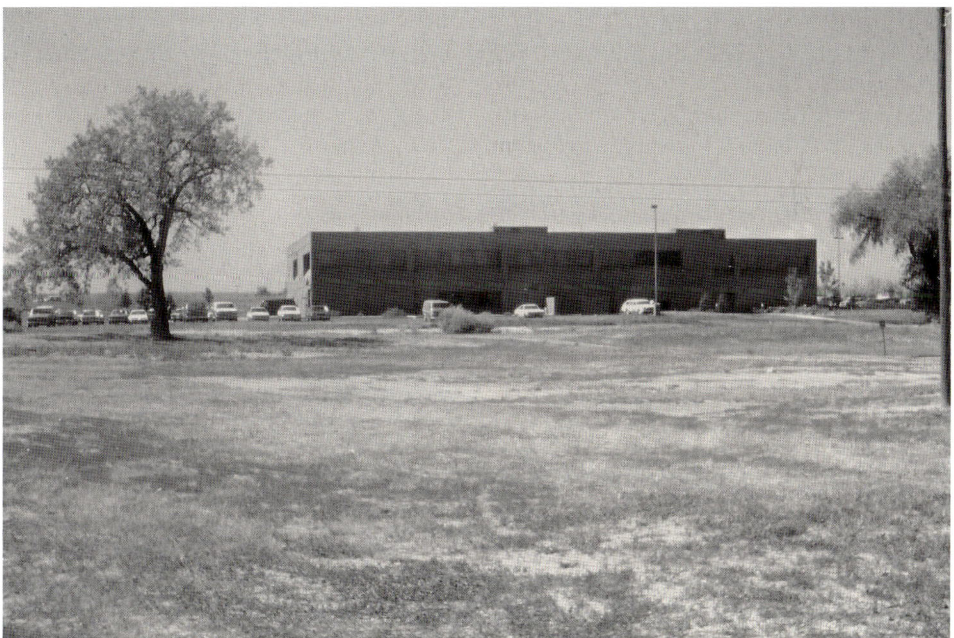

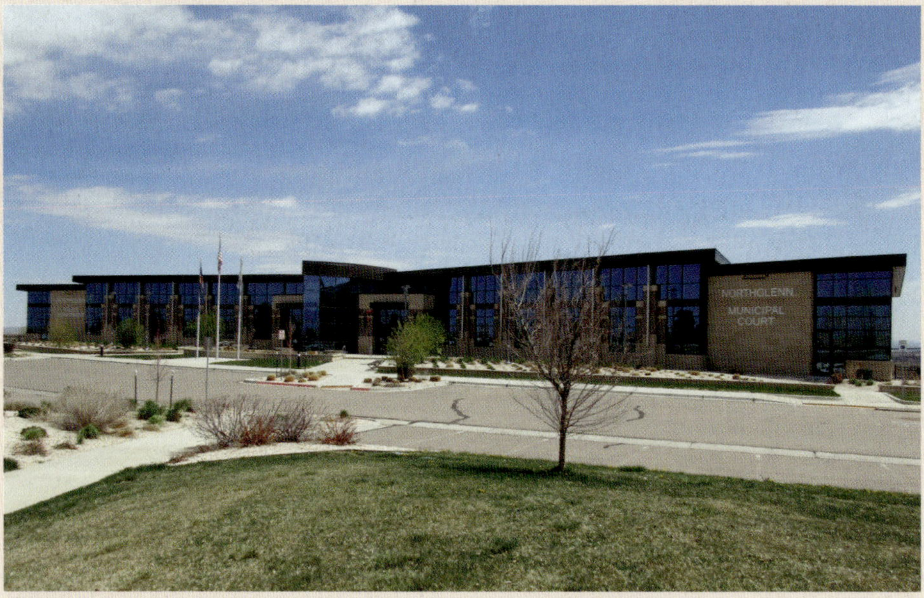

In the 1980s, this dirt field overlooking Interstate 25 almost became an exit from the highway to make it easier for police to respond to calls; however, residents voted against the exit. In 2015, a ground breaking was held for the Justice Center housing the police department on the same field. Designed by Hoefer Wysocki Architecture, the Justice Center held its ribbon cutting on September 11, 2018. The structure built in the shape of an eagle is designed to meet the city's justice needs for the next 100 years. (Past image, courtesy of Northglenn Police Department)

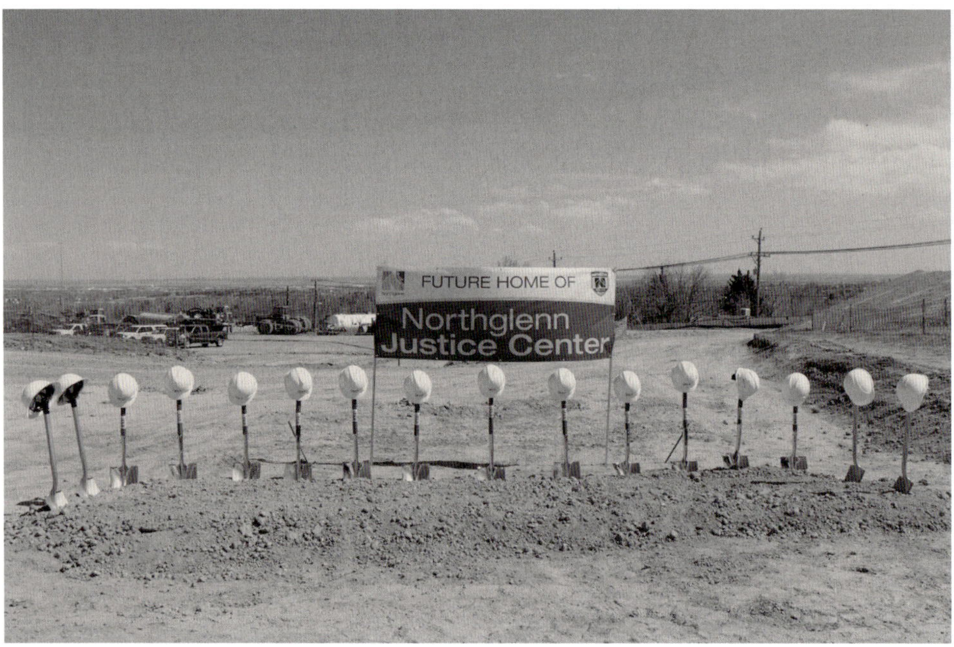

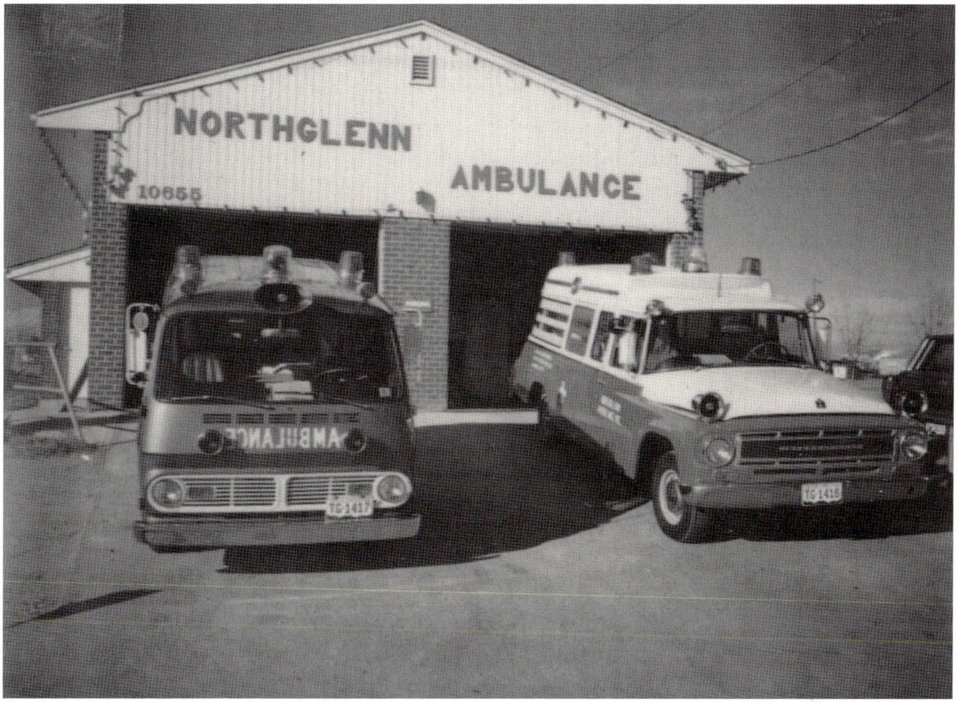

The Northglenn Ambulance Corp started as an all-volunteer service in 1962. Local businesses donated materials and the Northglenn Jaycees assisted with fundraising drives to help build a garage, designed by architects Wheeler and Lewis, at 10655 North Washington Street. In this January 1970 image, red ambulance 601 (right) and blue ambulance 602 (left) are ready for action. Sixty years later, Northglenn Ambulance continues to operate out of updated facilities at this location. (Past image, courtesy of City of Northglenn.)

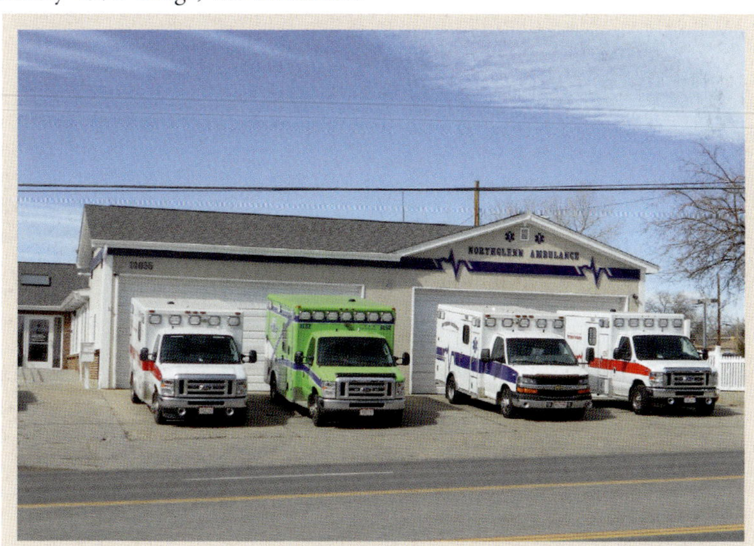

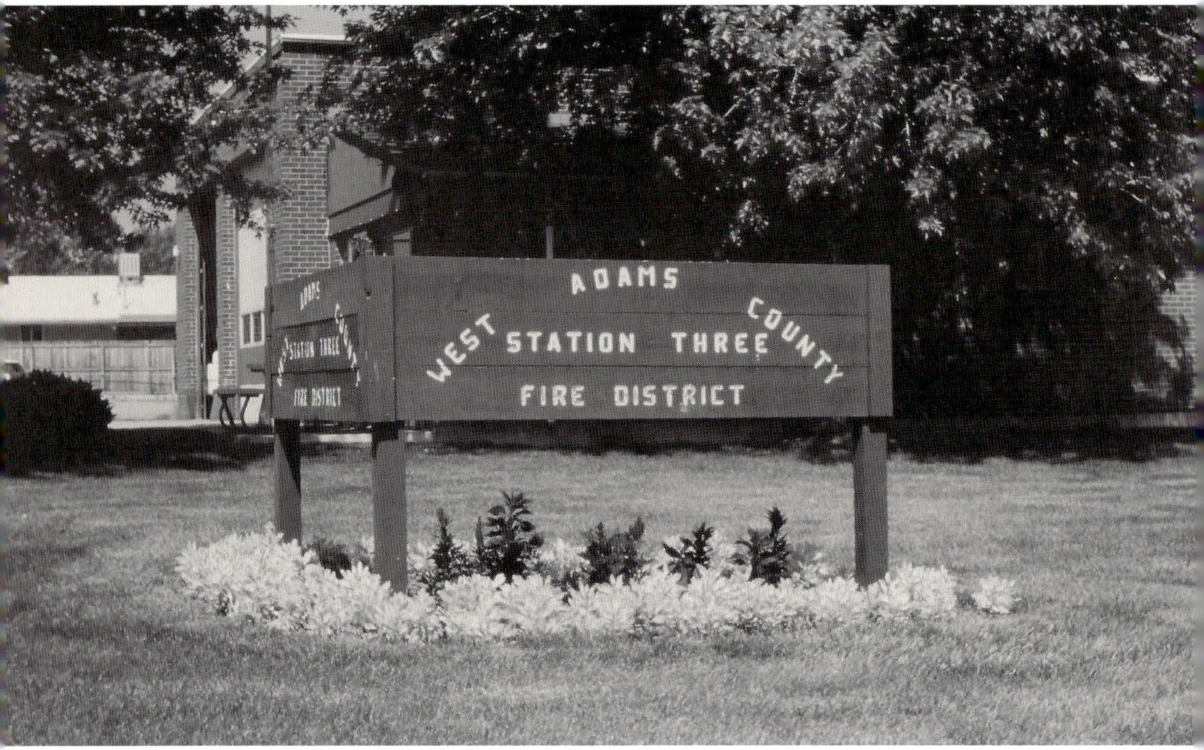

Originally part of the West Adams County Fire District, North Metro Fire Station No. 63, previously West Adams County Fire Station No. 3, was built in 1963 at the corner of Irma Drive and Muriel Drive. The building, seen in this c. 1984 image, was demolished in 2018. The enlarged two-story building constructed in 2018 features larger ambulance and fire engine bays that now open onto Irma Drive instead of Muriel Drive, along with a fitness center, additional office space, and safety upgrades. (Past image, courtesy of Northglenn Senior Center.)

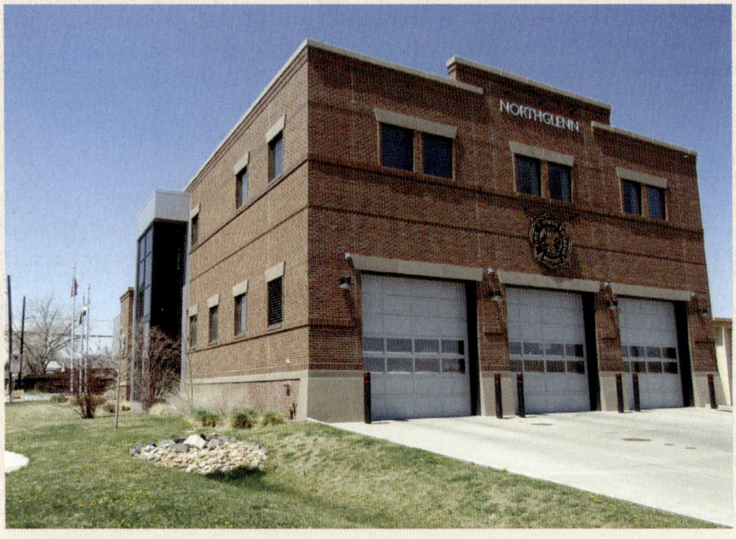

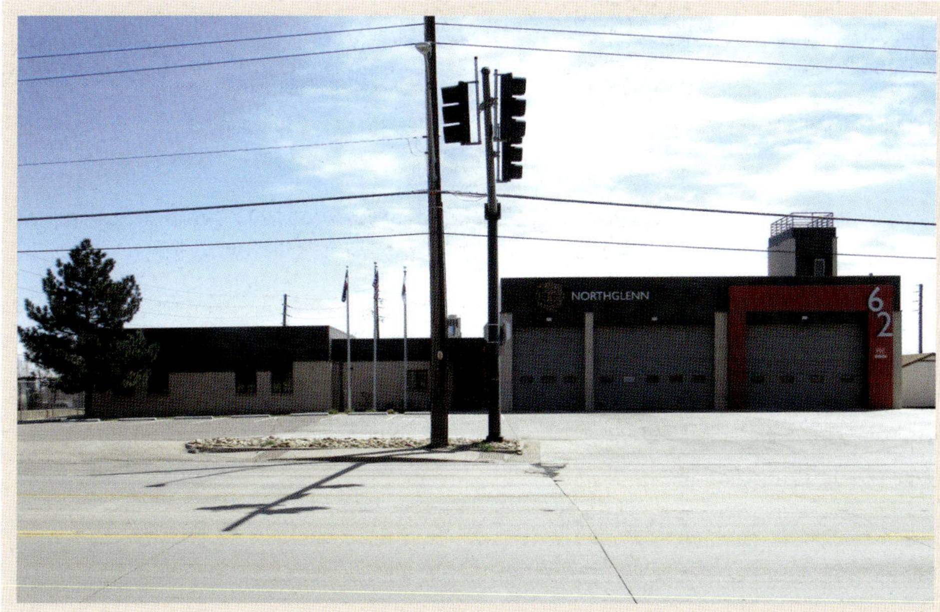

North Metro Fire Station No. 62, previously known as West Adams County Fire Station No. 4, was built at 10550 Huron Street in 1967. The building, seen in the past image in 1989, was remolded in 1989 and 2019. Although Station 61 responds to calls primarily in the western part of Northglenn, it is home to North Metro Fire's 75-foot aerial truck that responds to all structural fires in the district. (Past image, courtesy of City of Northglenn.)

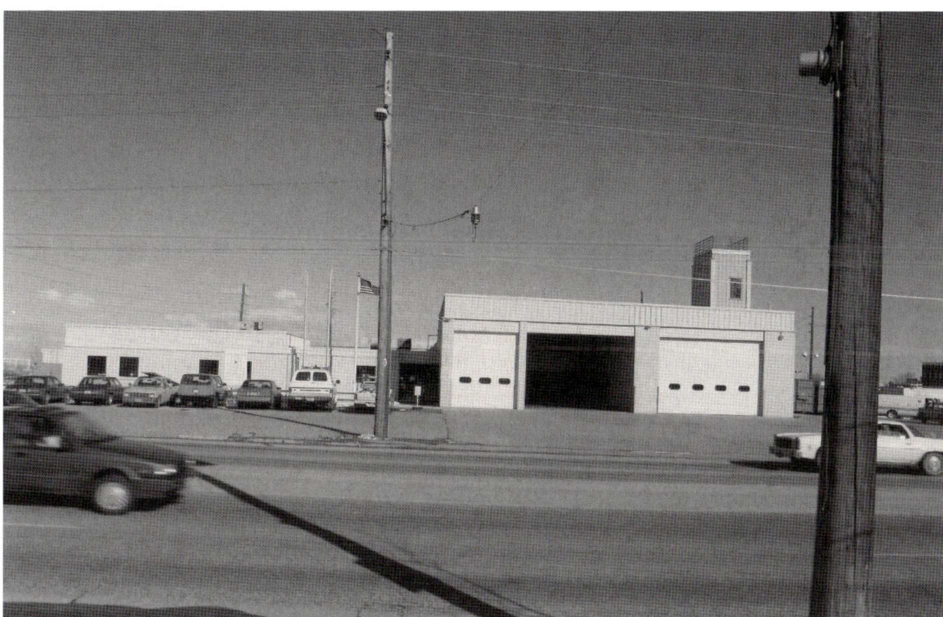

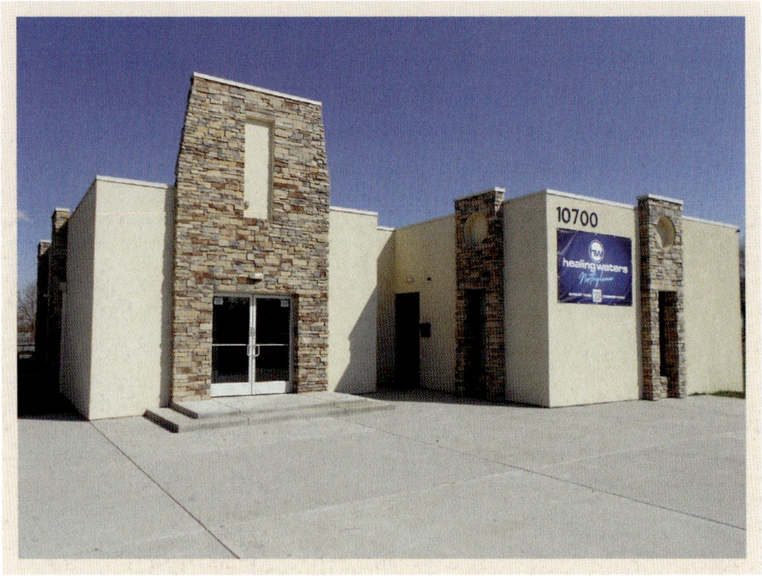

The Westview Neighborhood Center, originally a Perl-Mack model home sales office donated by Perl-Mack in 1967, was demolished in 1973. This 2,930 square-foot structure built on the original foundation at 10700 Pecos Street in 1973 was home to the Northglenn Senior Center. Westview closed its doors on February 22, 1982, when all activities were transferred to the Community Center Drive Recreation Center. Enhancements have been made to the building now used as the Northglenn campus of Healing Waters Ministries. (Past image, courtesy of City of Northglenn.)

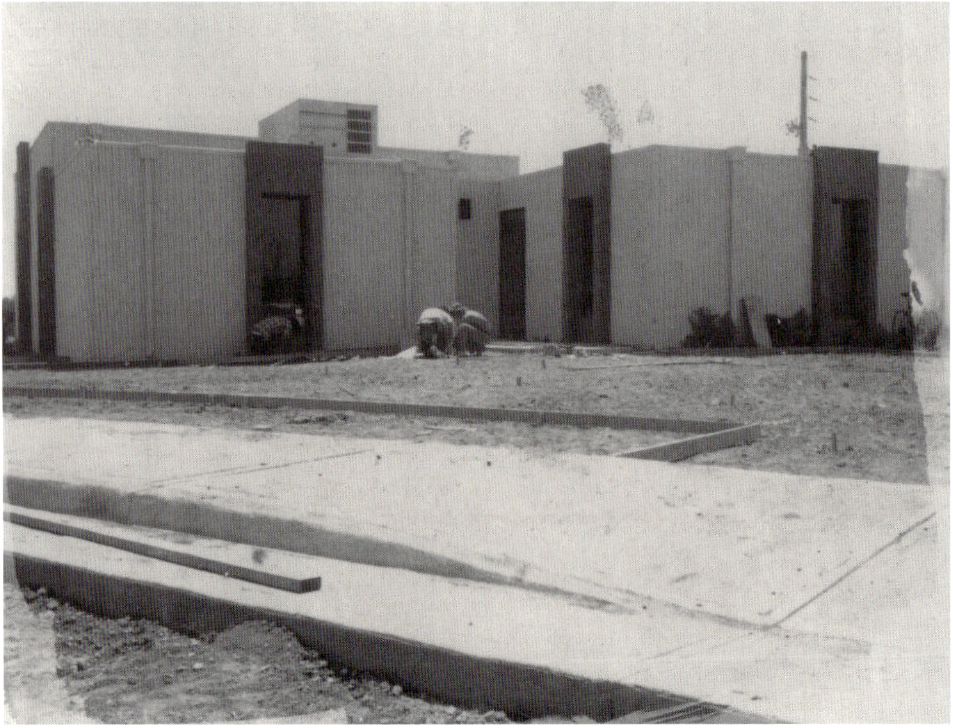

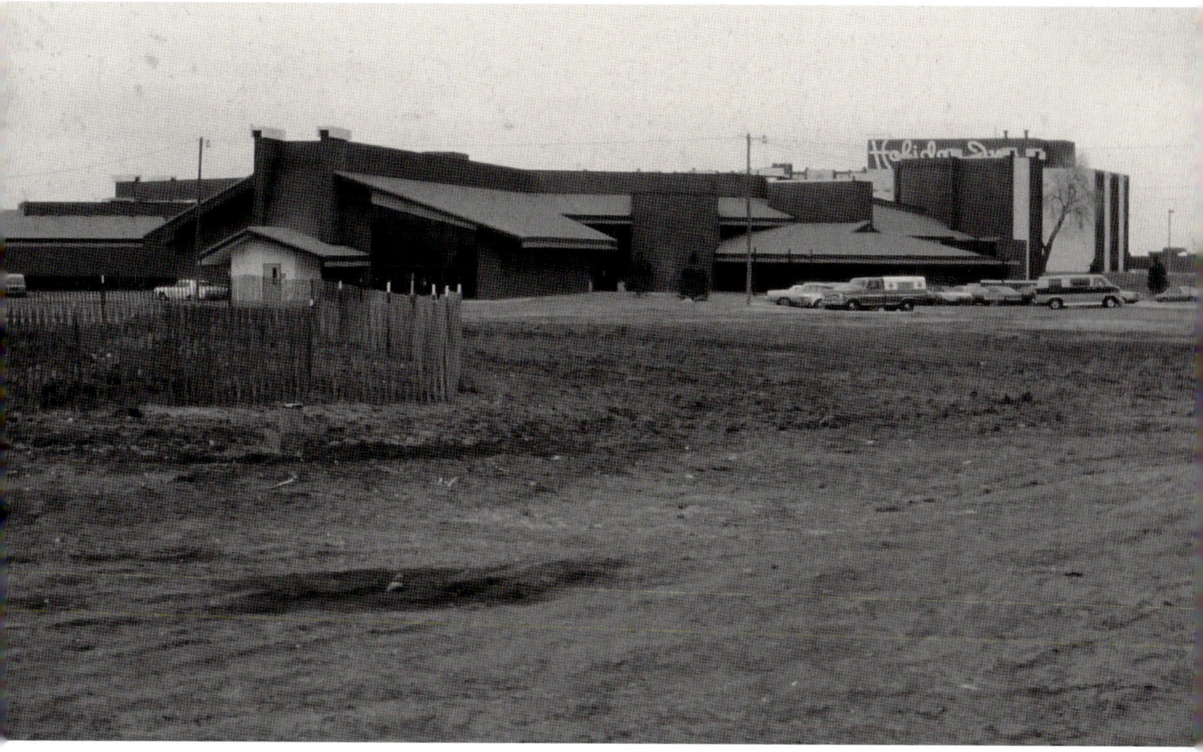

The Northglenn Community Center, pictured here in 1986, opened on November 22, 1975, and changed its name to the Northglenn Recreation Center in 1985. Architects Nixon, Brown, Brokaw and Bowen designed the building in the shape of a "Y." Constructed by Faith-Smith Contracting Corp, amenities included a swimming pool, theatre, gymnasium, office space, and meeting rooms. Closing its doors in 2021 when a new recreation center opened, the building is currently awaiting future development. (Past image, courtesy of City of Northglenn.)

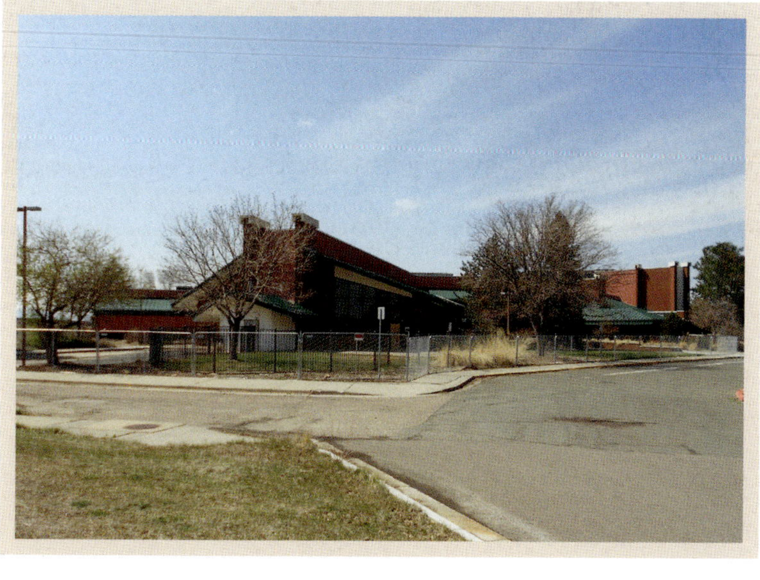

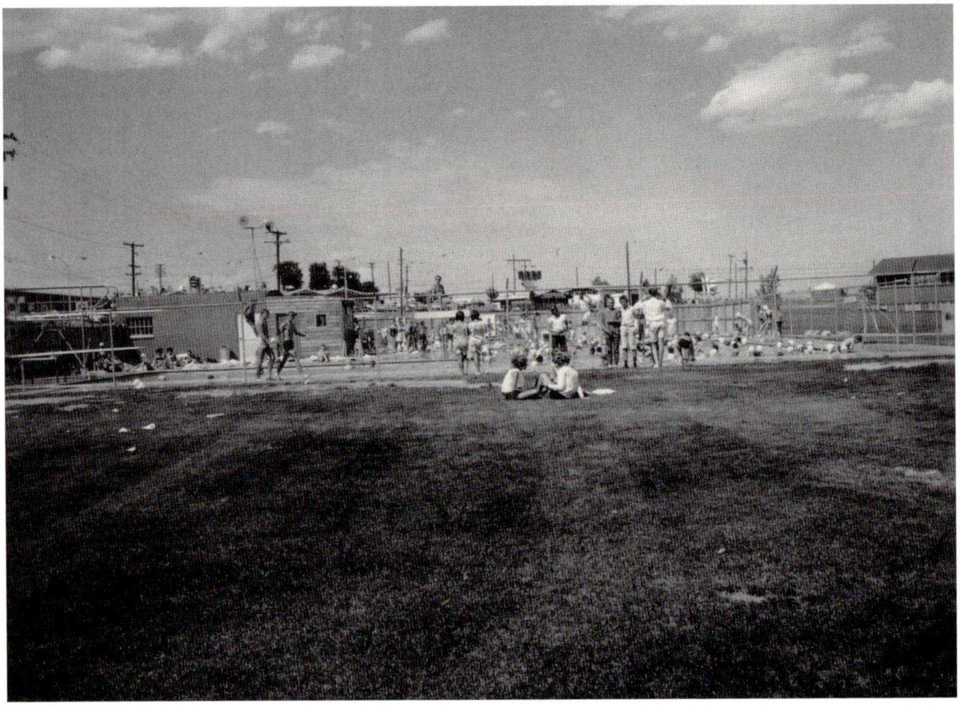

Kiwanis Pool was the first outdoor swimming pool in the area, opening in 1960. Located on Garland Drive, it was listed as a community amenity in Perl-Mack's promotional materials. Each summer, residents would flock to enjoy the pool from May to September. The locker room and concession buildings, seen center-left in the past image, were completely replaced as part of a 2020 renovation project. (Past image, courtesy of City of Northglenn.)

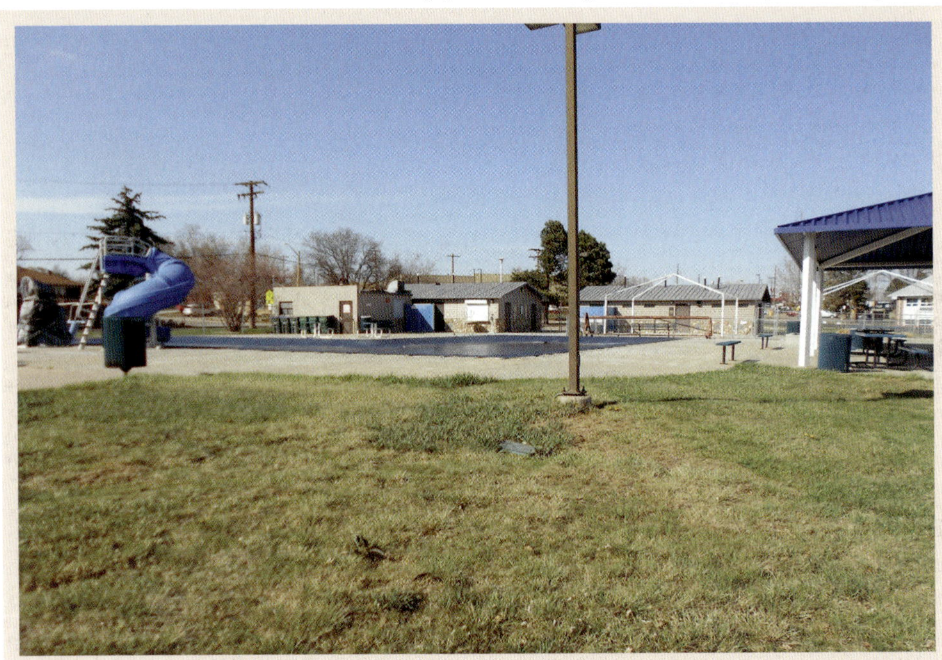

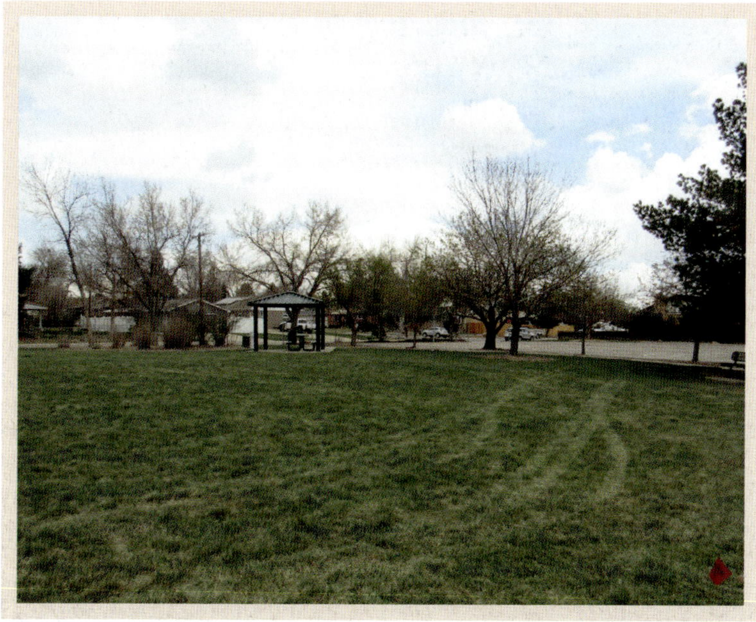

Larson Pool, at 112th Avenue and Larson Drive, the second outdoor swimming pool opening in 1963, contained no diving facilities, allowing for seven race lanes in the 42-foot-by-82-foot pool. The brick locker room and pool house can be seen behind swimmers in the past photograph. After operating for decades, the pool and pool house were in disrepair, resulting in them being demolished in the early 1990s and converted into the 1.3-acre Larson Glenn Park. (Past image, courtesy of City of Northglenn.)

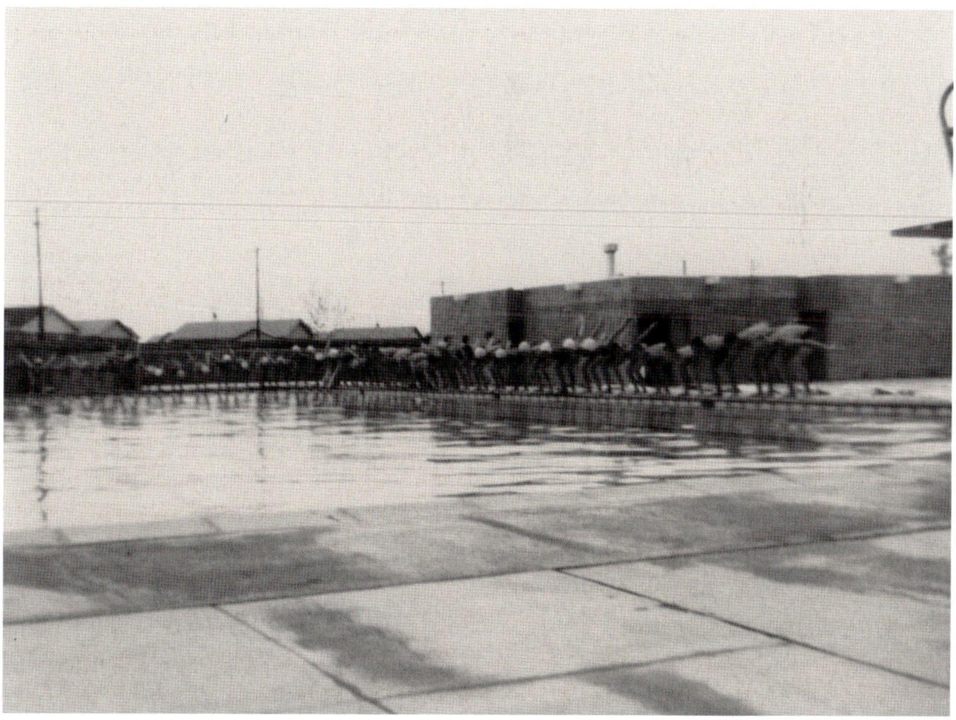

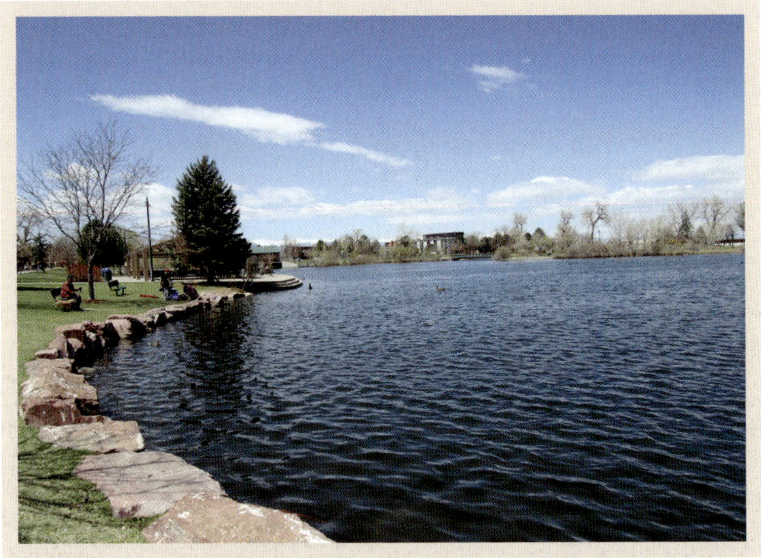

A variety of water activities necessitated the building of a boat dock, seen here in 1975 on the southeast side of Webster Lake. Webster Lake retained its name when the surrounding 28-acre park was renamed E.B. Rains Jr. Memorial Park in 1985 for a fallen Northglenn police officer. Undergoing several renovations, the park and lake remain a community gathering point for activities within the city, one of the largest being the annual Fourth of July celebration. (Past image, courtesy of City of Northglenn.)

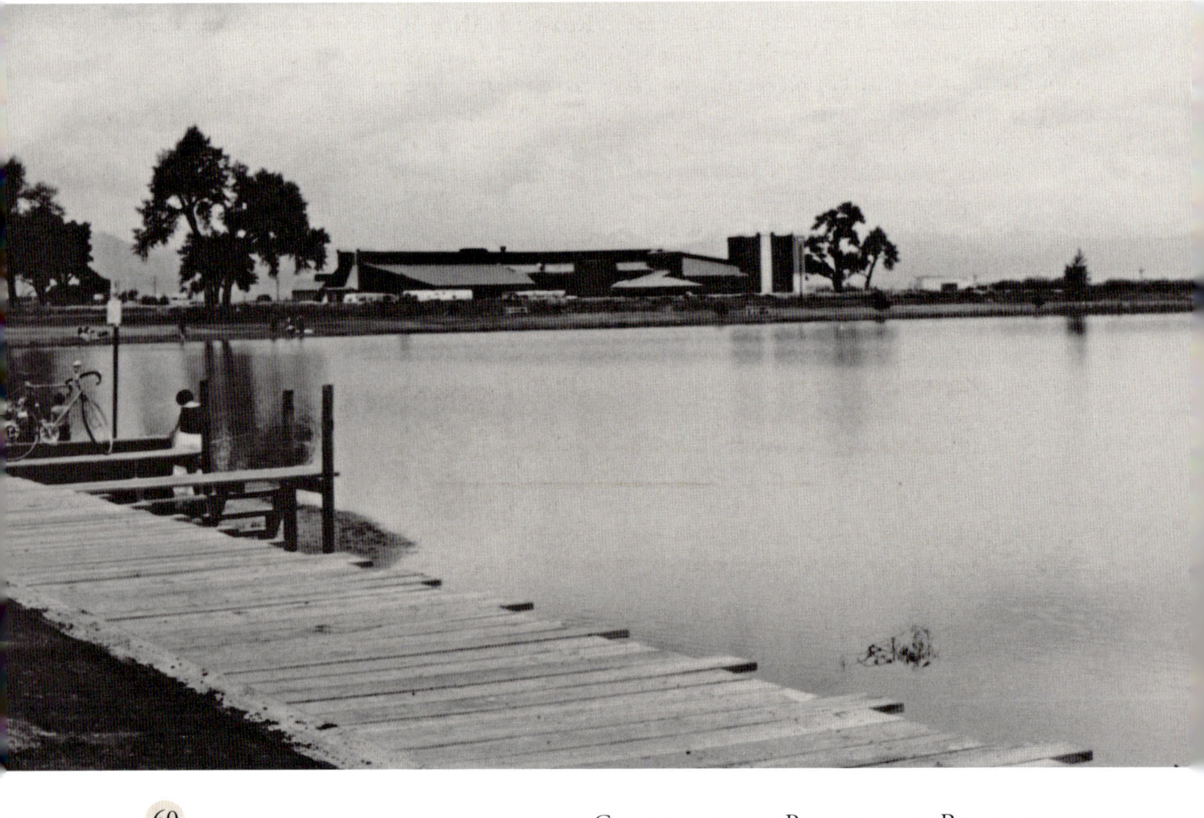

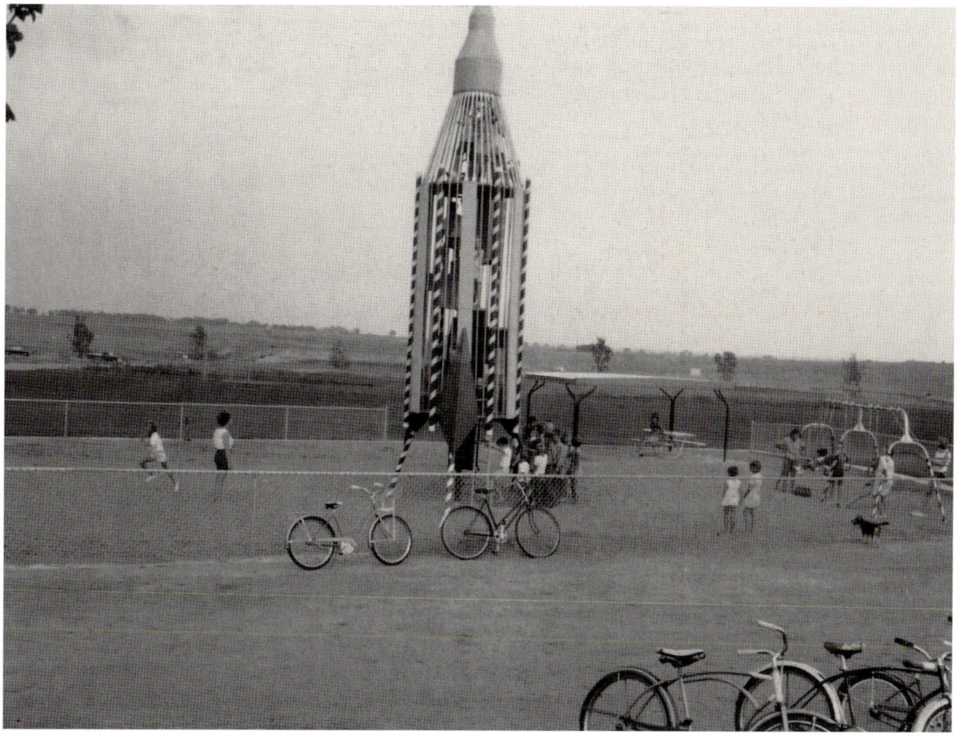

Situated where Rosalie Drive connects with Leroy Drive, Leroy Park was next to the Northglenn Recreation District administration offices. The rocket playground apparatus was a popular draw for children in the 1960s. The fields behind the playground were used for football and soccer games. Renamed Alvin B. Thomas Memorial Park in 1981, the playground equipment has been updated and the empty fields to the east are now filled in with businesses. (Past image, courtesy of City of Northglenn.)

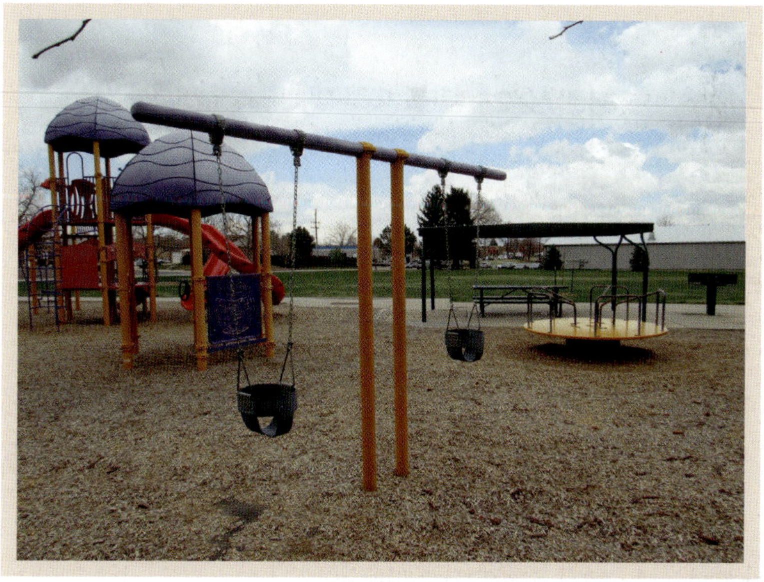

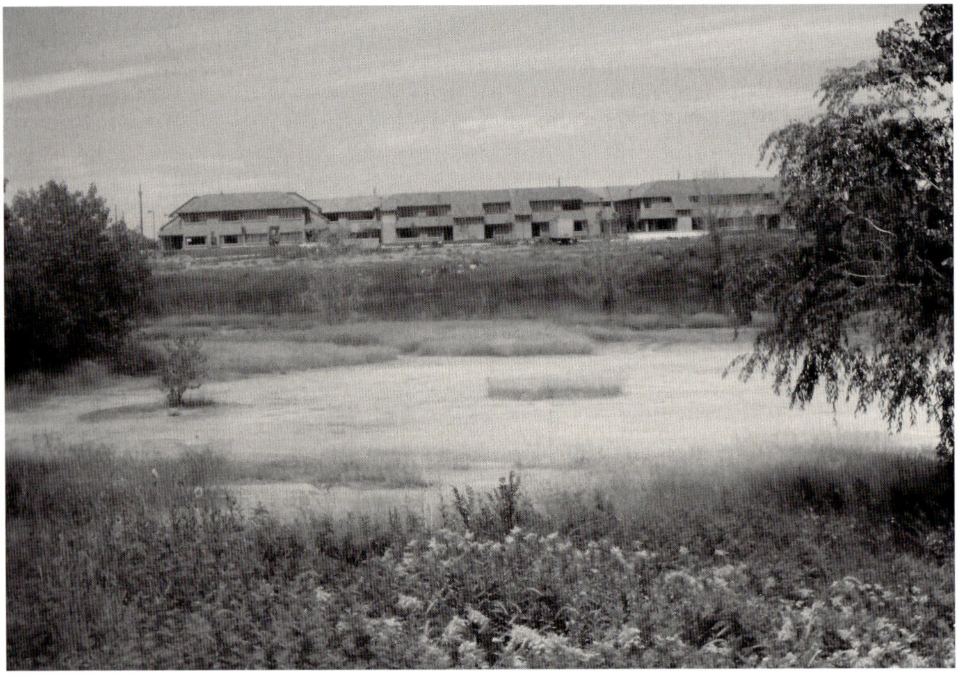

Winburn Park, formerly Huron Reservoir, is on Huron Street just south of Huron Office Plaza North and South on 112th Avenue. In 1987, Huron Reservoir was revamped into a park named for former mayor Charles Winburn. Prior to being mayor, Winburn was involved in the 1960 North Glenn Civic Association, served on the North Glenn Metropolitan Recreation District, and was a member of the board of education for Adams 12 schools. (Past image, courtesy of Northglenn Senior Center.)

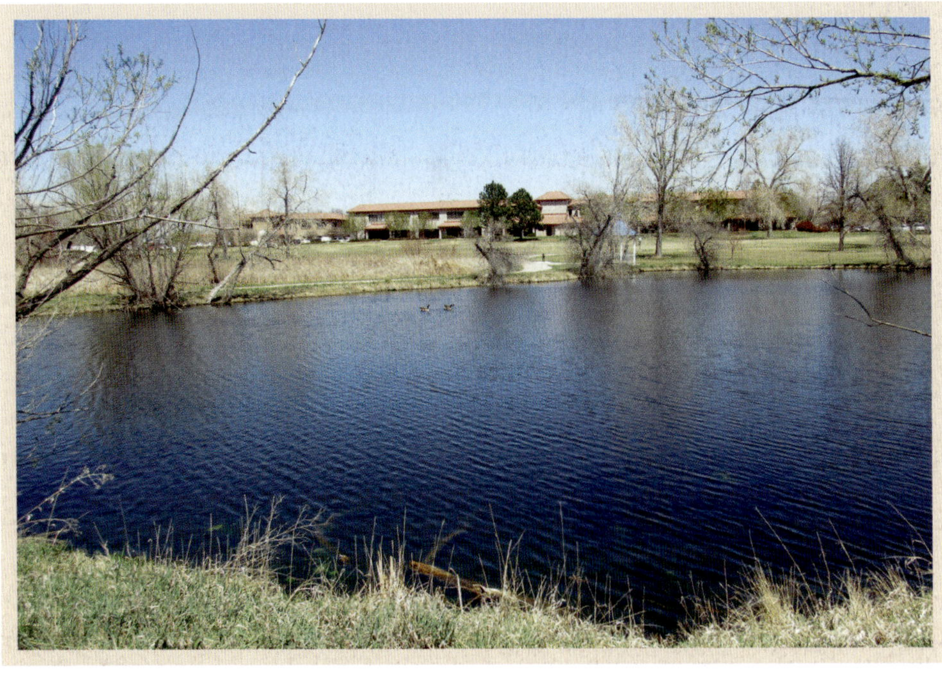

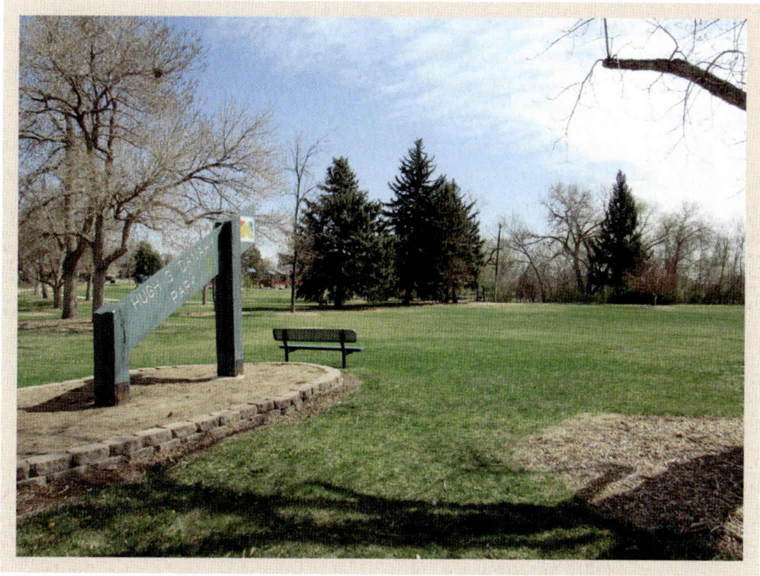

Livingston Park, formally dedicated in 1964, was renamed Hugh G. Danahy Memorial Park in 1975 in honor of Northglenn's first mayor. The park at the corner of Rosanna Drive and Livingston Drive connects with Croke Reservoir to create 4.87 acres of playground and nature walk areas. Today, the park includes playground apparatus, tennis courts, basketball courts, and picnic tables. Current renovations will upgrade the tennis courts on the northwest side of the park. (Past image, courtesy of City of Northglenn.)

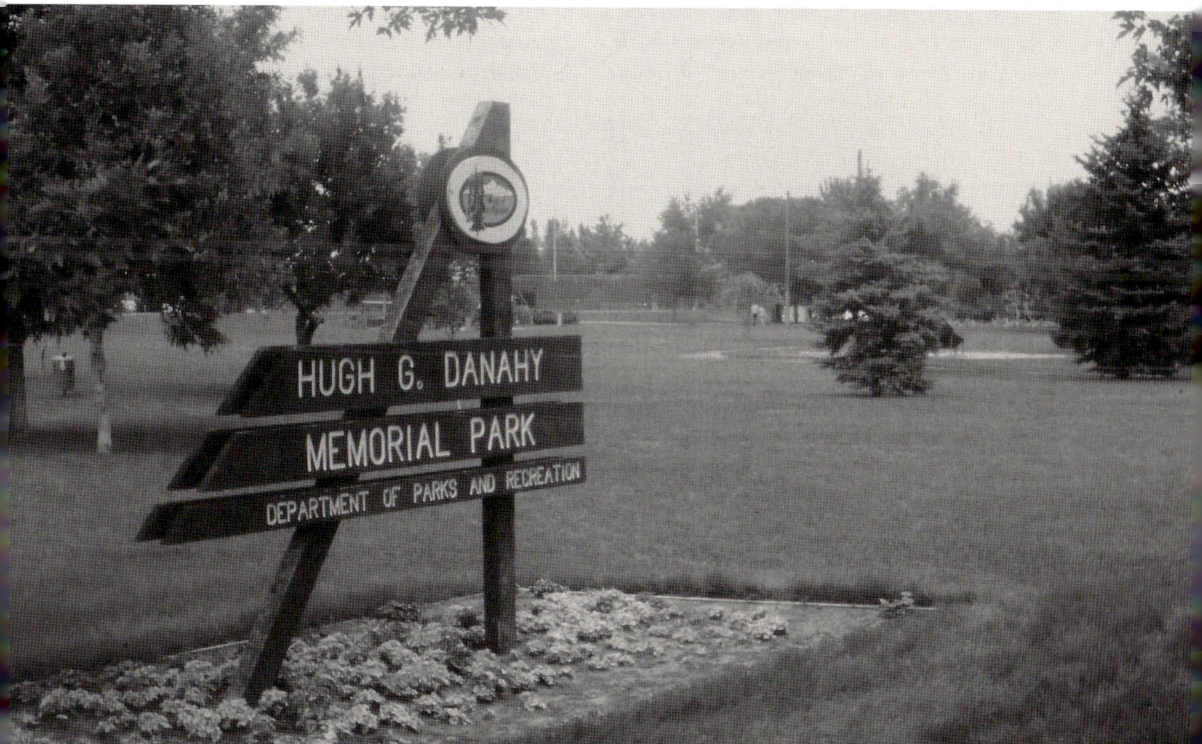

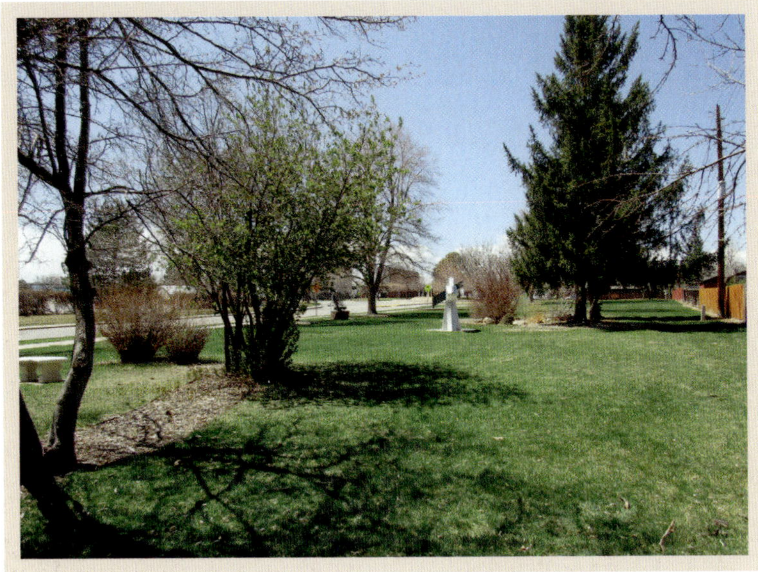

Eleanor Wyatt/Centennial Park, formerly Northglenn Civic Gardens, was dedicated by Mayor Al Thomas on November 11, 1976, to commemorate the nation's bicentennial. A time capsule holding city memorabilia and keepsakes was buried during the dedication and is set to be opened in 2026 and again in 2076. Multiple pieces of public art have since joined the concrete sculpture Liberty Bell by artist John L'Argent and concrete flag by Northglenn American Legion Post 22 member Lloyd Holyoak that were part of the 1968 dedication. (Past image, courtesy of City of Northglenn.)

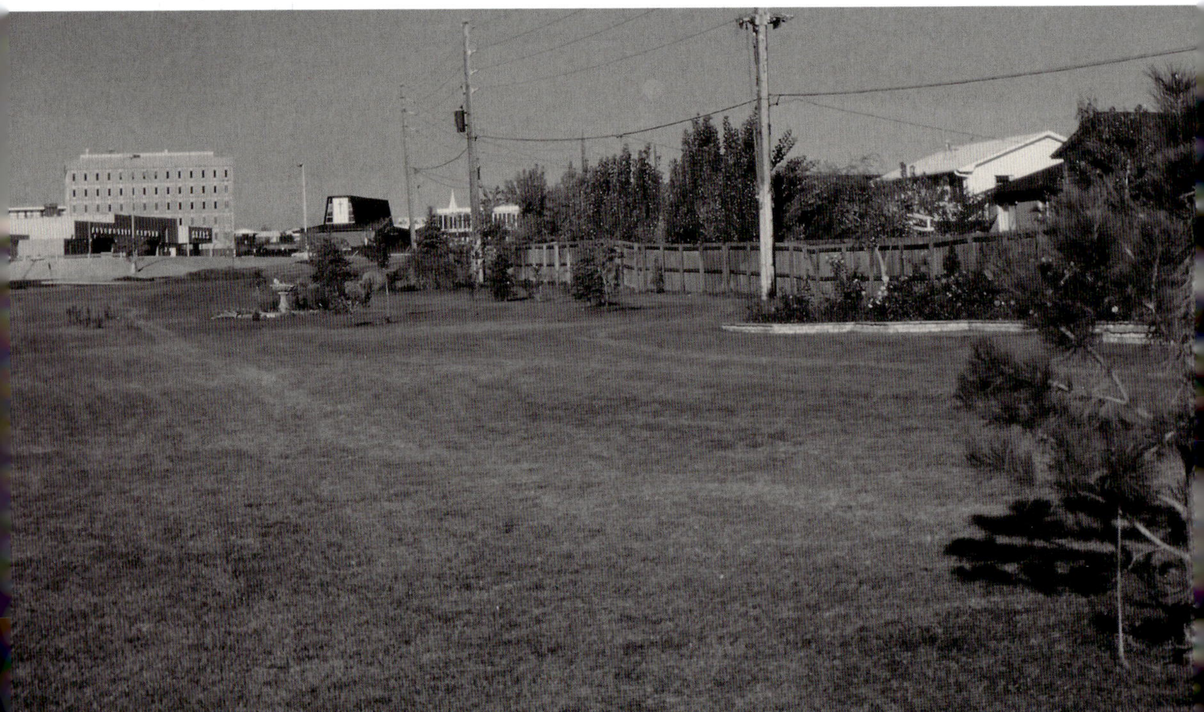

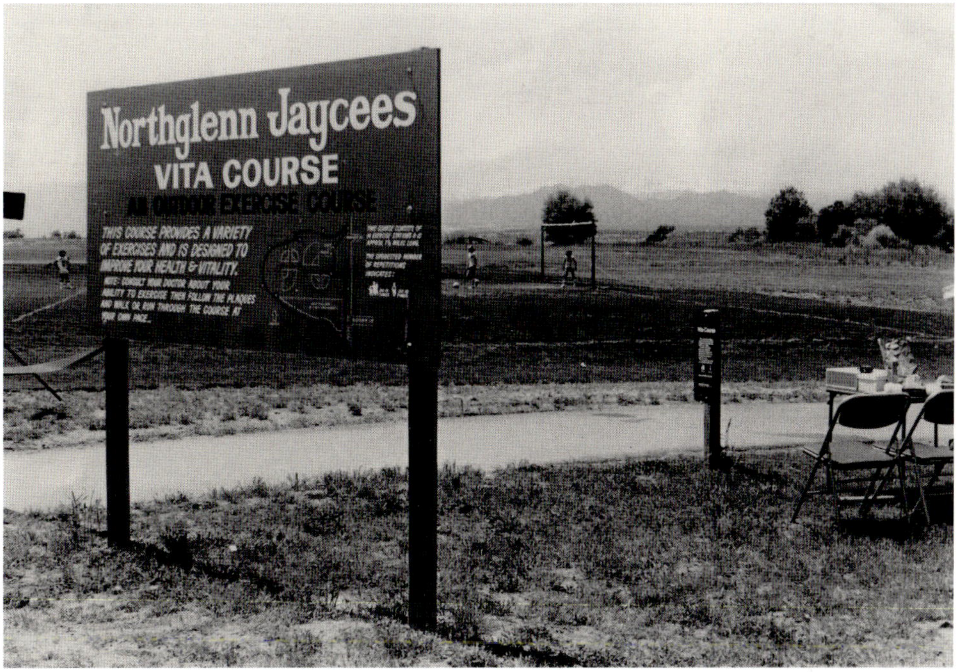

Northwest Open Space, a 50-acre athletic complex, is utilized throughout the year for various recreation needs including soccer, football, cross-country, baseball, and softball. In the 1980s, the Northglenn Jaycees Vita Course encouraged people to utilize the space as a self-paced outdoor exercise course. North of the soccer fields is the Oscar Arnold Nature Area where a host of wildlife inhabits the wooded and wetland areas. The sign may be gone, but residents still use the park for daily exercise. (Past image, courtesy of the Northglenn Senior Center.)

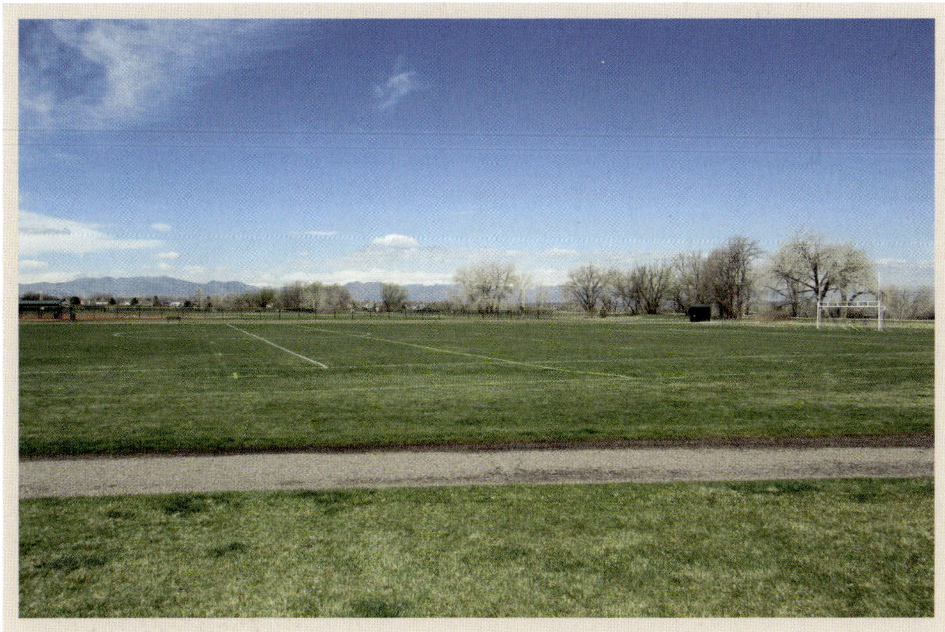

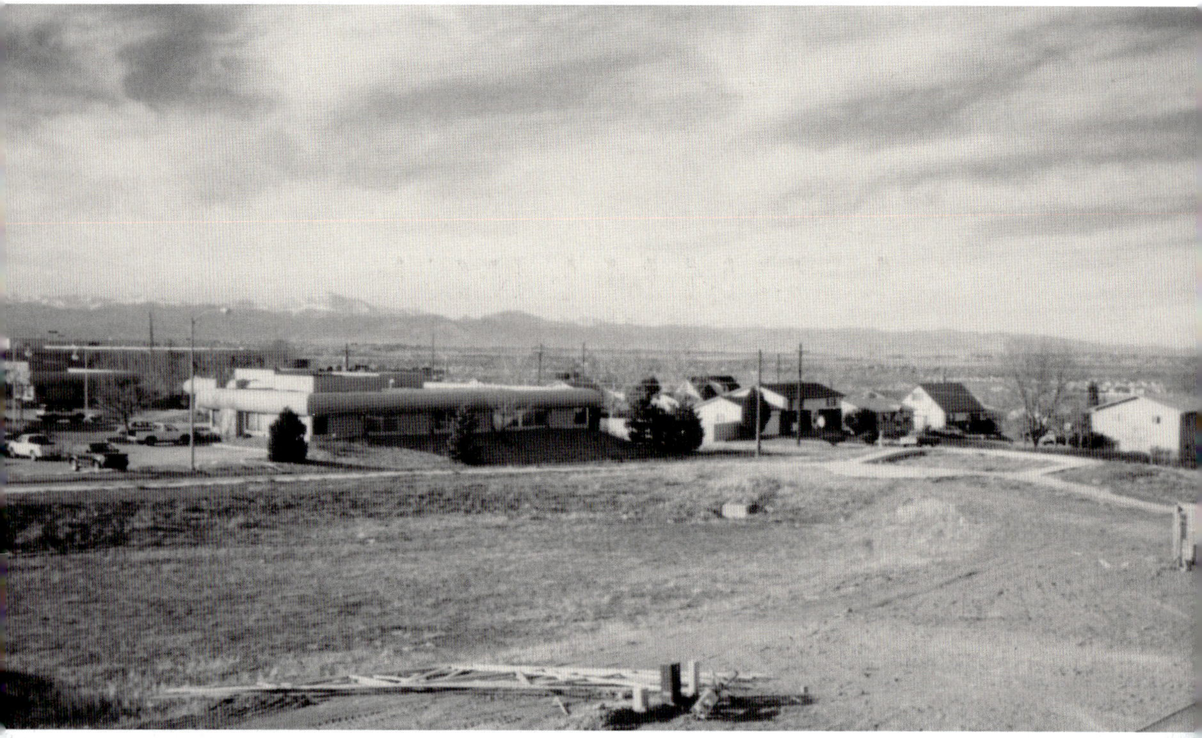

Huron Crossing Park remains a small neighborhood park tucked between the businesses at North Point Business Park, seen to the west of the park in this late 1990s image, and the houses in Huron Heights. After construction, the park's amenities included a basketball court, a gazebo, playground equipment, a picnic table, and an outdoor ping-pong table. The trees in the two-acre park now partially obscure the nearby businesses and houses. (Past image, courtesy of Northglenn Senior Center.)

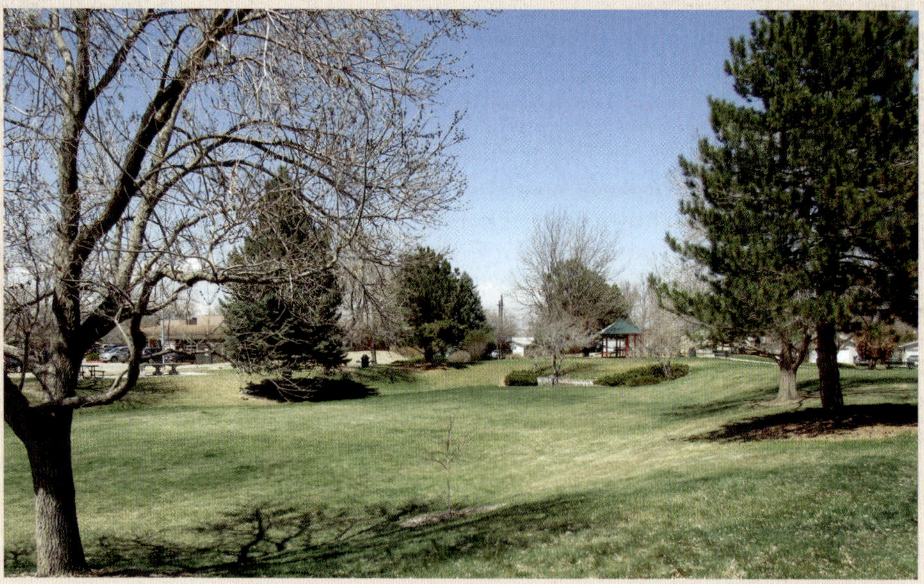

CHAPTER 5

Commerce and Industry

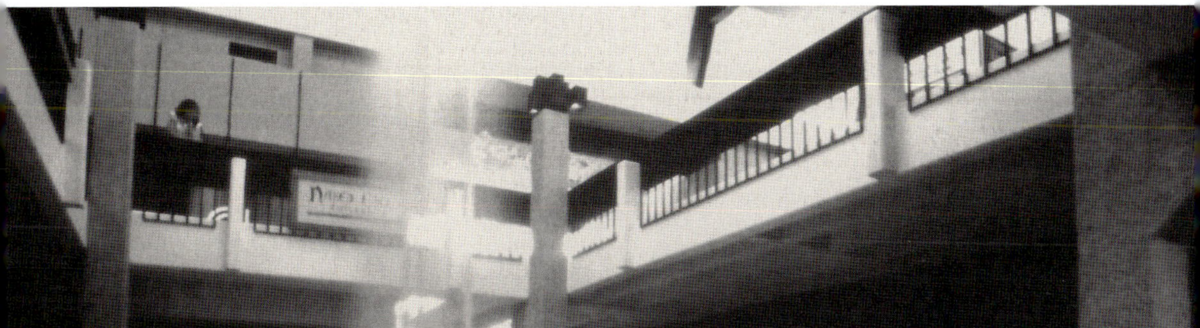

Northglenn Mall, constructed in 1968, was designed by Warren A. Flickenger & Associates who won awards for their "imaginative and creative" use of Western lumber that provided the trusses for the framework of skylights and railings. A person stands at the rails watching the colors change on the fountain lights below, perhaps making a wish on a coin thrown into the pool. (Courtesy of Northglenn Senior Center.)

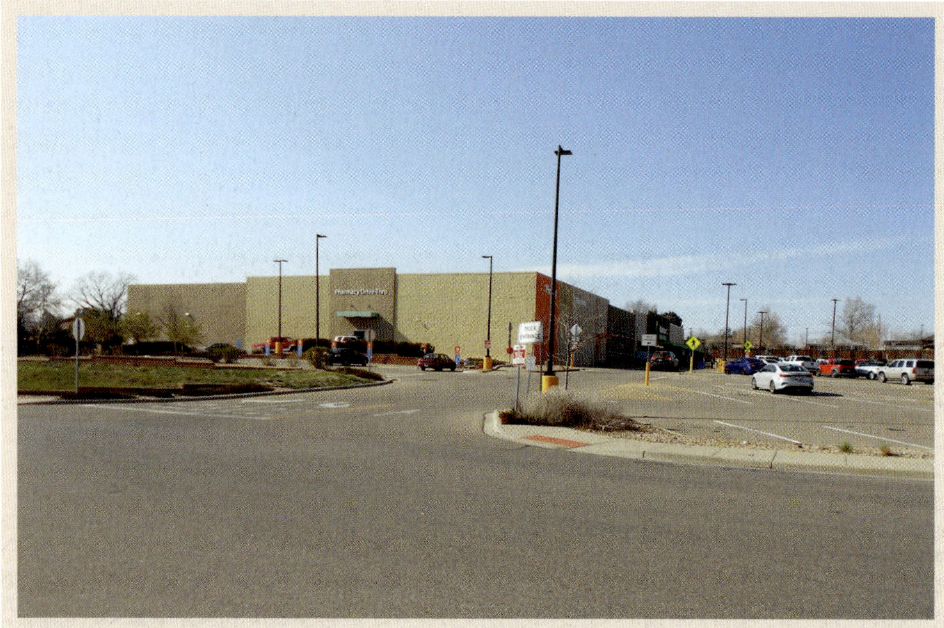

Garland Shopping Center, a 40,000-square-foot structure designed by Warren A. Flickenger & Associates and constructed by Abe Perlmutter Construction Company, had a three-day grand opening event in July 1961 as Northglenn's first indoor shopping center. Original businesses included Safeway, Duckwall's, Owl Drugs, Gambles, a barbershop, a dentist's office, and the *Northglenn News*. The aging building seen in this 1961 image was demolished in 2014 and a Walmart Neighborhood Market was built on the site. (Past image, courtesy of Gethsemane Lutheran Church.)

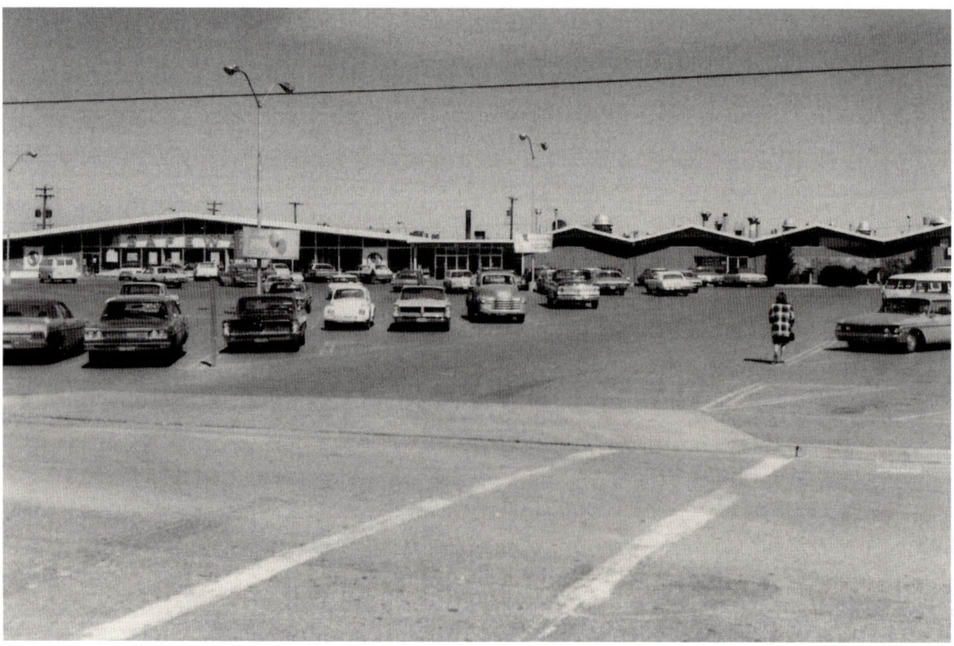

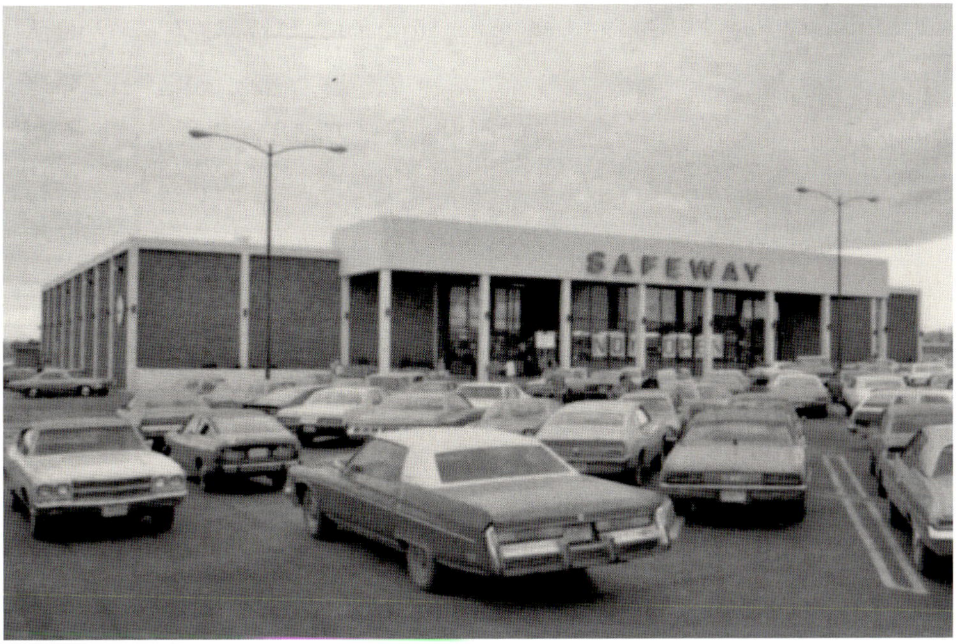

Opening on January 18, 1976, this 40,000-plus-square-foot Safeway was the largest in Denver. The earth-toned structure was built with exterior walls made of multi-hued natural aggregate panels separated by monolithic pilasters. The plate glass and column entryway provides access to the store that showcased a second-story lounge and office area. An anchor building for a shopping center at 112th Avenue and Washington Street, the building is now occupied by a thrift store. (Past image, courtesy of City of Northglenn.)

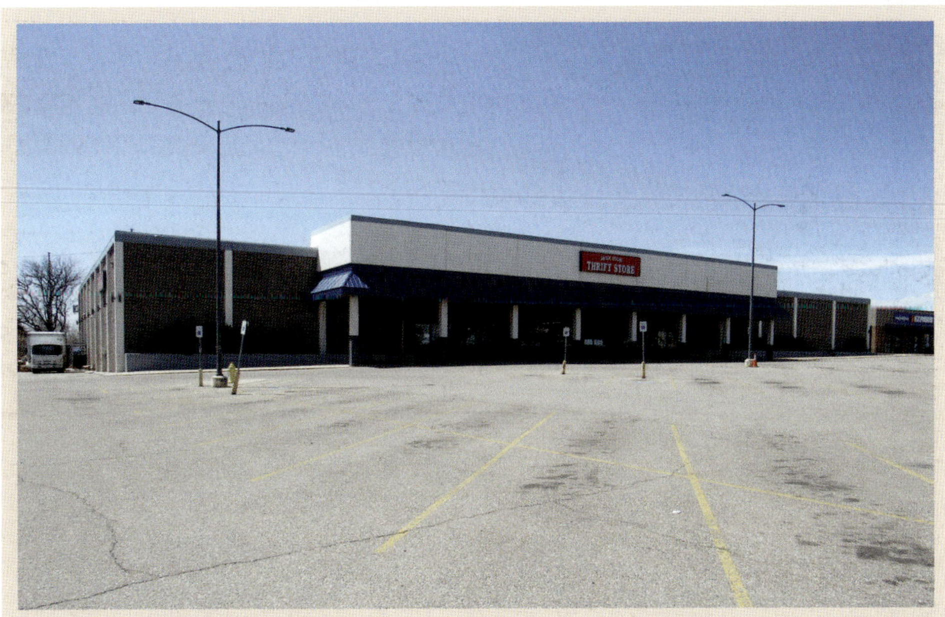

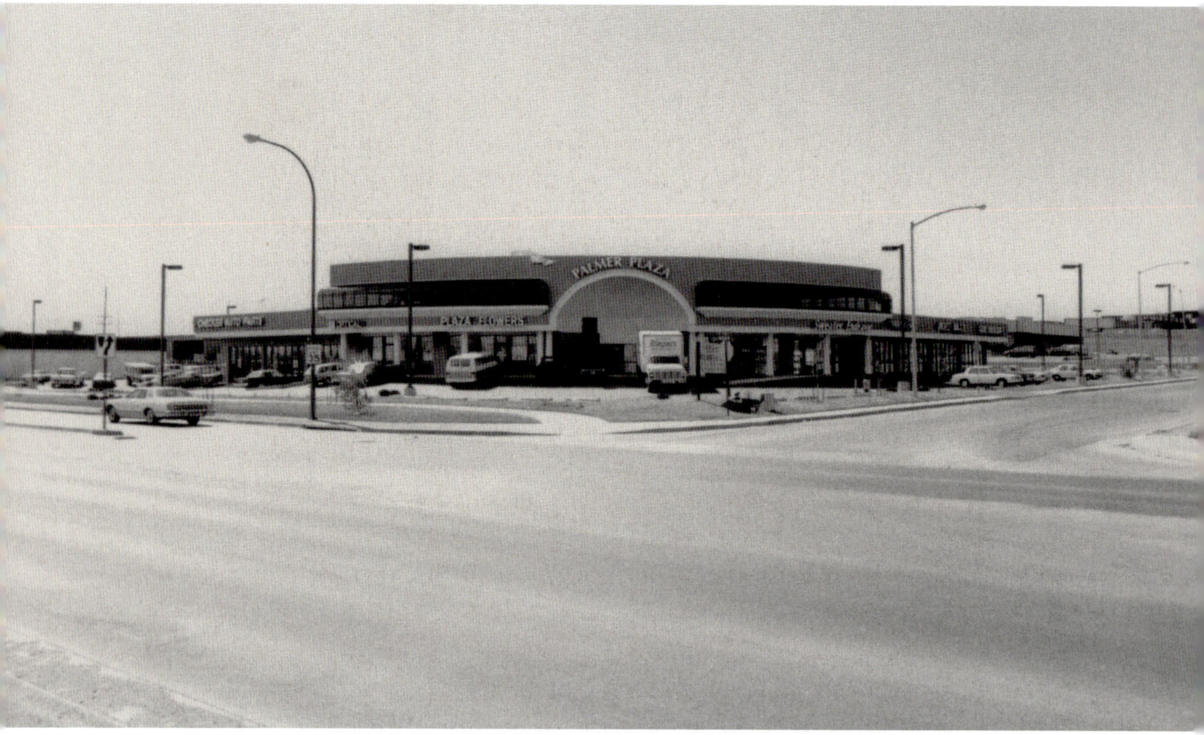

The 16,320-square-foot Palmer Plaza was constructed on the corner of Washington Street and East 114th Court in 1987 for mixed-use retail and office space. Various stores including Fantastic Sams, Abbey Carpet & Tile, Sherwin Williams, Checkers Auto Parts, and Plaza Flowers have called this location home. Receiving a 2019 NURA grant for property improvements, the east-facing, rounded-corner edifice remains largely the same today. (Past image, courtesy of City of Northglenn.)

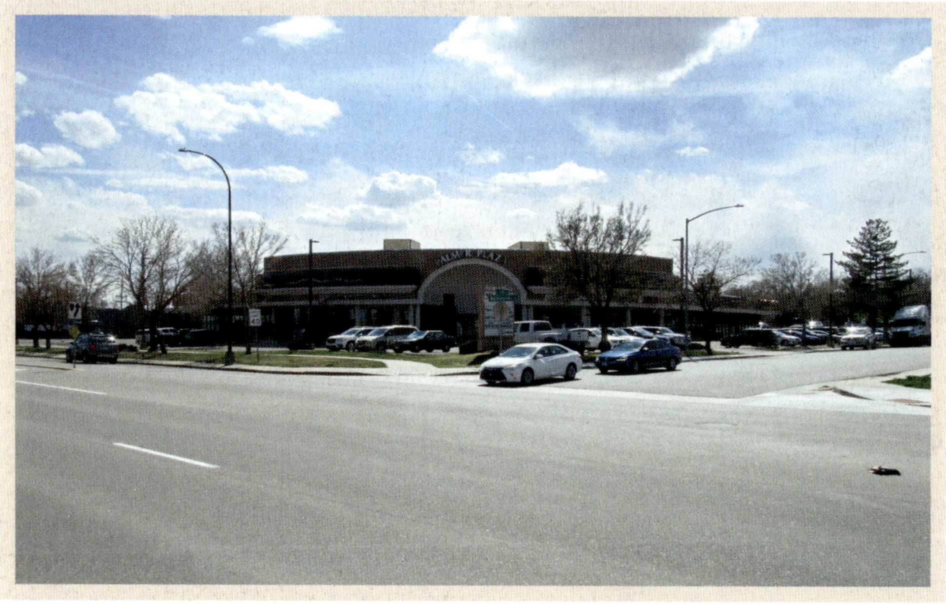

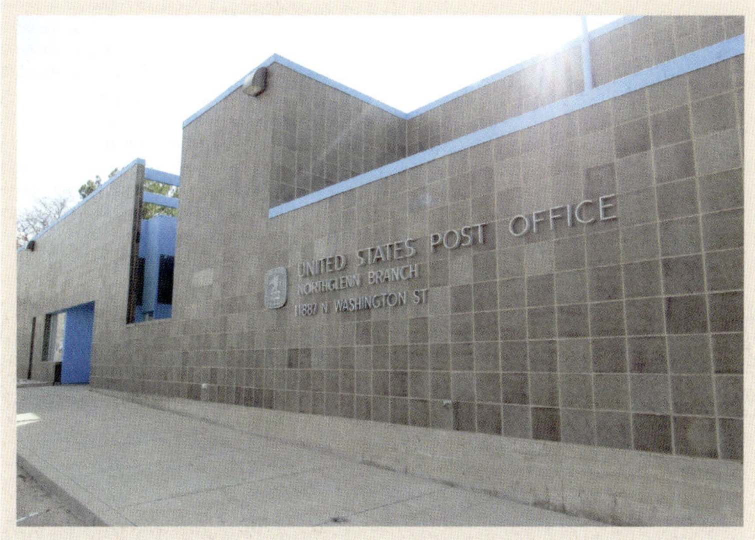

Multiple challenges arose in getting this post office building completed in 1976. A one-acre lot at a different location was originally procured by the US Postal Service in 1972. A change in growth expectations led to the city agreeing to trade the post office's one-acre with the city's two acres at this location on Sylvia Drive and Washington Street. General contractor Cyrus Delano used steel beams, concrete blocks, and porcelain panels in the construction of the structure. (Past image, courtesy of City of Northglenn.)

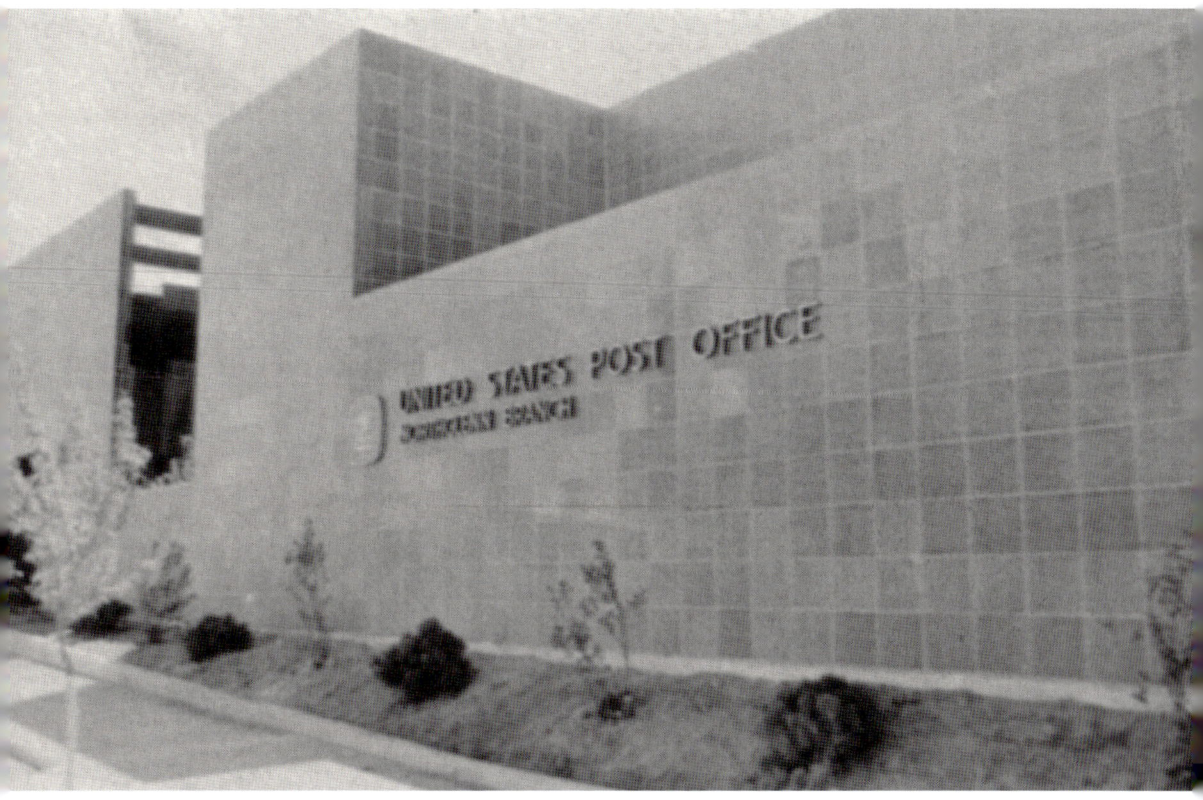

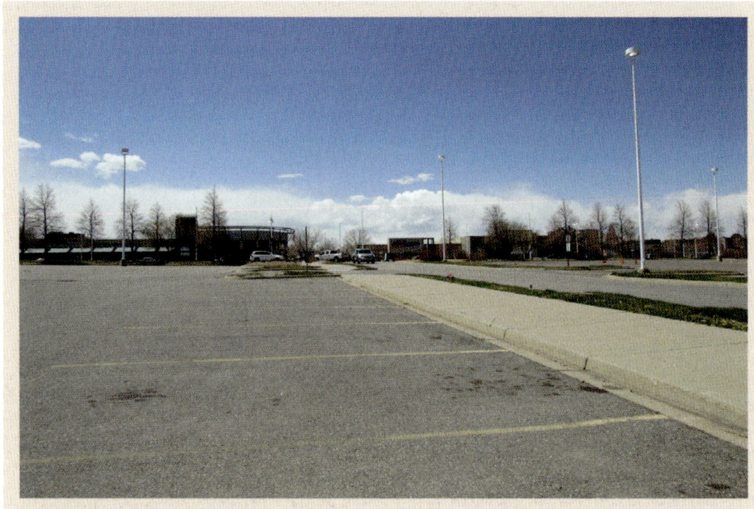

When the Denver Dry Goods Company agreed to be included in the 1968 opening of Northglenn Mall, it was its biggest branch at 139,000 square feet. The building boasted two levels of shopping with a third level dedicated to executive offices. In addition to shopping, the second floor housed a tea roomette where up to 65 patrons could enjoy limited food options. The building was demolished in 1998. (Past image, courtesy of Beck Archives of Rocky Mountain Jewish History, University of Denver Libraries)

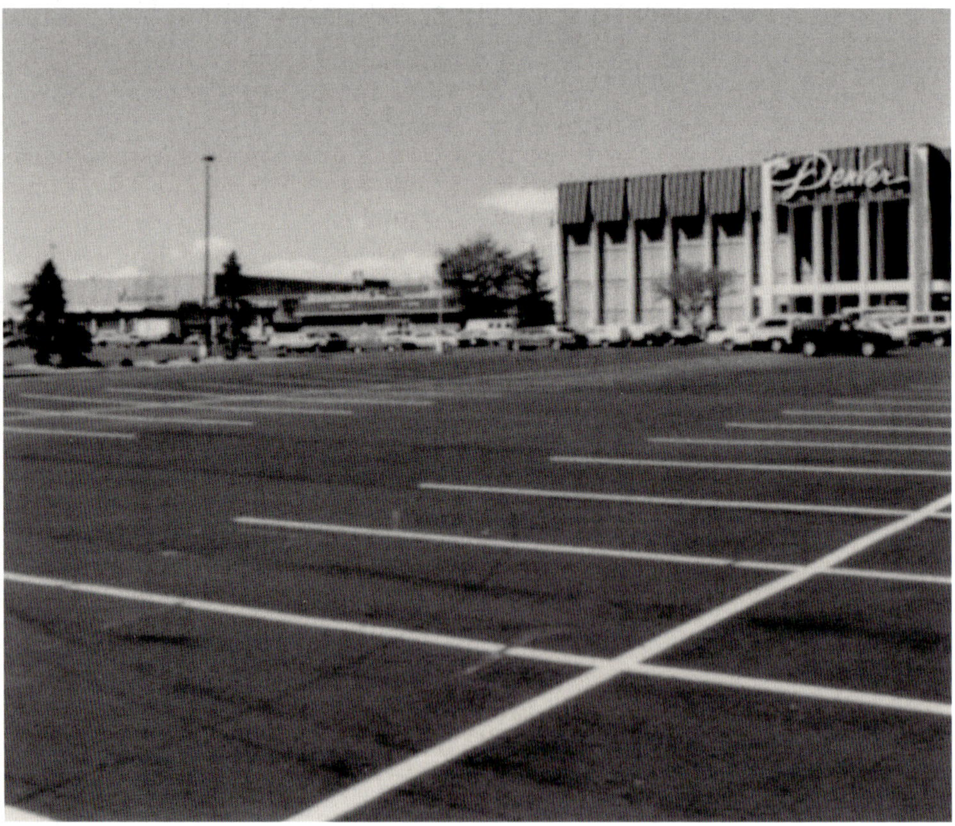

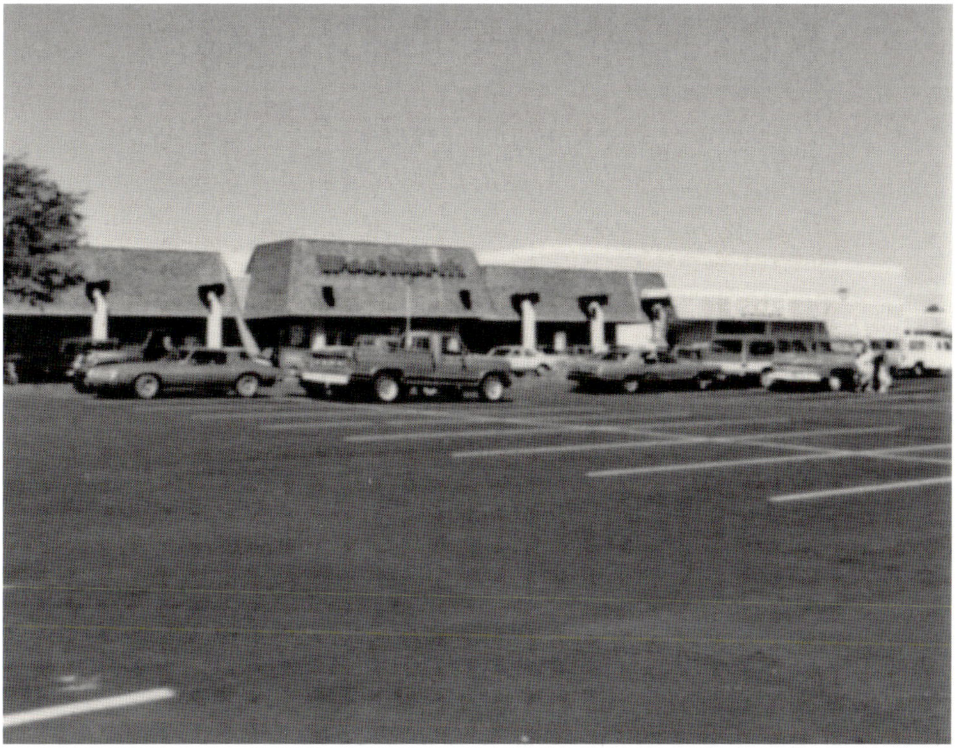

When F.W. Woolworth Co. signed a lease with Perl-Mack to open a new 60,000-square foot store on the east side of the mall, Northglenn Mall was still called North Glenn regional shopping center. The store, including its popular lunch counter, was demolished in 1998 along with the rest of the mall, and the area was revitalized by original developer Jordon Perlmutter into the U-shaped, outdoor Northglenn Marketplace. (Past image, courtesy of Beck Archives of Rocky Mountain Jewish History, University of Denver Libraries.)

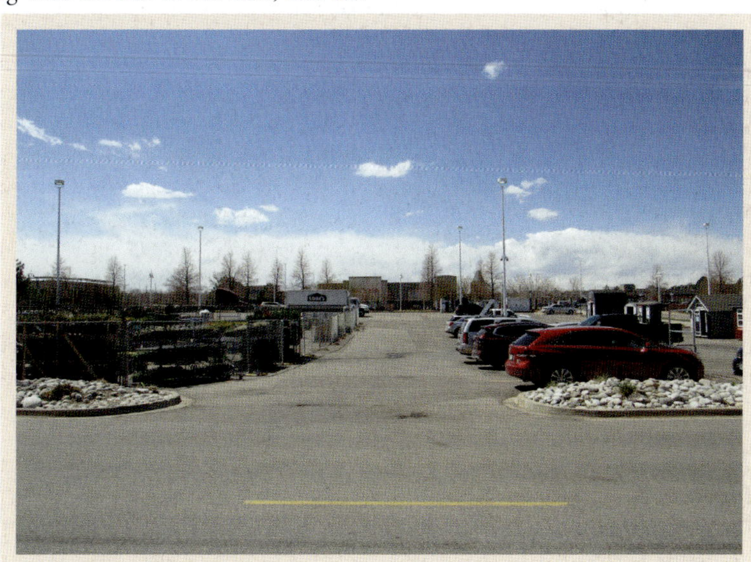

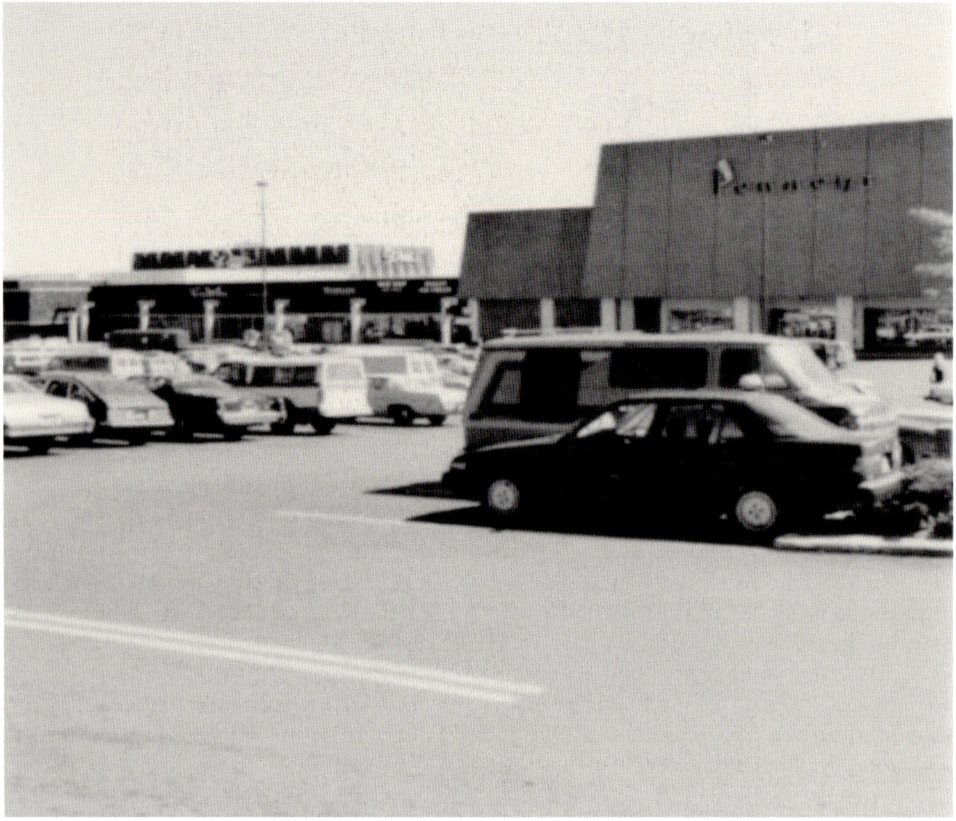

The J.C. Penney store on the south end of Northglenn Mall was one of 70 stores that participated in a ribbon-cutting ceremony attended by mall developers, company executives, local government representatives, and residents in March 1968. Penneys included an all-new home improvement department designed for the growing community. Restaurants and parking for Northglenn Marketplace now occupy the area after the 1998 mall demolition. (Courtesy of Beck Archives of Rocky Mountain Jewish History, University of Denver Libraries.)

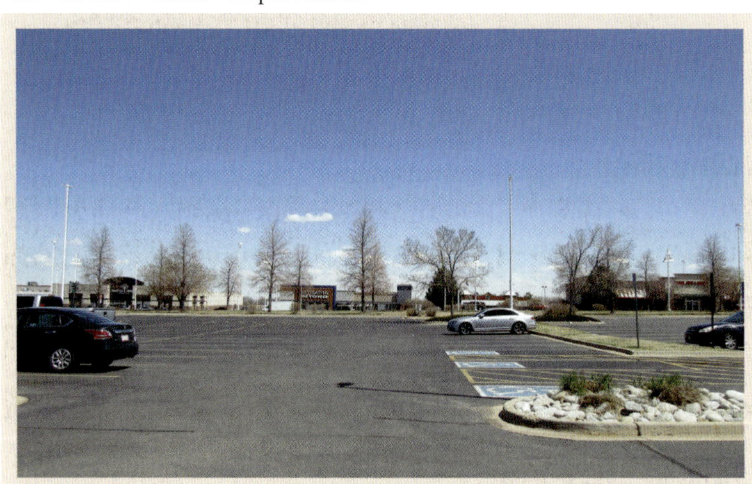

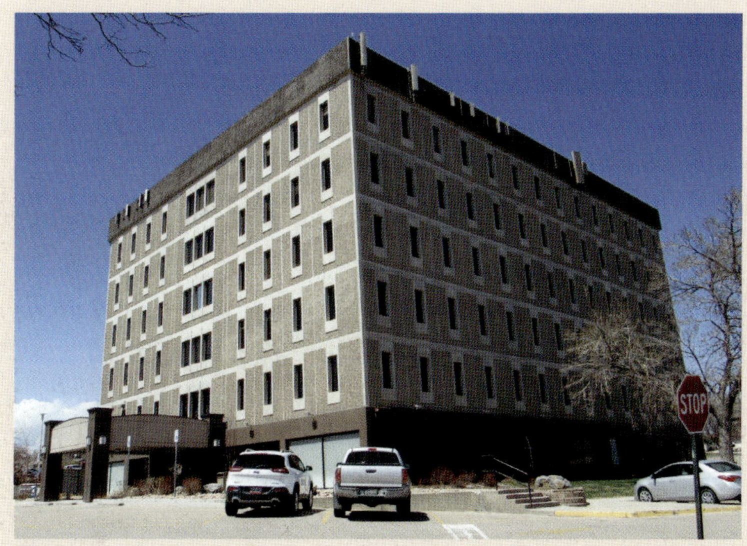

Perl-Mack began construction on this six-story office building in 1971. The 53,000-square-foot building designed by Donald R. Roark and Associates had tinted bronze glass windows, acoustical ceilings, and recessed fluorescent lighting. The central core design with loop corridors allowed the designer to meet any design request by floor. For many years, the main level was occupied by various banks, until the most recent bank vacated the building in 2022. (Past image, courtesy of Beck Archives of Rocky Mountain Jewish History, University of Denver Libraries)

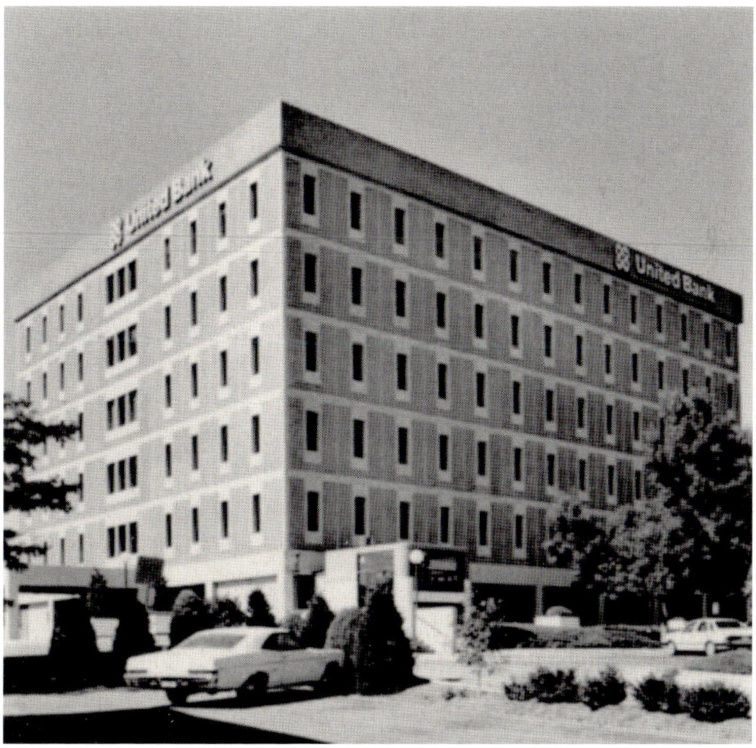

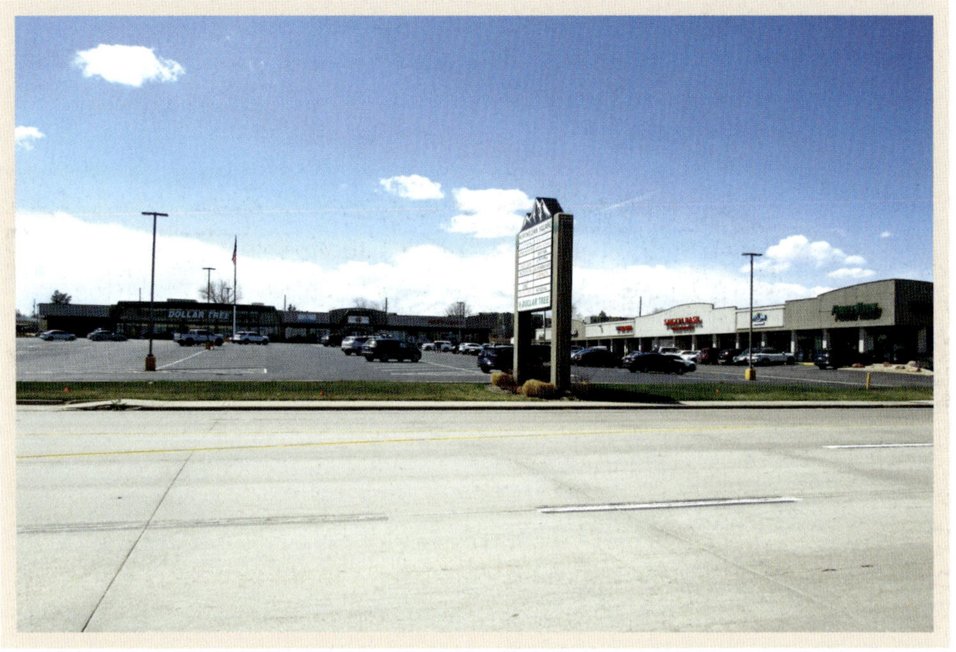

The 73,000-square-foot Northglenn Square strip mall on Melody Drive drew consumers from the neighboring Northglenn Mall. The anchor store on the left was occupied by Playworld from 1982 through 1995, at one point making the news for a roof collapse during a winter snowstorm. The complex has been renovated since this 1989 image and is still home to a variety of retail and restaurant establishments. (Past image, courtesy of City of Northglenn.)

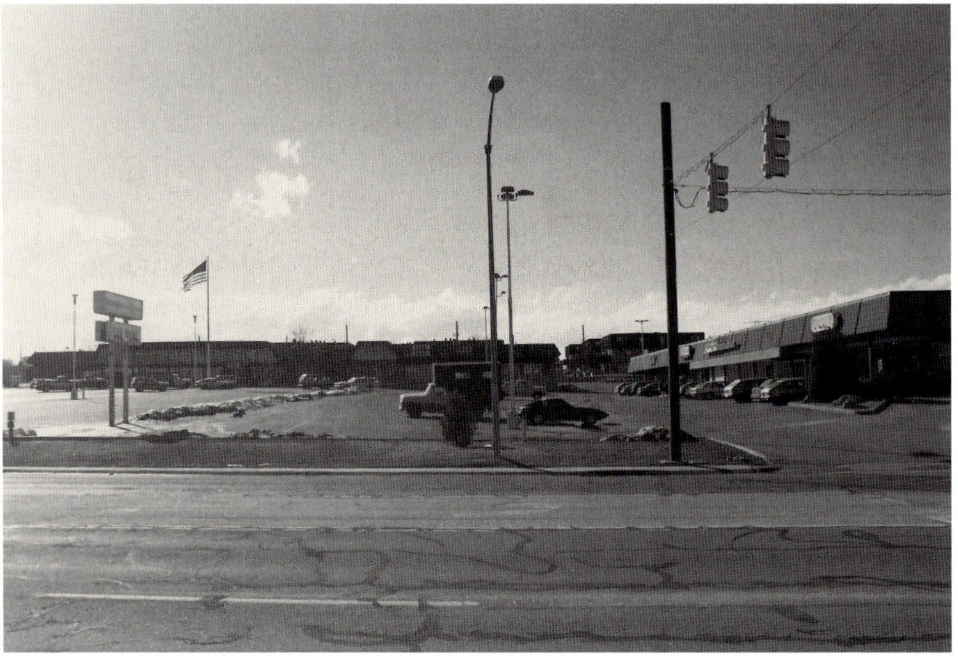

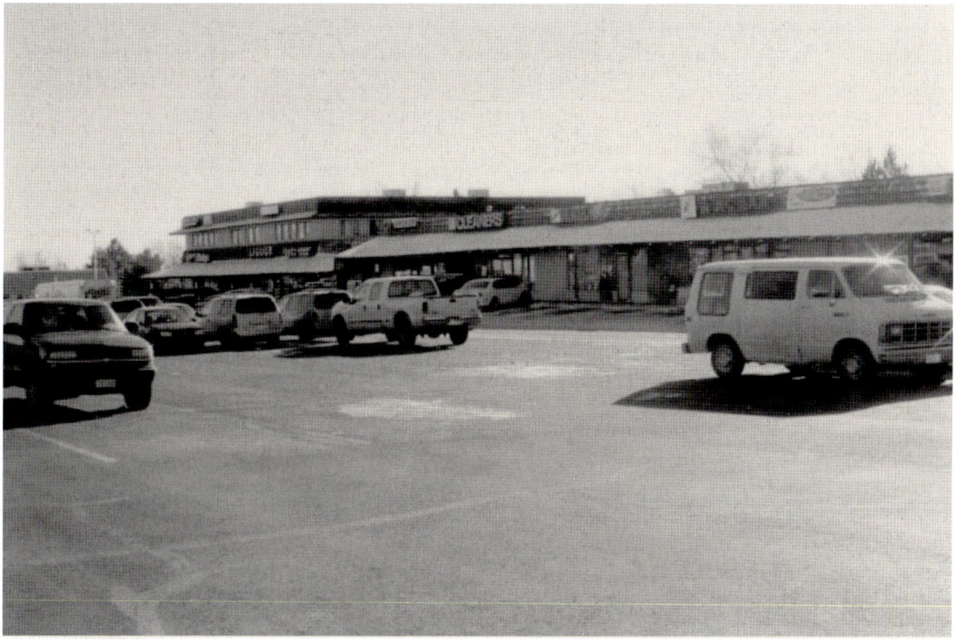

The acreage that Hillcrest Plaza now occupies was zoned for residential use by Heftler Construction Company, which was building the homes in the Hillcrest subdivision. After an initial Northglenn annexation bid was defeated, the area was rezoned for commercial use, making way for Hillcrest Plaza to be built in 1972 at 104th Avenue and Pecos Street. One of the first city flags was ordered from a fabric store in Hillcrest Plaza, which today remains commercial mixed-use. (Past image, courtesy of City of Northglenn.)

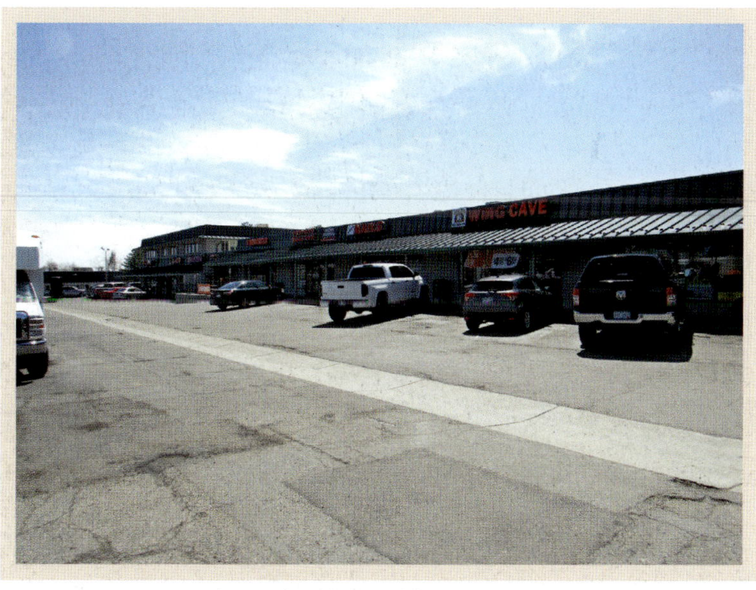

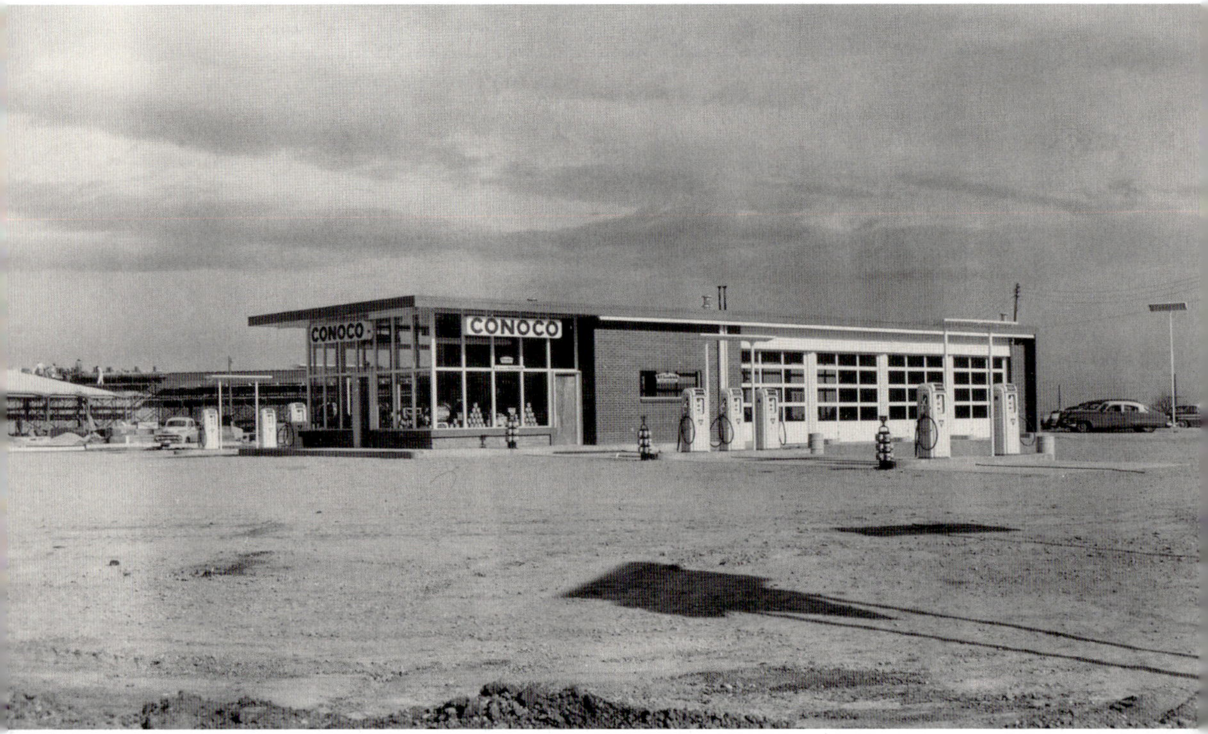

The Badding family property extended along 104th Avenue to the Valley Highway (now Interstate 25). After the property was sold to Perl-Mack in 1960, a Conoco gas station was built there. In the past photograph, workers can be seen building what would become the Royal Inn. Over the years, additional gas stations have occupied this location, which today is once again a Conoco. (Past image, courtesy of Caron Horner.)

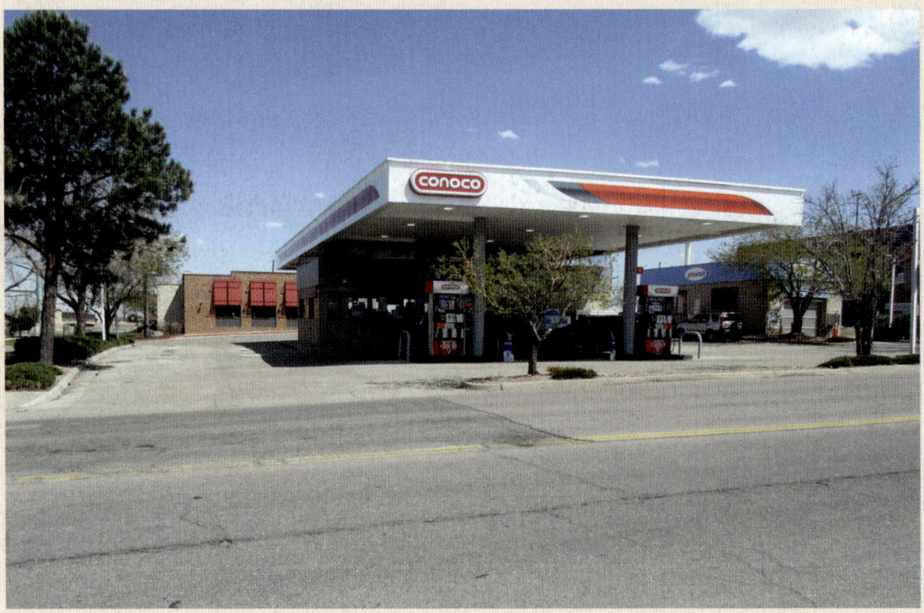

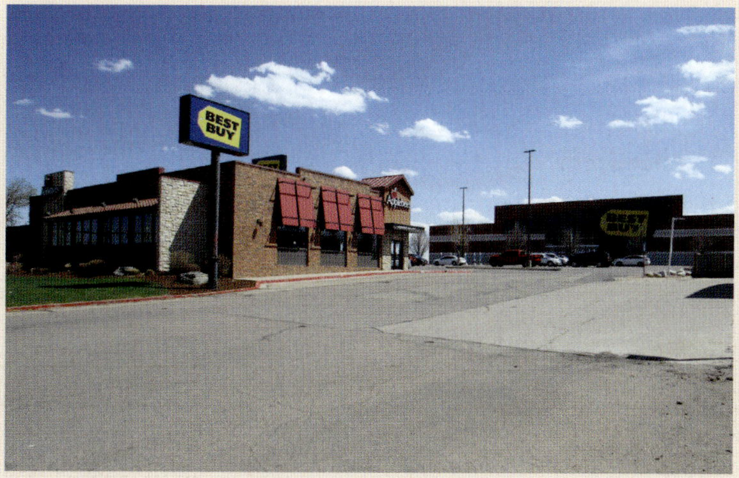

City officials, developers, and executives held a ground-breaking ceremony on August 6, 1969, for the 100-room Royal Inn of America hotel and adjoining Jolly King Restaurant on 104th Avenue near Interstate 25. The Royal Inn was renamed the Bronco Inn in 1973, and by the time of this 1989 image, the Jolly King Restaurant had become the Huddle. Both were demolished in 2007 to make way for Best Buy, and in 2012, an Applebees. (Past image, courtesy of City of Northglenn.)

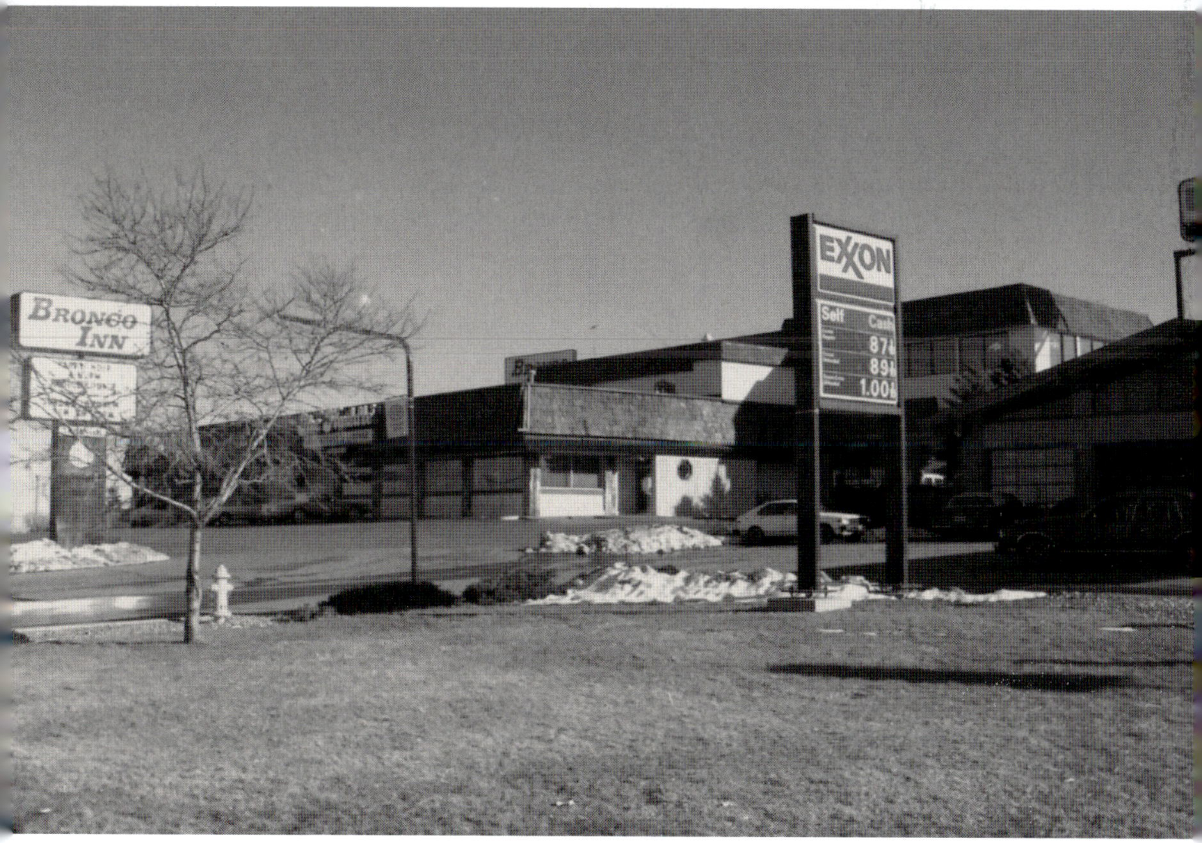

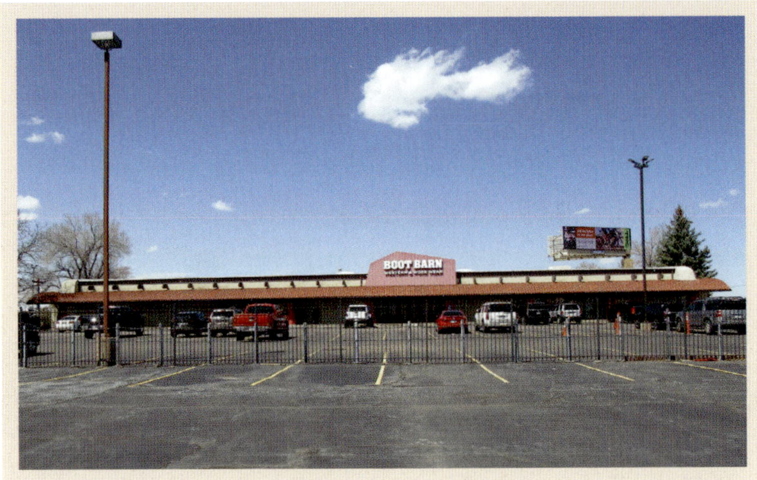

The past image taken in 1969 shows a portion of the mini-golf course north of the fairways of the nine-hole golf course originally marketed as part of the recreational amenities of Northglenn. After a three-year court battle with the City of Northglenn, Perl-Mack was successful in re-zoning the golf course from open space to commercial, allowing them to build a commercial building at this site along with space for overflow from O'Meara Ford. (Past image, courtesy of City of Northglenn.)

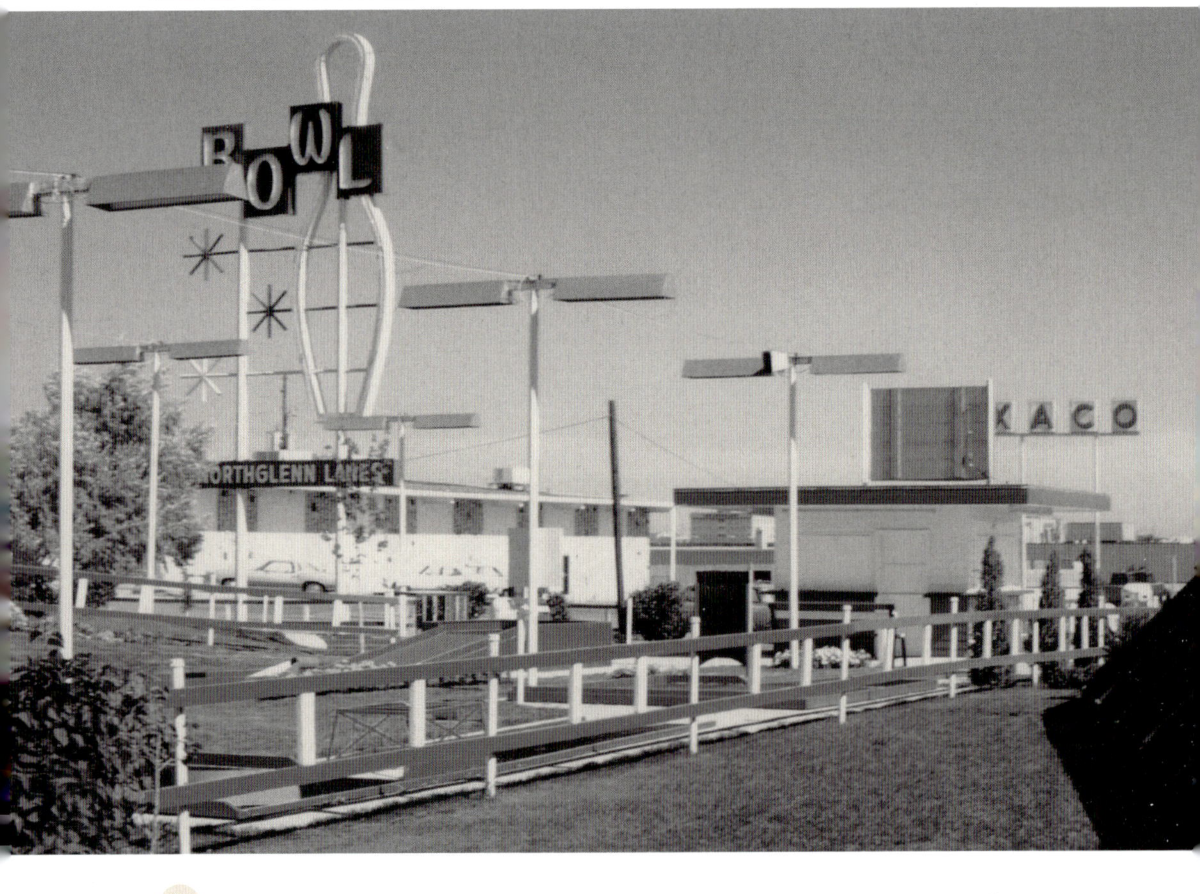

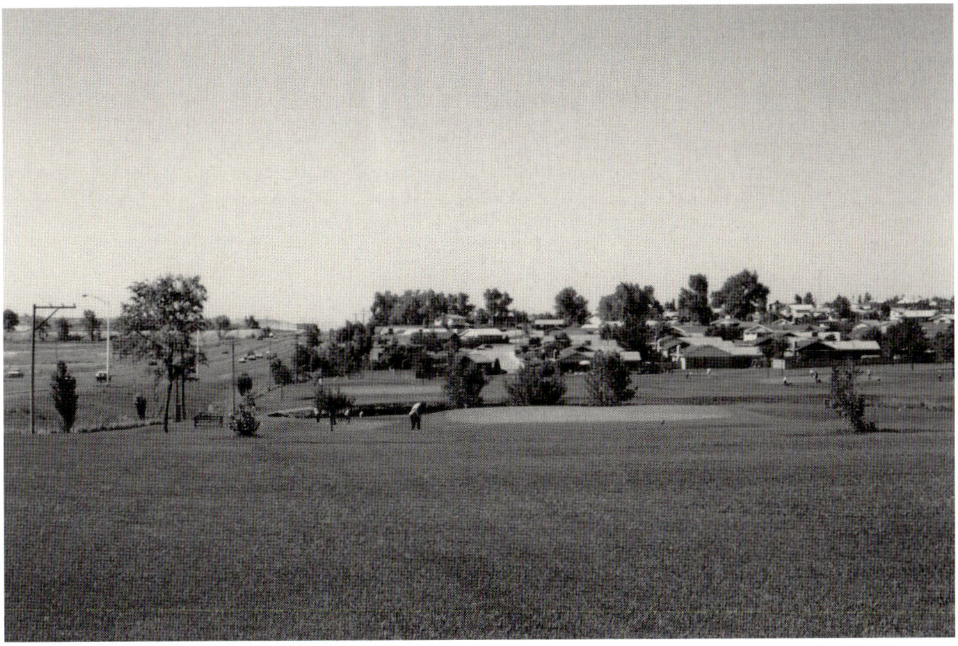

Early promotional materials from Perl-Mack listed a nine-hole golf course, seen here around 1969, as an amenity for the new community of Northglenn. Opened in 1960 adjacent to the Valley Highway (current Interstate 25), the golf course was later rezoned for commercial use. Despite resident objections, Perl-Mack succeeded in its court case against the City of Northglenn in 1977 to rezone the property as commercial and built an office building on the fairways. (Past image, courtesy of City of Northglenn.)

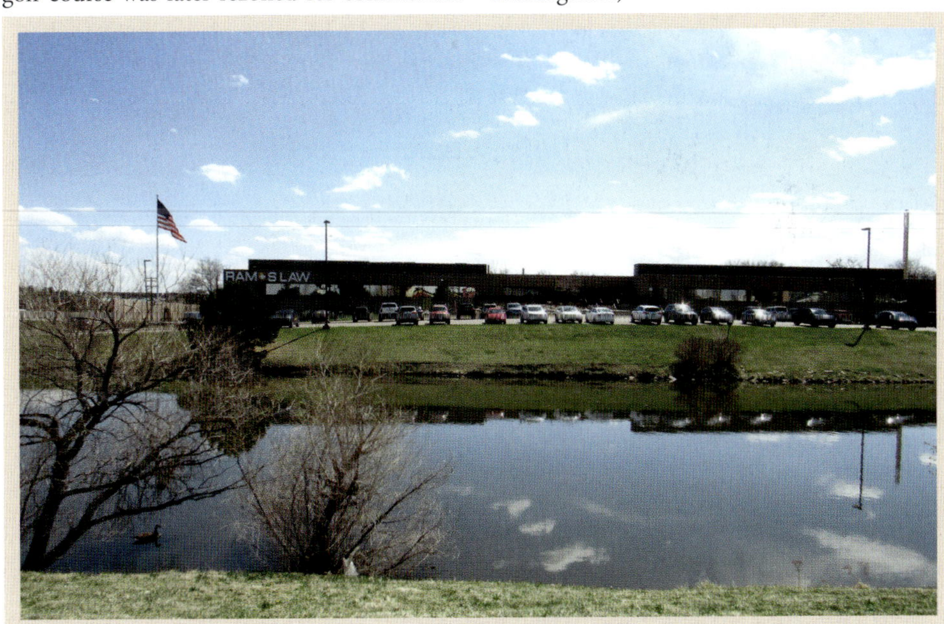

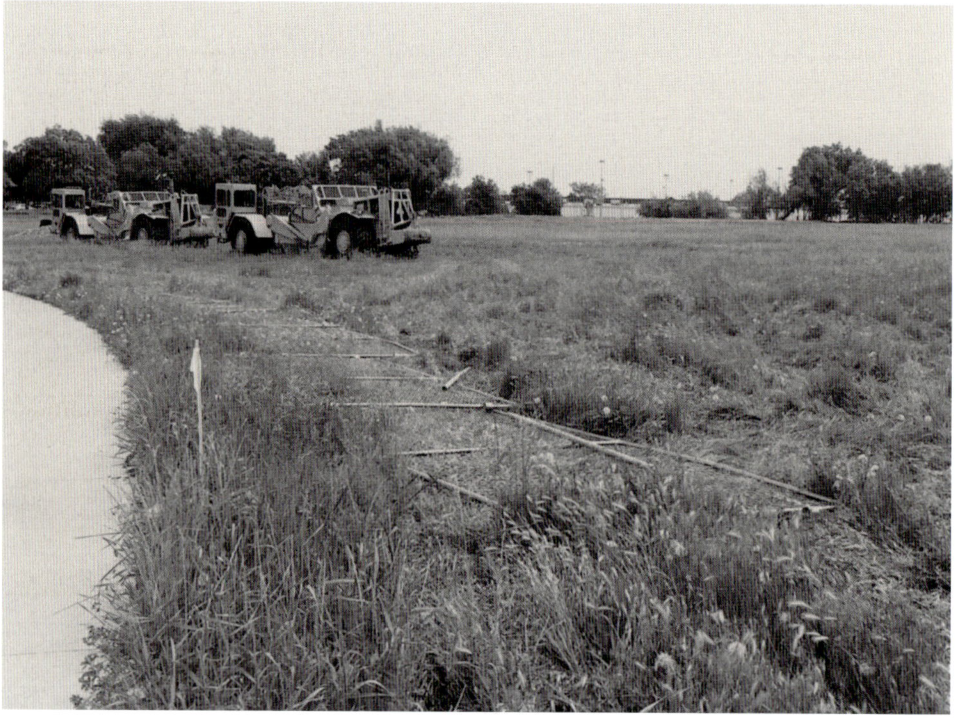

Early master plans for Northglenn called for a hospital near 120th Avenue and Washington Street. While that building never materialized, SCL Health Saint Joseph was built on this empty field at 11900 Grant Street just north of E.B. Rains Memorial Park. The three-story structure built in 2016 is 55,528 square feet and provides local residents access to medical facilities and a full-service emergency room. (Past image, courtesy of City of Northglenn.)

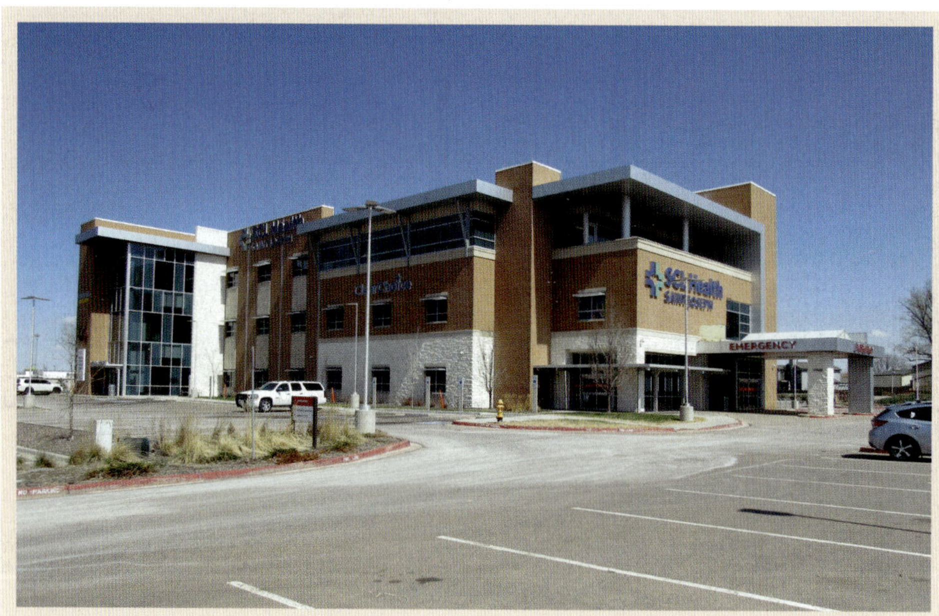

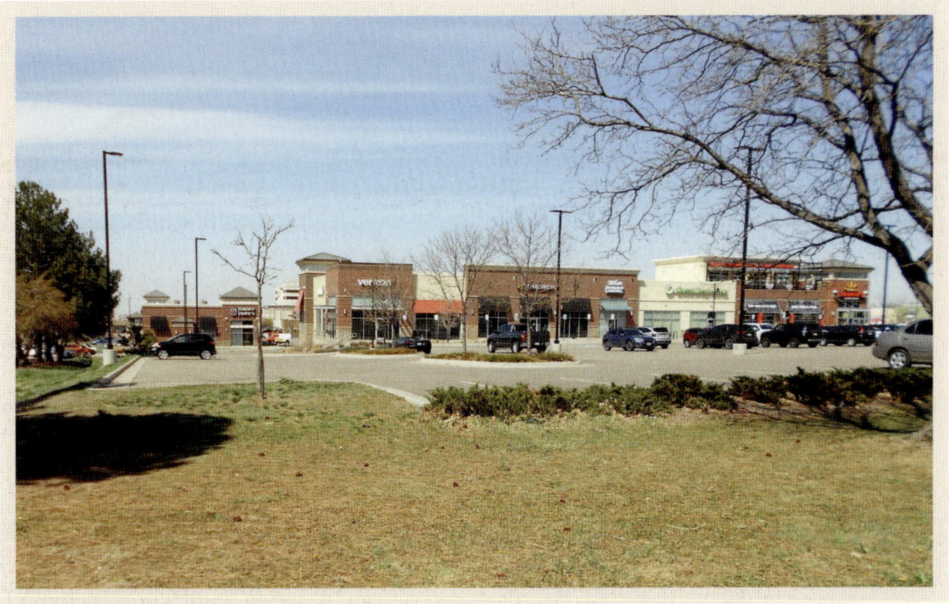

Looking north from the recreation center, a 10-acre empty field lay just south of 120th Avenue while an office building is being constructed north of 120th Avenue in this past image. The Northglenn Urban Renewal Authority's plan to develop this lot into Webster Lake Promenade included a mix use shopping center with restaurant, medical, and retail establishments. Completed in 2015, the promenade was successfully leased prior to breaking ground. (Past image, courtesy of City of Northglenn.)

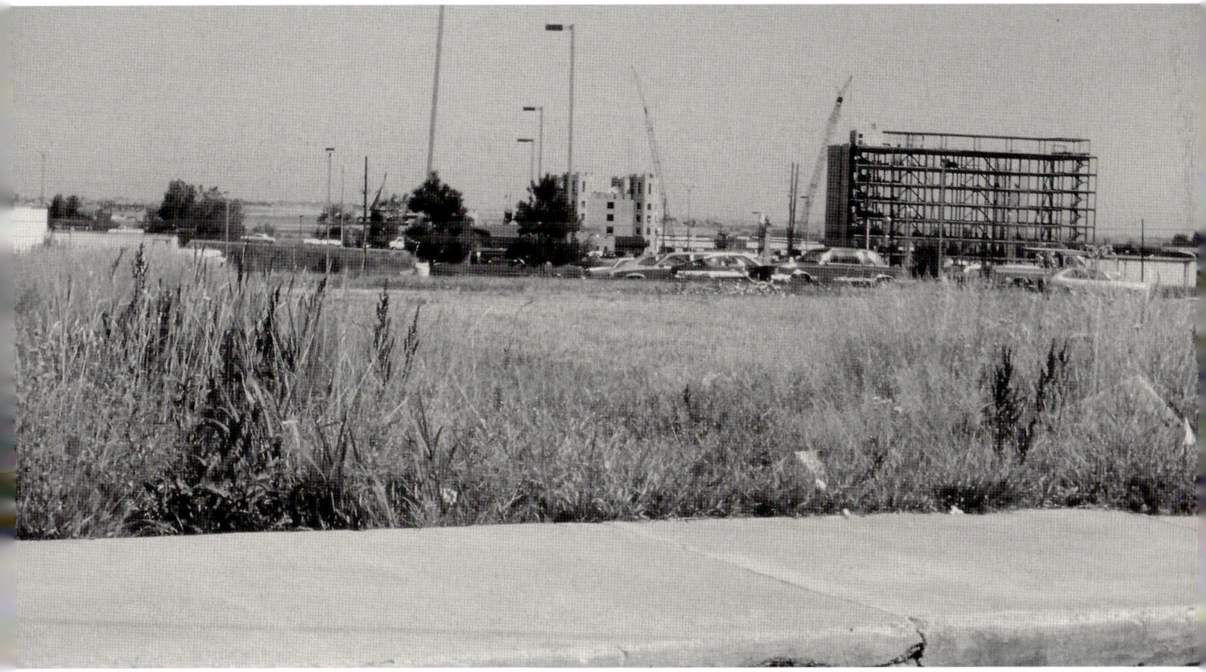

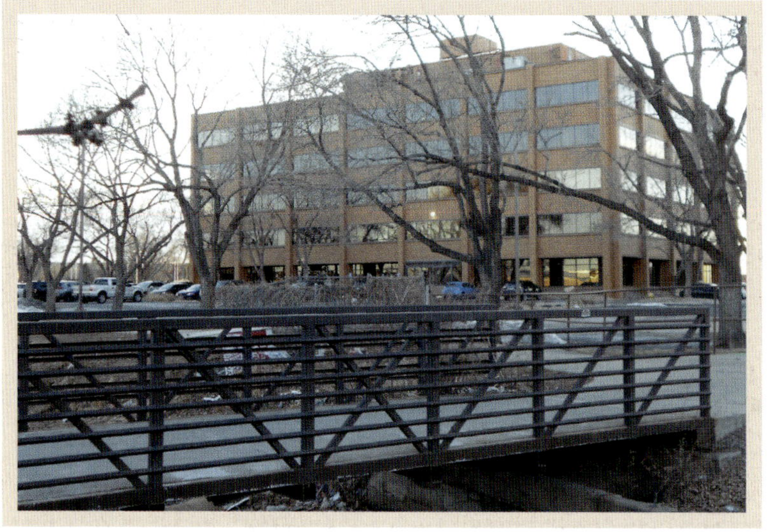

Built at 11990 Grant Street in 1983, this 86,000-square-foot office building is ideally placed on the northern border of Northglenn near Interstate 25. Originally referred to as the Grant Street Building, now called the Metro North Office Building, the five-story structure has housed a variety of businesses. Among the minimal alterations done to the site, in 1995, public works employees installed a pedestrian walkway on the northeast corner of the property, making passage safer along 120th Avenue. (Past image, courtesy of Northglenn Senior Center.)

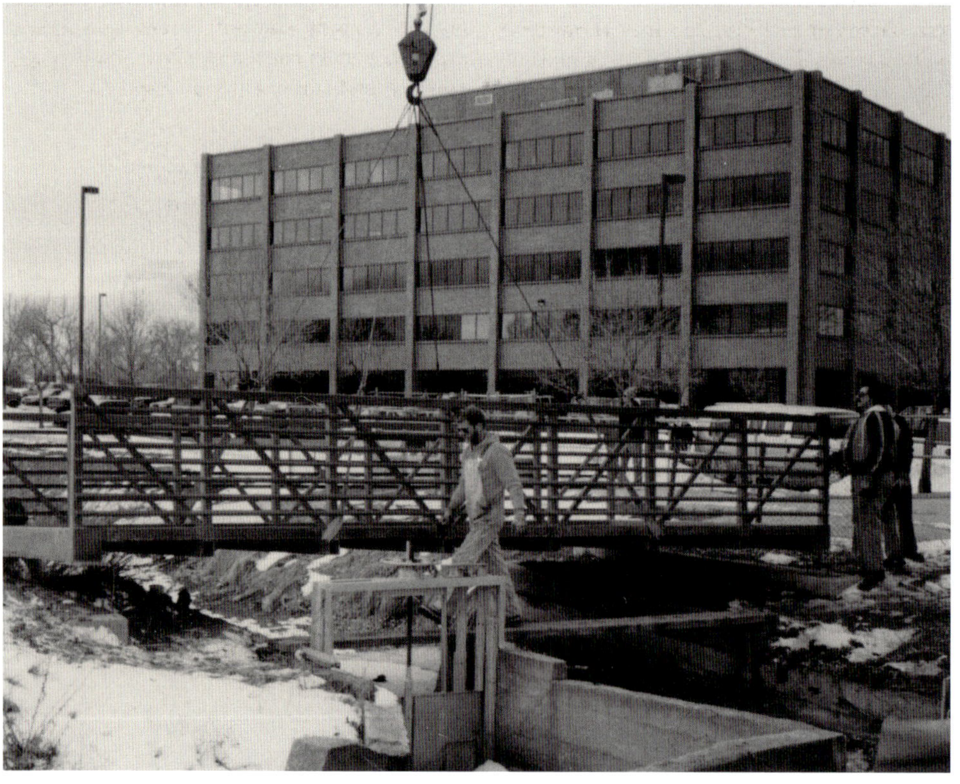

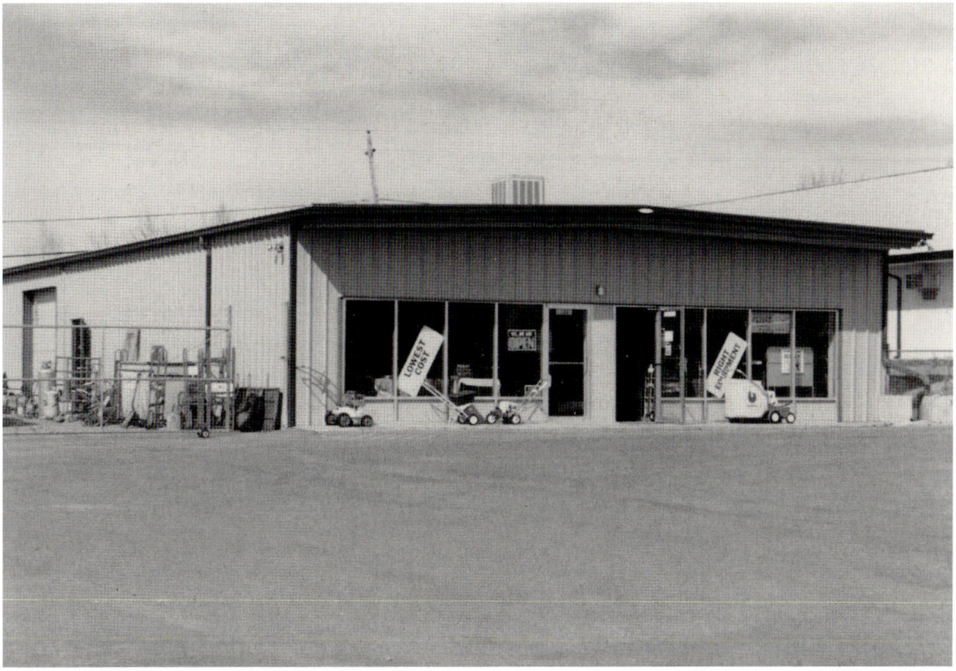

The structure at 11081 Irma Drive was a hardware store when American Legion Post 22 purchased the building in 1988. The post, chartered in 1968, had met at previous locations in Thornton and Northglenn. They remodeled the building, named it the "Ranch", and held a deed burning ceremony on June 16, 1990. Through their multiple charitable activities, the members of Post 22 are still actively engaged in serving veterans and residents in the community. (Past image, courtesy of American Legion Post 22.)

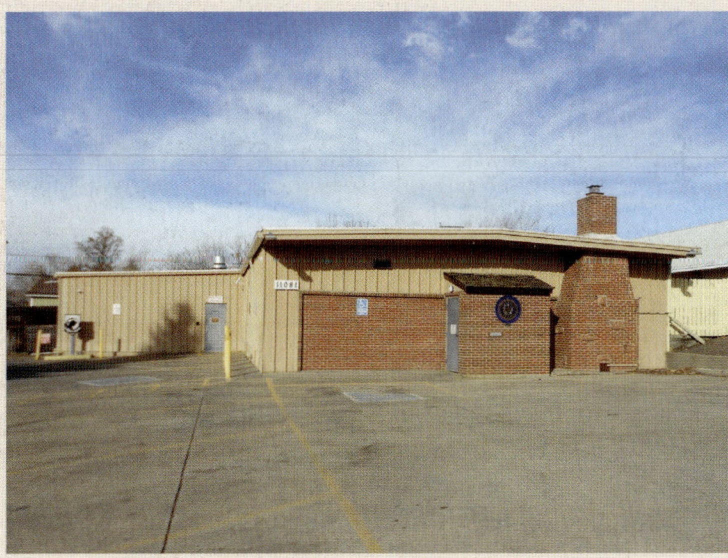

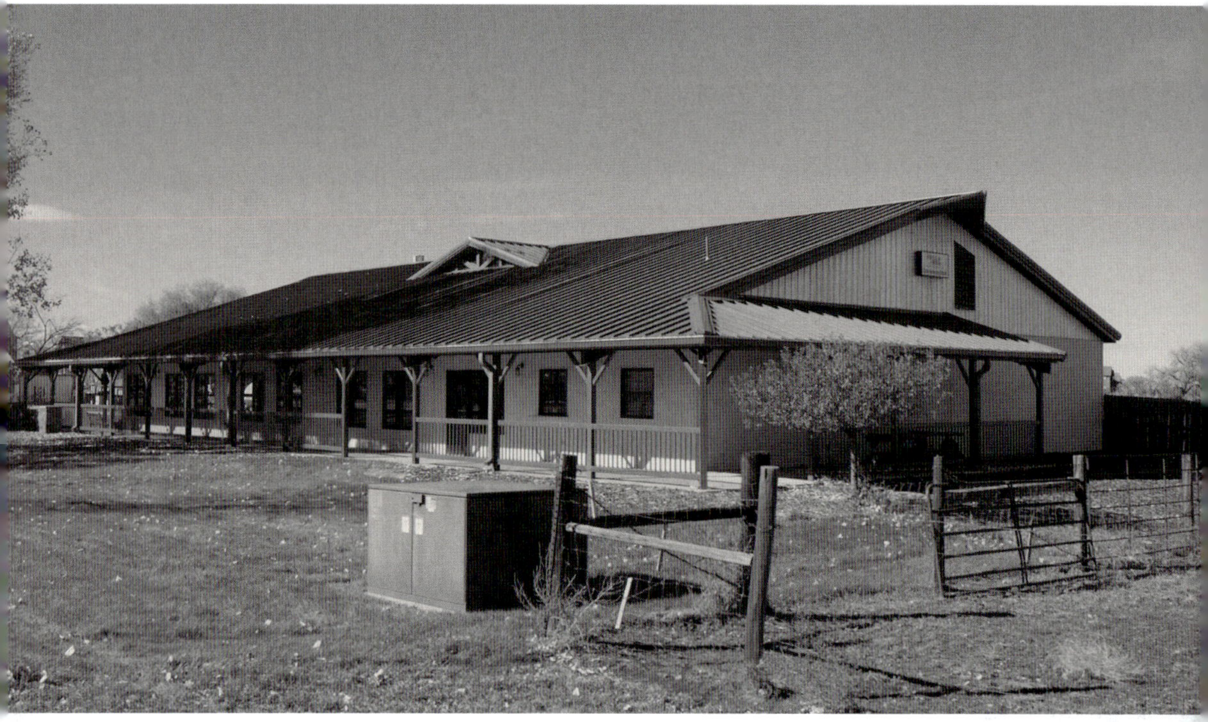

The Hinkhouse family, owners of Karl's Farm Dairy since 1947, opened a country store on 120th Avenue and Irma Drive in 2002 to sell a variety of products including the dairy's milk. After 65 years of operation, the dairy and store closed on June 20, 2012. The store building was used for various other industries until 2022, when it was demolished to make way for the Karl's Farm Development Project. (Past image, courtesy of City of Northglenn.)

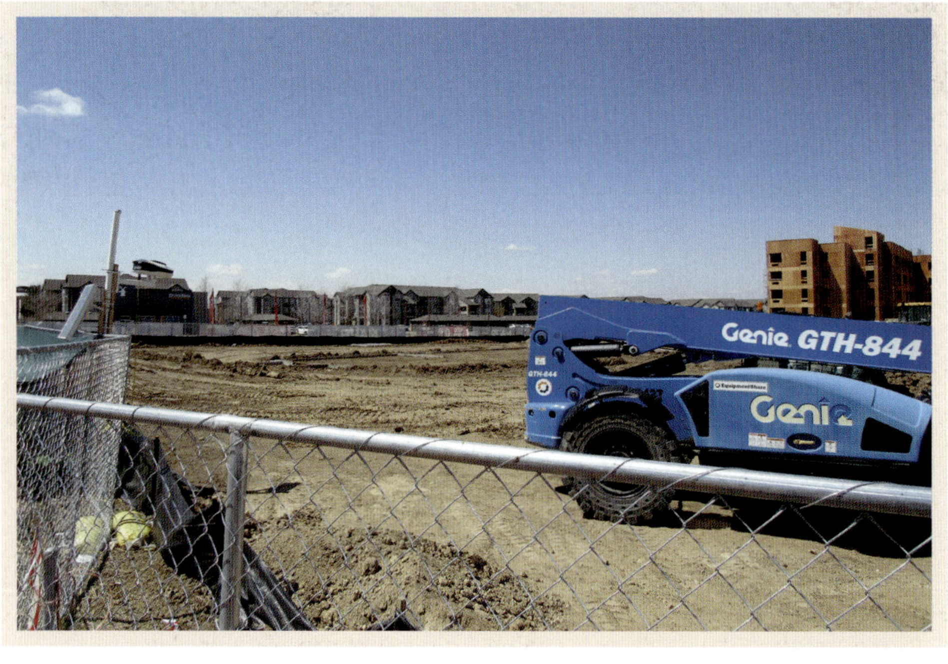

CHAPTER 6

STREET SCENES

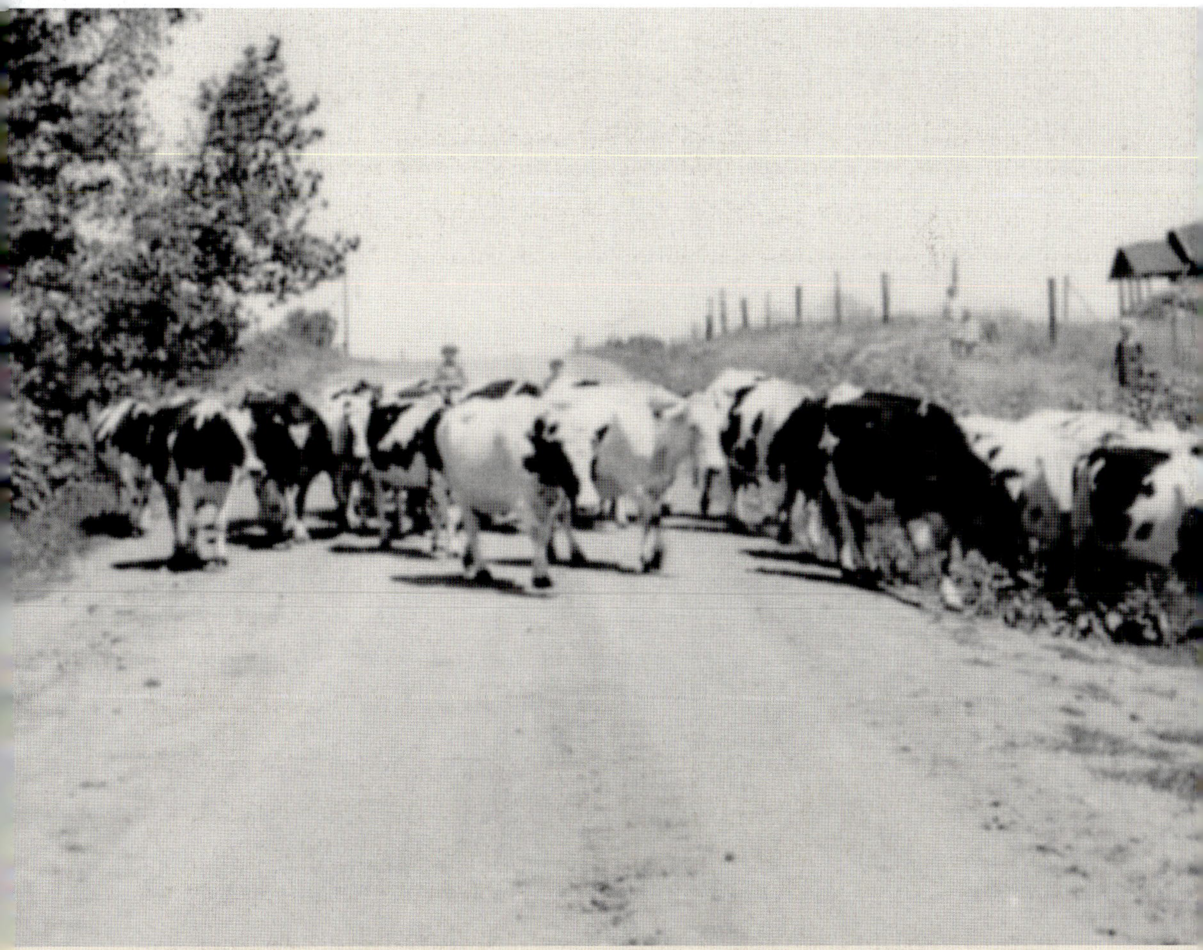

The Badding Farm was bordered on the west by Huron Street. In this c. 1938 image, the Badding children can be seen herding cows along Huron Street when it was a dirt road. The cows were moved from the west portion of their land, across the Valley Highway, currently Interstate 25, to the east part of their property along Washington Street. The family would stop traffic to allow the cows to cross safely. (Courtesy of Caron Horner.)

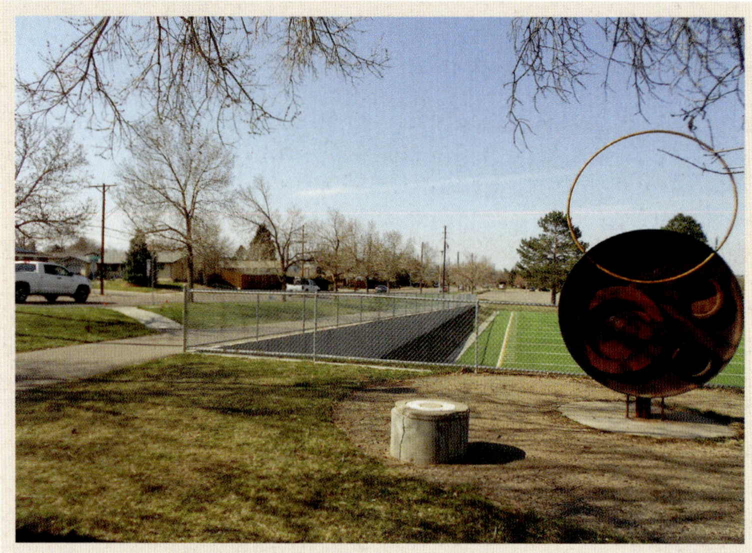

This view looking north along Huron Street at 100th Place highlights the first public artwork commissioned in Northglenn. While working on the piece in 1974, artist Angelo De Benedetto encouraged residents to stop by High School Park, now Norse Glenn Park, and comment on the modernist-style steel structure that he viewed as "the people's project." Benedetto appreciated this location so that drivers could see a work of art while going to or from work. (Past image, courtesy of Northglenn Senior Center.)

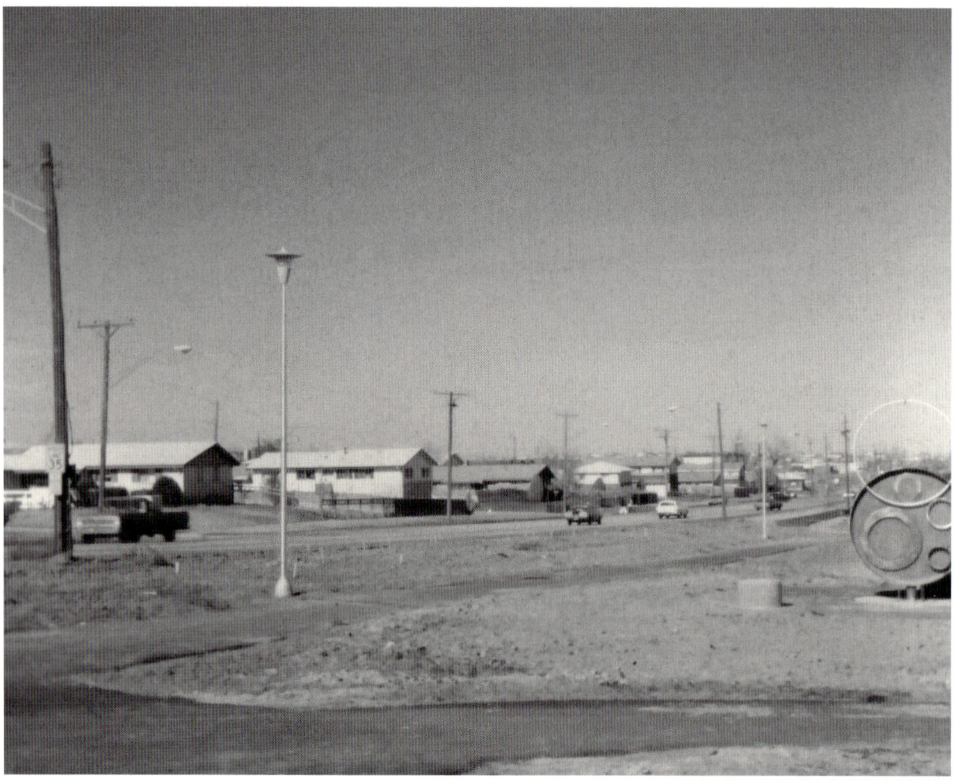

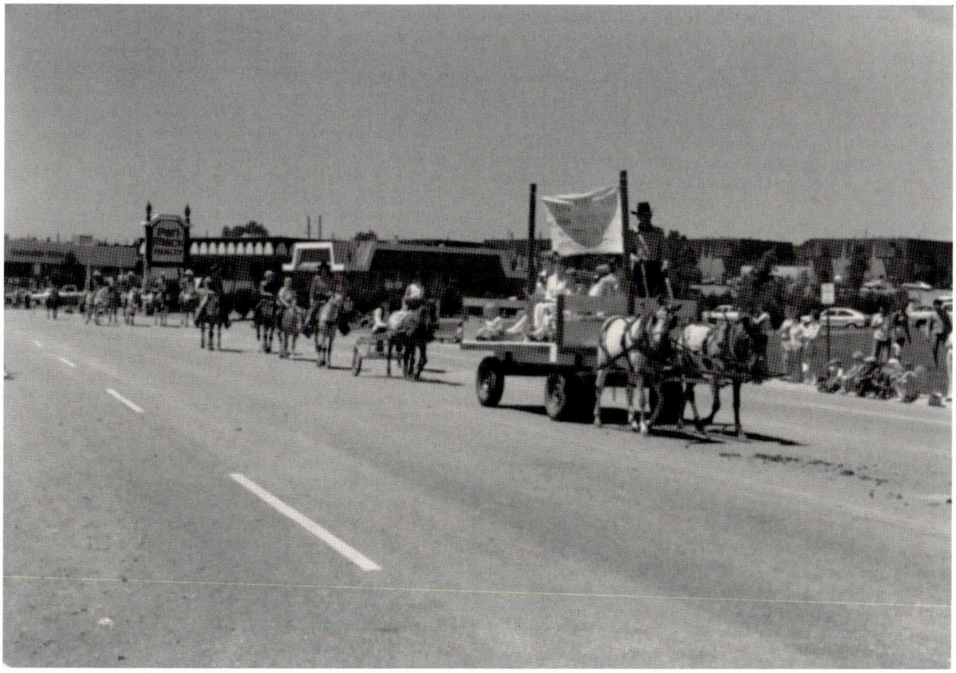

Melody Drive from 104th Avenue to Kennedy Drive on the west side of Northglenn Mall, now Northglenn Marketplace, was the site of several city parades. In this past image, taken during the 1976 festival days, horses and carriages delight onlookers as they make their way north toward Kennedy Drive. The Perl-Mack Realty building, seen at center, has been home to multiple realtors and is currently a European market. (Past image, courtesy of City of Northglenn.).

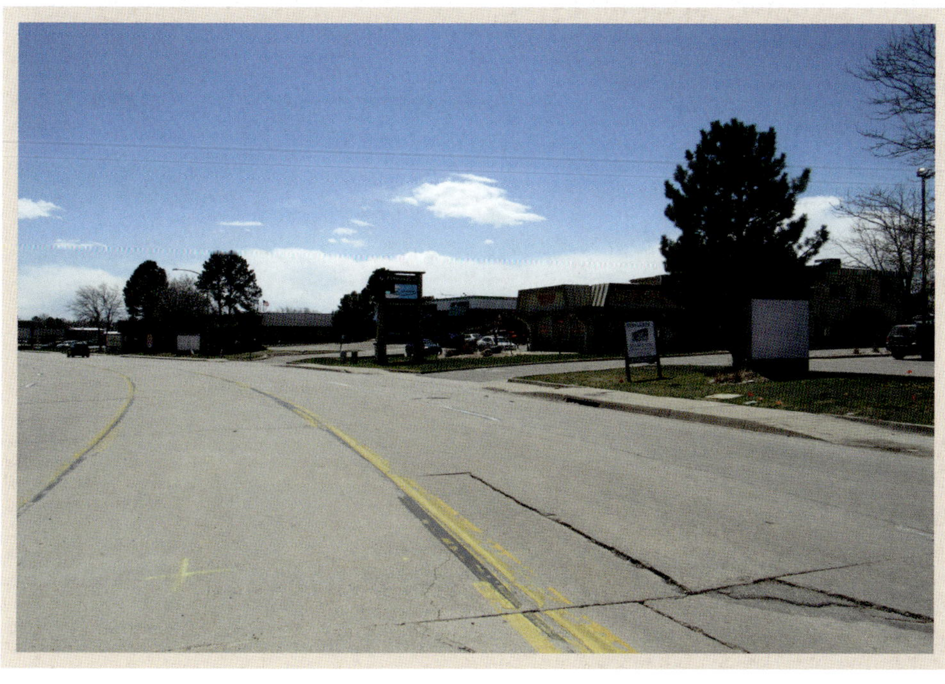

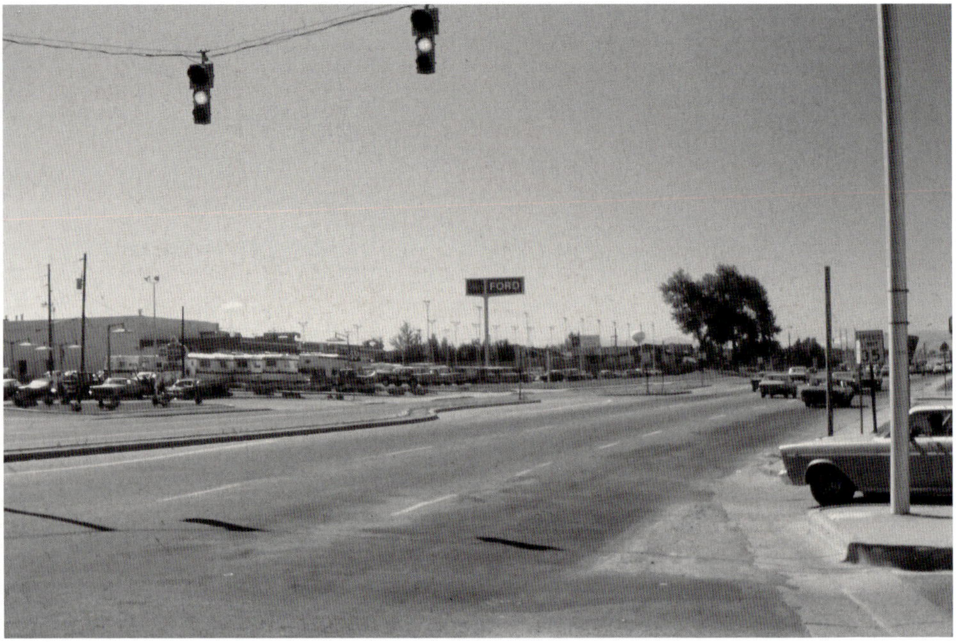

Once a two-lane dirt road, today 104th Avenue remains a main east-west thoroughfare in Northglenn. In this 1976 image, 104th is shown looking west from what is now the entrance to Northglenn Marketplace. O'Meara Ford can be seen on the south side of the road. In 1968, O'Meara Ford built a 30,000-square-foot building on a five-acre lot across from Northglenn Mall. Remodeled in 2003, O'Meara still operates from this location today. (Past image, courtesy of City of Northglenn.)

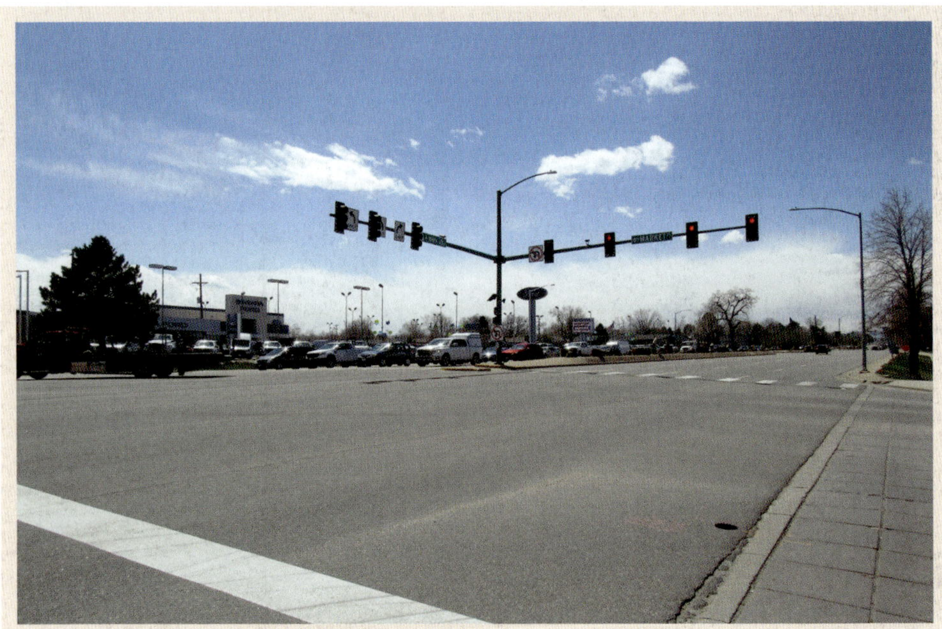

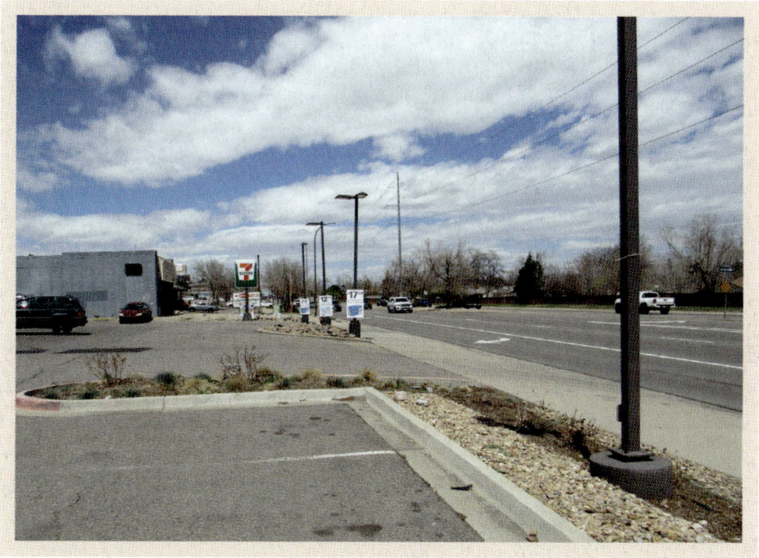

A 1989 image shows the corner of Washington Street and Malley Drive looking north. Washington Street remains a main thoroughfare through the city. The Texaco was demolished and a dentist office building was constructed on the site. Medians were added to Washington Street to assist the flow of traffic. The 7-11 remains in the same location. On the right side of the image, the top of the dome of Northside Baptist Church is barely visible. (Past image, courtesy of City of Northglenn.)

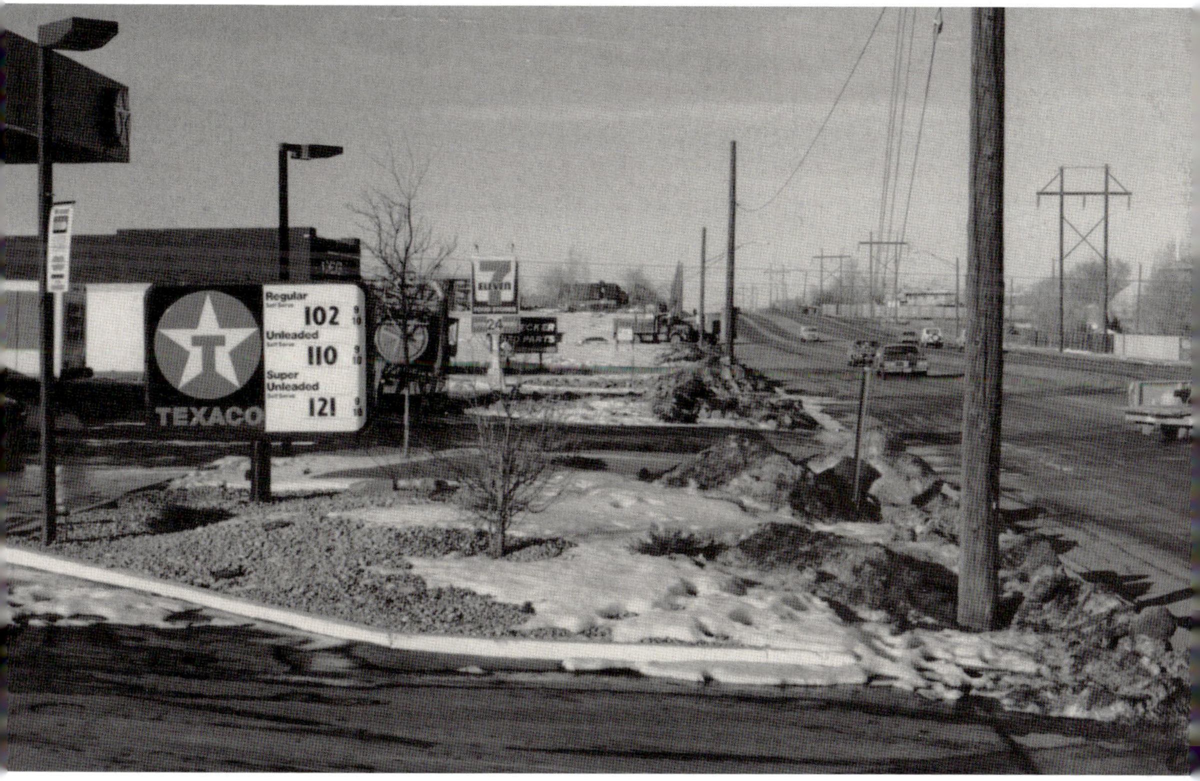

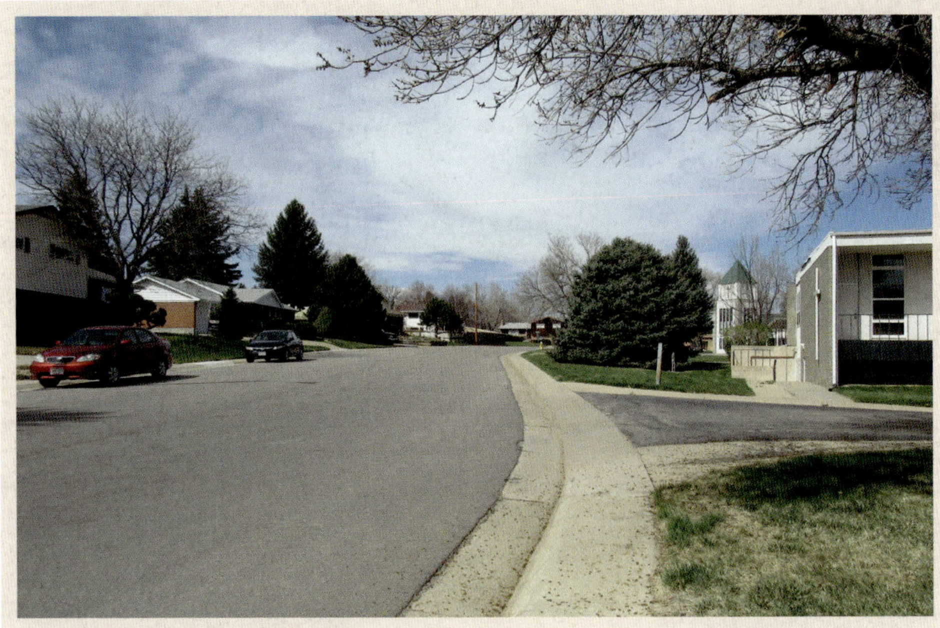

In July 1966, as seen at left, 106th Avenue already had houses on the south side of the street, and Northglenn United Methodist Church had opened the doors to its first building (right). To the west is an open view of the mountains before houses were built along Quivas Street. The view of the mountains is now partially obscured by mature trees. (Past image, courtesy of Northglenn United Methodist Church.)

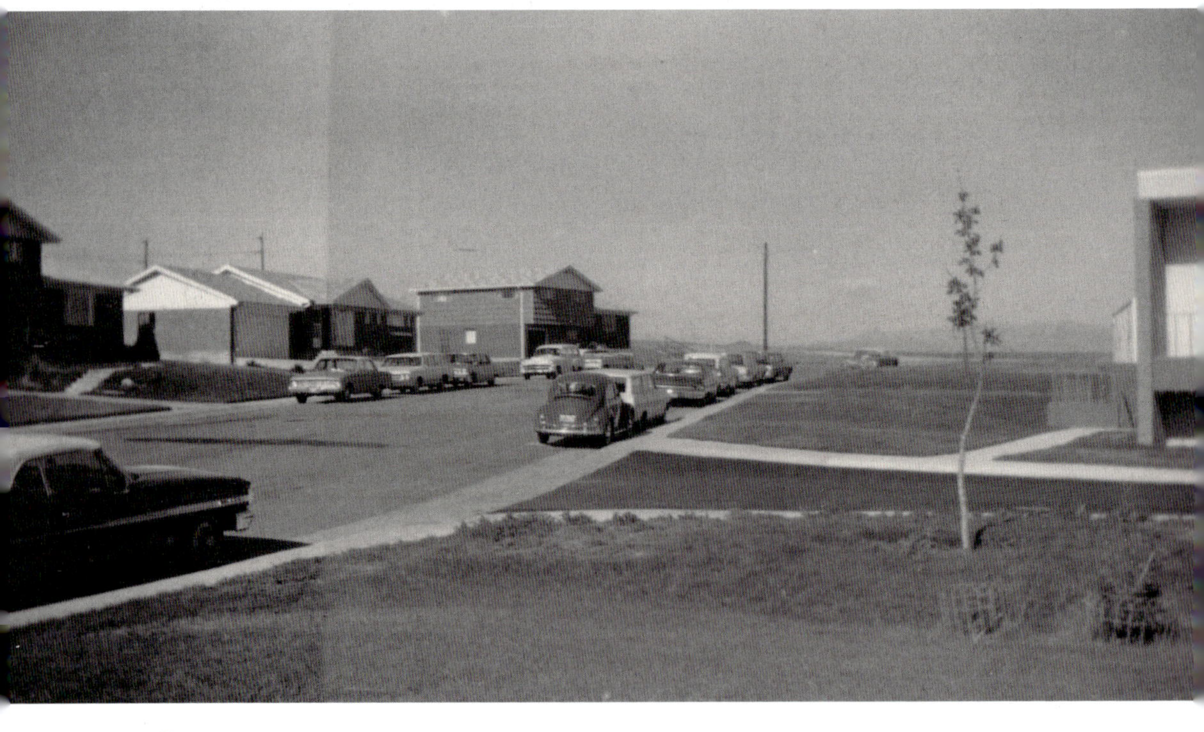

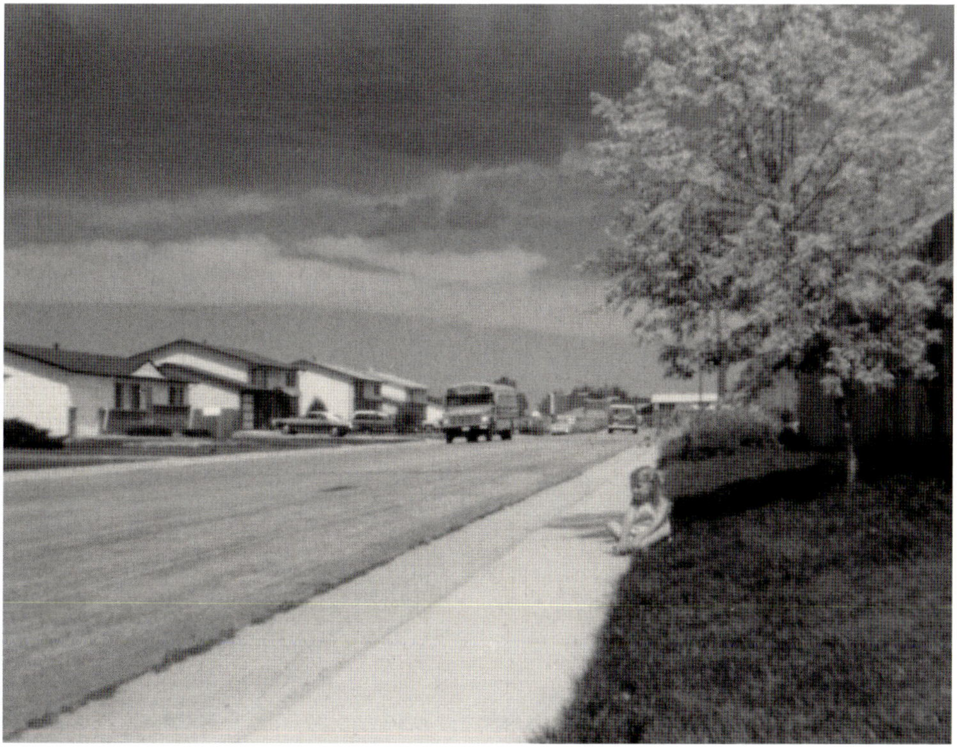

Tara Carney sits in the grass on the north side of her house in Huron Heights waiting for the bus to bring her three brothers home from school. This 1970s image of 118th Street near Melody Drive shows various styles of homes built by B&B Builders. In the past image, the Northglenn Recreation Center can be seen in the background. A noise-reducing wall was installed to mitigate noise from traffic on Interstate 25. (Past image, courtesy of Phil Carney.)

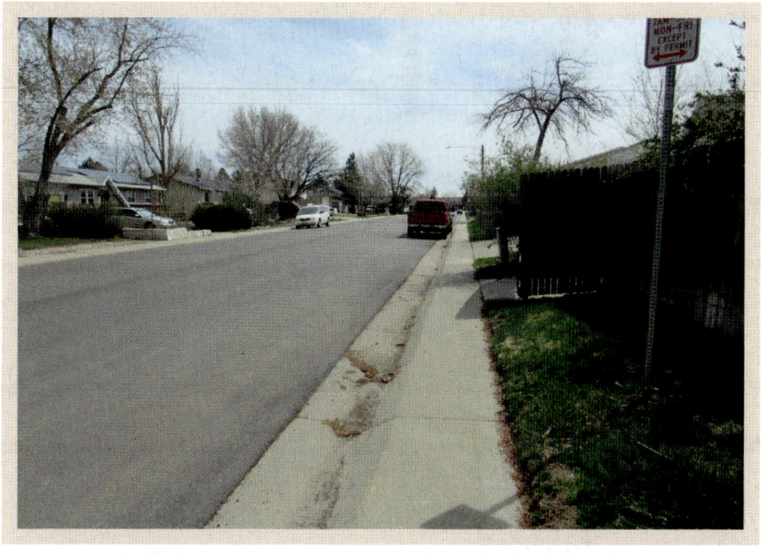

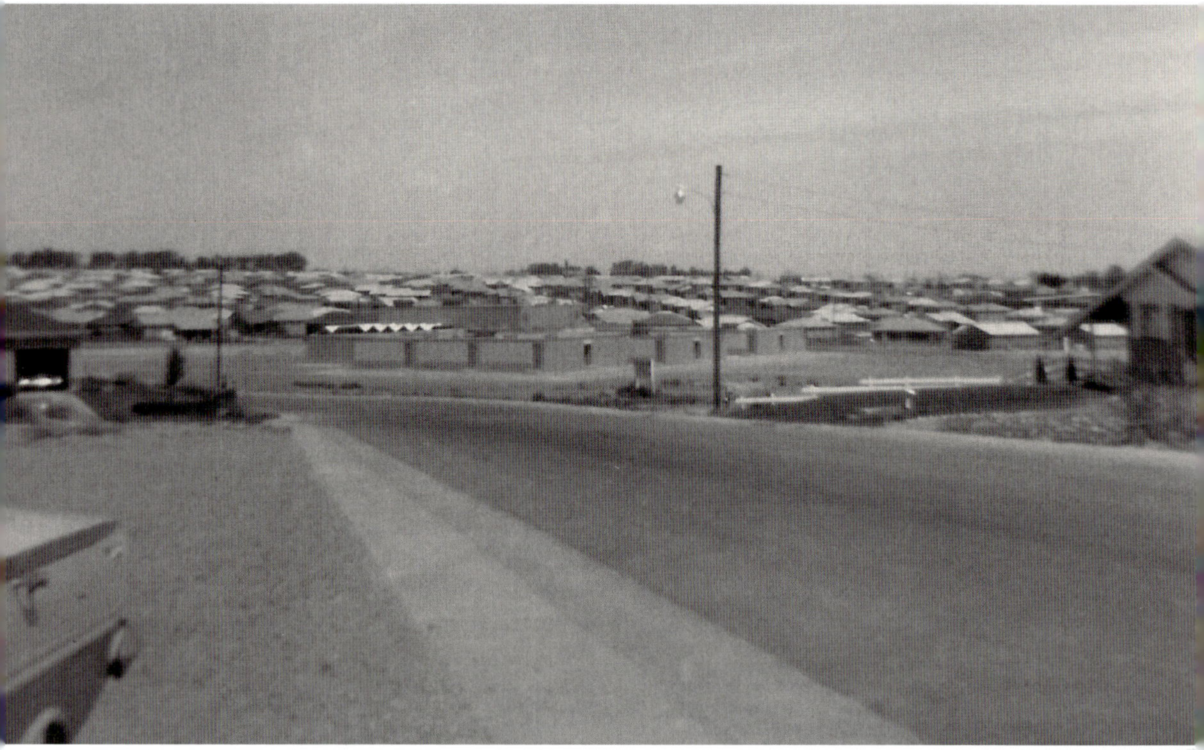

Visitors to the Perl-Mack sales center next to the original model homes on Grant Drive had this view looking north. The Northglenn United Church of Christ (center) was designed by John Anderson and was the first officially chartered congregation in Northglenn. Hulstrum Elementary School, named for education board member Ted Hulstrum, designed by Atchison, Kloverstrom, Saul and Atchison, built in 1961, is seen behind the church. Hulstrum, now the Studio School, was the first school building completed in the city. (Past image, courtesy of Lillian Frey.)

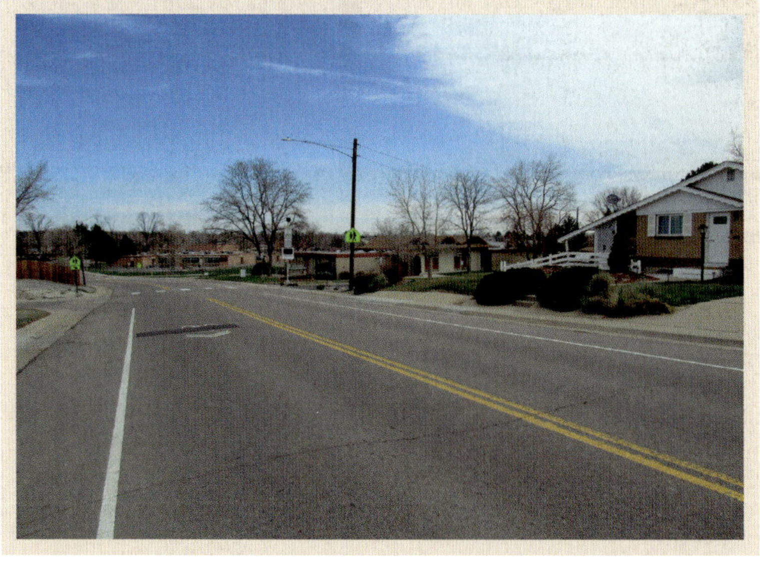

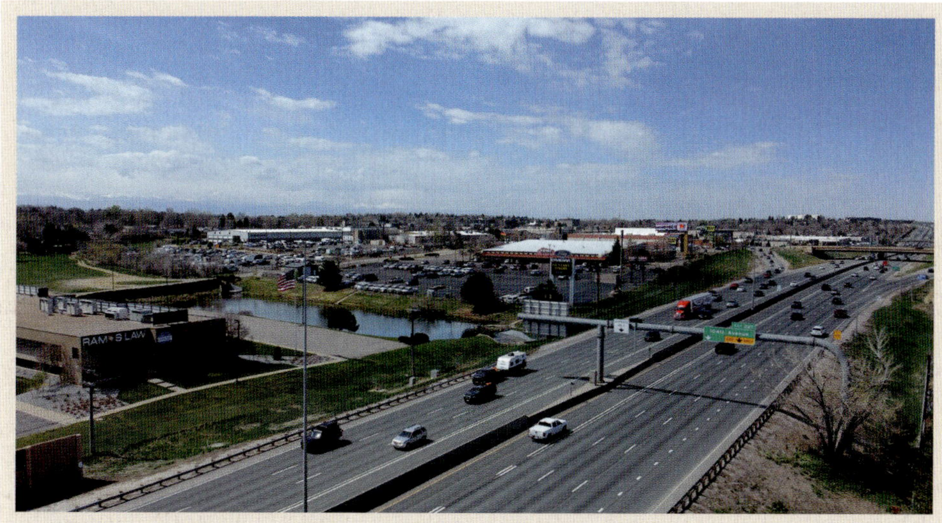

Perl-Mack developers knew that the Valley Highway, present-day Interstate 25, was the main artery for Northglenn. In their promotional materials, they used drive times instead of miles to show how close Northglenn was to major places in the metro area. In this mid-1980s image, it is easy to see the growth of the city with an office building where the golf course once sat south of the Bronco Inn. (Past image, courtesy of City of Northglenn; present image, courtesy of Xavier Culp.)

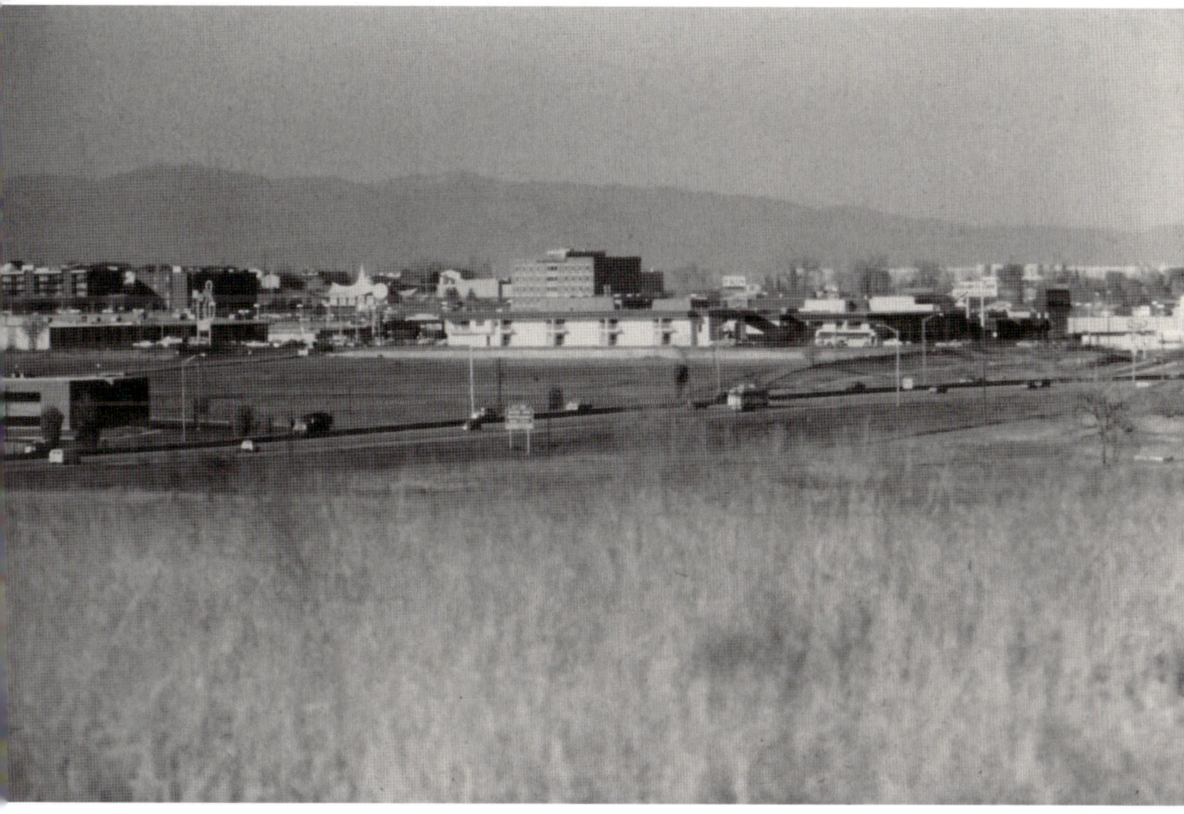

Consistent with our mission to preserve history on a local level, this book was printed in South Carolina on American-made paper and manufactured entirely in the United States. Products carrying the accredited Forest Stewardship Council (FSC) label are printed on 100 percent FSC-certified paper.

MADE IN THE USA